Guide to
Czechoslovakia

Simon Hayman

BRADT PUBLICATIONS, UK
HIPPOCRENE BOOKS USA

First published in 1987 by Bradt Publications, 41 Nortoft Rd, Chalfont St Peter, Bucks SL9 0LA, England. Distributed in the USA by Hippocrene Books Inc, 171 Madison Ave, New York, NY 10016.

British Library Cataloguing in Publication Data

Hayman, Simon
    Guide to Czechoslovakia
    1. Czechoslovakia—description
    and travel—1978— Guide-books
    I. Title
    914.37′044   DB2022

    ISBN 0 946983 10 0

Maps by the author
Photos courtesy of Čedok, London
Cover photo: Pernstejn Castle

Lasermasters coordinated in UK by Scriptmate, London

Printed and bound in Great Britain by A.Wheaton and Company Ltd, Exeter, Devon.

This book is dedicated to my mother

ACKNOWLEDGEMENTS

Thank you to all the many people in Czechoslovakia who helped me with my research, to Hugh Matthews for offering his word processor, and to Eva Jenson for putting up with me getting up at 6am every morning to write!

The publisher would like to thank Čedok of London, and especially Jane Ashton, for much valuable help and for supplying the photographs in this book. Grateful thanks, too, to Dagmar Barrett for Czeching.

TABLE OF CONTENTS

Part 1: General Information

Part 2: Guide to the Regions

PRAGUE 61

WEST BOHEMIA
Cheb 83 Františkovy Lázně 84 Karlovy Vary 85 Mariánské Lázně
89 Plzeň 91 Domážlice 94

SOUTH BOHEMIA
Šumava 97 Český Krumlov 103 České Budějovice 105 Třeboň
108 Tábor 109

NORTHERN BOHEMIA
Terezín 113 České Švýcarsko 113 Poděbrady 119 Český Ráj
120 Krkonoše 120

MORAVIA
Brno 129 Jihlava 137 Žďárské Vrchy 137 Znojmo 137 Moravský
kras 138 Podyjí 139 Strážnice 141 Buchlovice & Velehrad 142.
Gottwaldov (Zlín) 142 Northern Moravia 143 Bílé Karpaty 115

WEST SLOVAKIA
Bratislava 145 Bratislava to Žilina 159

MOUNTAIN REGIONS OF SLOVAKIA
Malá Fatra 161 Čičmany 166 Vélká Fatra 167 Orava including
Chočské Vrchy & Západné Tatry 167 Nízke Tatry 171. Vysoké
Tatry 179 Muránska Planina 191

EAST SLOVAKIA
Slovenský Raj 193. Levoča 198 Spišské-Podhradie 199 Prešov
200 Slovenský Kras 202 Košice 210 Zemplínská Širava & Vihorlatské vrchy 213. Kremenec & the Polish Border Area 215 The
Tokai Region 216

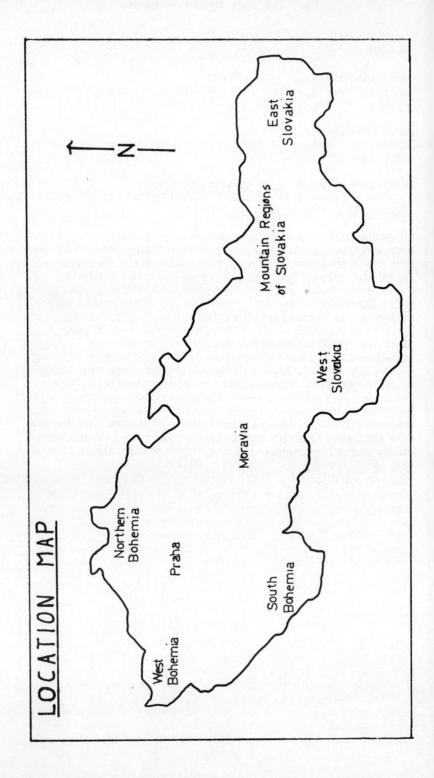

LOCATION MAP

West Bohemia

Northern Bohemia

Praha

Moravia

South Bohemia

West Slovakia

Mountain Regions of Slovakia

East Slovakia

N

PART 1

INTRODUCTION

Czechoslovakia, lying in the heart of Europe, is a country with an immense variety to offer, but a country entirely neglected by most travellers. Most people never go there. Those who do always want to return.

Czechoslovakia is not only a treasure-trove of all the attractions Europe is famous for (cathedrals, castles, and beautiful old buildings, to name but a few), but it also has something sadly lacking in many countries of Europe: fantastic natural scenery. In fact, as the Czechoslovak tourist authorities like to boast, Czechoslovakia has everything except the sea!

I have tried to give specific information and not just the general glossy descriptions you find in travel brochures. This sort of information can of course change over time, so please write and tell me if you have further information or suggestions. Write to: Simon Hayman, c/o Bradt Publications. Prices in Czechoslovakia don't tend to go up very often, but when they do, they go up with a bang! So remember to allow for possible increases.

BASIC FACTS
Czechoslovakia is situated in the centre of Europe, a long narrow country made up of Bohemia, Moravia and Slovakia, about 800 km from west to east. Its population of 15 million live in an area of 128,000 sq. km. Since 1969 Czechoslovakia has been a federal state of two republics, the Czech republic (Bohemia and Moravia), and the Slovak republic. The capital city is Prague.

Time: CET. One hour ahead of Greenwich Mean Time. i.e. the same as most of western Europe. Summer time from April 1 to September 30.

HISTORY
There is archaeological evidence of habitation of Czechoslovakia from prehistoric times. Later, the Celts inhabited the land. One of the Celtic tribes, the Boi, gave that part of Czechoslovakia known as Bohemia its name. The Celts were driven out by Germanic tribes towards the end of the 4th century A.D.

The first Slavs, the predecessors of the present population of Czechoslovakia, arrived in the 5th century. By the 9th century, the Slav tribes had united to form the Great Moravian Empire, which included Bohemia, Moravia, Slovakia and part of Austria. In 863 A.D. two Greek monks, Cyril and Method (Metoďej) brought Christianity to Moravia. They created the Slav alphabet, and translated the bible and Christian literature into Slav.

In 929 the first of the Přemysl princes, Václav 1 (920 - 929), was murdered by his brother. He became the patron saint of the Czechs, and is the 'King Wenceslas' of the carol we know so well.

In the beginning of the 10th century the Magyars invaded Slovakia, putting an end to the Great Moravian Empire. Slovakia remained annexed to Hungary for the next thousand years.

In 995 the Czech lands were united under the rule of the Přemysl princes. In the 14th century, there remained no male Přemysl successor to the throne, and the female successor, Eliška Přemyslid, married John of Luxembourg who annexed the Czech lands to the German Empire. Their son, Charles (Karel) IV, became the Holy Roman Emperor, and so for a period, Prague became the capital of the empire. Charles has been remembered with a warm heart by the Czech people, as the father of their land. Many of the fine works in Prague date from his time, and it is said that he loved the Czech people and their language.

The 15th century saw the rise of the Hussite movement. Jan Huss was a clergyman who tried to reform the church and society. In 1415, with both the Roman Catholic Church and the Holy Roman Empire against him, he was burnt at the stake at Constance as a heretic. The Hussite movement lasted 20 years before it was finally crushed, and the Hussites were driven out to northern Europe.

The 16th century saw the beginning of a period of 400 years of Hapsburg rule over most of Central and South Europe. In 1618 the Czech nobility rebelled. This rebellion resulted in a crushing defeat for them at the Battle of White Mountain in 1620, and the loss of the Czech lords' independence. In 1621, 27 of the leaders of the rebellion were executed in the Old Town Square in Prague. The Hapsburgs forcibly re-Catholicized the land, and suppressed the Czech language and culture. Many left the country, including the famous Comenius (Jan Ámos Komenský, the great teacher). 1618 also marked the beginning of the Thirty Years War, which saw the Swedes in Bohemia before it finished in 1648.

1805 Napoleon defeated the Russian and Austrian armies in the Battle of Austerlitz (Slavkov). Frightened by the French Revolution, Kaiser Franz II suppressed all freedom movements and put all public life under police surveillance. In 1866 war between Austria and Prussia took place on Czech soil, with the Czechs fighting loyally on the Austrian side.

During the First World War, the Czech and Slovak peoples' sympathies were on the Allies' side. In London, Paris and Washington, Masaryk, Beneš and others worked hard for the Czechoslovak cause. On the 28th October, 1918, the Czechoslovak Republic was proclaimed. Masaryk became its first president until Beneš succeeded him in 1935. Czechoslovakia suffered during the depression, with many unemployed and poor.

Hitler stirred up trouble in the Sudetenland, and encouraged

Slovak separatism. In 1938 the British and French 'sold out' Czechoslovakia to the Nazis, by agreeing that the border regions of Czechoslovakia had to be ceded to Germany. Chamberlain said he had obtained 'Peace in our time'. In March 1939, Germany invaded. Bohemia and Moravia became a German 'protectorate', and Slovakia achieved a satellite sort of independence.

In 1942, the German 'Protector', Reinhard Heydrich, was assassinated by Czech patriots. The Nazis razed the Central Bohemian village of Lidice to the ground, and shot all its men, in reprisal. The only large scale armed resistance during the war was an uprising in Slovakia in 1944, which was brutally crushed by the Nazis. The backbone of the Slovak National Uprising, as it came to be known, was the communist resistance movement, and it was supported by the Soviet Union and the Allies .

On the 5th May, 1945, there was an uprising in Prague. A few days later the Red Army reached the city. The U.S. army had orders to stop at the demarcation line near Plzeň, according to the Yalta Agreement. During the war a government in exile was set up in London under Beneš. After the experience of 1938 there was not much trust of the West, and a treaty of friendship was signed with the Soviet Union in 1942. As part of this treaty, the Soviet Union agreed that its troops would not remain on Czechoslovak soil after the war.

A new government was formed at Košice in March 1945. Beneš was the head of a four party coalition until the Communists took over in 1948 during a Cabinet crisis. Beneš resigned and was succeeded by Gottwald. Then followed a Stalinization period, when many were imprisoned, including leading Slovak communists, who resented centralized Prague rule, and including the present President, Gustáv Husák. In 1960, Czechoslovakia was proclaimed a socialist republic.

In 1967 a liberalization process commenced. In 1968, Novotný was succeeded as party secretary by Alexander Dubček on January 4, and as president by Ludvik Svoboda on March 31. The period known as the 'Prague Spring' began, with an attempt to shape 'socialism with a human face', as it was called. Censorship was removed, and a lively public debate started. On the 21st August, 500,000 Warsaw Pact troops from the Soviet Union, Bulgaria, Poland, Hungary and East Germany entered Czechoslovakia, putting an end to the liberalization. They were met by non-violent resistance. The official explanation for the troops was that the country was on the verge of a counter-revolution. The Czechoslovak government reintroduced censorship, and increased party and police control. During autumn the Warsaw Pact troops withdrew, with the exception of the Soviet army, which still remains in Czechoslovakia.

In 1969 Gustáv Husák became first secretary of the Czechoslovak Communist Party, and in 1975 he also became president, succeeding Ludvik Svoboda.

MINORITY GROUPS AND CHANGING BOUNDARIES
Historically Czechoslovakia is made up of Bohemia, Silesia, Moravia, Slovakia and Carpathia (Podkarpatská Rus).

A lot of the old Silesia is in Poland, the rest is now part of Moravia.

Moravia itself is normally lumped together with Bohemia, as part of the Czech speaking part of the country, (a fact that gets many Moravians' backs up!)

In the inter-war period Czechoslovakia bordered Romania. This eastern part of the country, 12,000 sq km with 725,000 inhabitants, was given to the Soviet Union after the war.

There is a Ukranian minority (Subcarpathian Ruthenians), particularly in East Slovakia. Slovaks sometimes complain that they are ruled by Ukranians, many of whom have government jobs.

The Spis region of Slovakia was devastated by the Tatars. The Hungarian rulers called new immigrants, mostly from Saxony, into the depopulated land. There was a large German minority living in the border regions of Bohemia. They were Hitler's pretext to enter Czechoslovakia. After the war about 3 million Germans were deported to Germany.

There is a large Hungarian minority (about 600,000) in Slovakia, especially in the south. During the Second World War part of Slovakia was handed over to Hungary, but returned to Slovakia after the war.

There is a gypsy minority of about 100.000 (nobody knows how many) in Slovakia. They managed to escape the Nazi gas chambers, because Germany only truly occupied Slovakia from October 1944 until January to April 1945.

There is also a Polish minority.

THE COUNTRY

Czechoslovakia offers a landscape varying from the Danube lowlands to the only alpine mountains between the Alps and the Caucasus, and almost everything you could think of in between.

It lies on the watershed between the Baltic, North and Black Seas. The main rivers are the Danube (Dunaj), Elbe (Labe) and the Vltava (Moldau). Nearly 10 per cent of the country has some type of nature protection status.

One third of the country is covered in forests and mountains and lakes are everywhere. Many of the lakes, especially the larger ones were created as storage for hydro-electric power stations, or as fishing dams. They are open for recreational use. In the mountains are beautiful natural tarns.

There are still remnants of Europe's near extinct wildlife in Czechoslovakia, particularly in Slovakia, where 500 brown bears live in the mountains. Though your chances of seeing a bear may be rather slim, your chances of seeing wild deer in Slovakia are much better. There are also wild boar, wolves, lynx and foxes. Wildlife of a smaller kind in some areas at some times of the year, so insect repellant can be very useful!

There are fascinating limestone areas with caves open to the public, areas of sandstone carved into remarkable shapes by the elements, and even boiling mudpools and geysers.

Castle enthusiasts will be enthralled with Czechoslovakia, where there are several thousand castles and chateau, ranging from those which have been restored and are now interesting museums, to ruins atop deserted rocky outcrops in the forest.

   As well as the indescribable beauty of the heart of Prague, there are many well preserved historical towns, with their fascinating old buildings and narrow cobbled lanes.

   On the negative side, rapid industrialization has polluted air and water, and Czechoslovakia is suffering badly from the European-wide problem of acid rain. Firs are dying in all woods, but the problem is especially great in Bohemia. The Krušné Hory and Krkonoše are almost dead. As with other European countries, Czechoslovakia tends to blame its neighbours instead of getting to the root of the problem. The high sulphur content of the coal burned is one of the problems. Desulphurization is expensive. But today there does seem to be a growing awareness of the problem of pollution.

LIFE & PEOPLE

You meet people of all shades of political opinion, from ardent capitalist to ardent communist, and it can be very interesting talking with them. The people tend to think in economic rather than political terms when comparing east with west (e.g. how well off people are). If you speak only English, communication can be difficult, but it is worth making the effort. There is not the freedom of expression that we are used to, so don't expect that people will necessarily talk openly with you, especially in public places.

   Many Czechs have a rather rosy picture of the west, and do not realize that many of the problems they blame on 'the system' are also endemic in the west. But they also fear that American and Russian actions may lead to war, with Europe as the battlefield.

   If you come from some distant country (such as New Zealand where I come from), you may cause a minor sensation in places where people are not so used to seeing foreigners.

Work: There is no unemployment problem in Czechoslovakia. Everyone is guaranteed work. Both husband and wife usually work. In fact everyone, except students, must work: it is an offence not to. Czechoslovakia complains it does not have enough workers. Many of the Vietnamese you'll undoubtedly notice in the country are working there on temporary work permits. (They must promise that they will not marry a Czechoslovak.)

   Czechs and Slovaks normally get up very early in the morning to go to work. The working week is Monday to Friday, plus some Saturdays which are designated as working Saturdays. The working tempo tends to be slower than in the west. I have been told that in Czechoslovakia one *goes to work* from Monday to Friday (and some Saturdays), but one actually *works* at the weekend, when people are busy with private work. I mentioned this to others, who remarked, 'How did you know our secret?'

   If someone has a foreigner visit them at work, they are supposed to write a report on the visit. So many people prefer that you don't visit them at work.

Births: There is both social and governmental pressure to have children. The birth rate is high by European standards. In 1977 it was 18.7, as compared with 11.8 in Great Britain. However, contraception is available and it has recently become easier to obtain an abortion.

Housing: Flats are rented from the State or are collectively owned. Rent is low by western standards. Some of the newer complexes are rather frightful. Privately purchased houses are relatively very expensive, even those built by the owner.

Travel: Czechoslovaks may not travel freely to the west. One of the easiest countries for them to travel to is East Germany. For a seaside holiday it is popular to go to Bulgaria. They are subject to some of the same restrictions as western travellers if they wish to travel to the Soviet Union, but do not need a visa. In theory they may travel to the west once in 3 years, but the practice is more restrictive, with travel to the west restricted for both political and economic reasons. Czechoslovakia has limited convertible currency reserves and it is difficult to get permission to purchase foreign currency.

Religion: Religion is frowned upon by communist ideology, but freedom of religion is guaranteed by the Czechoslovak constitution. The Roman Catholic church is the largest of the different sects. The proportion of the population that are Christian varies from one part of the country to another. There is some discrimination against Christians, for example when it comes to allotting places in educational institutions. From a tourists' point of view, many churches are only open for mass.

Compulsory Military Training: Normally every male must undergo compulsory military training for a period of 2 years. For students the period is 1 year, with a half day a week of their studies as army day.

THE ARTS

Some of the famous names in Czech literature are Karel Čapek (1890-1938), through whom the Czech word robot became internationalized, Jaroslav Hašek (1883-1923), who wrote *The Good Soldier Schweik* and Franz Kafka (1883-1924), who lived in Prague but wrote in German. Slovakia didn't get its own written language until the middle of the 19th century and its writers are not well known outside the country.

The most famous Czech composers are Janáček, Martinů, Friml, Smetana and Dvořák. Bedřich Smetana (1824-1904) is especially well known for his work 'Má vlast' (My Fatherland), which includes the movement 'Vltava' (Moldau), which follows the river Vltava on its course across Bohemia. Antonín Dvořak (1841-1904) is best known for his Symphony from the New World.

An international film festival is held in Karlovy Vary every second year. The most famous Czech film director today is probably Miloš Forman.

The wonders of Czechoslovak architecture of earlier centuries are around you all the time. In the interwar period there was a progressive school in Germany. Many of the members were Jews, so they came to Bohemia to avoid Hitler, helping to create good architecture in this period. After the Second World War art suffered under 'socialist realism' and architecture tends to be either very drab and functional, or designed as showpieces.

FALSE MYTHS

Some people have rather weird illusions about Czechoslovakia because it has a communist government. There are no Russian spies following you around and you are free to travel as you wish. You may find the propoganda placards and banners everywhere rather irritating. But generally it is a pleasant country to travel in.

Another myth is about shortages and queues. Consumer goods are not nearly as available as in western Europe, but most of what you will need you can easily buy.

Prague - cobbled street in castle area

RED TAPE

VISAS

A visa is required to enter Czechoslovakia. These cannot be obtained at the border, and must be obtained in advance from a Czechoslovak embassy or consulate. Although this might sound inconvenient, visas are normally issued very quickly—in my experience between 15 and 45 minutes if you go to the embassy yourself. You can also apply by post, but in this case allow a few weeks. You'll need a passport which is valid for at least 3 months after the date you will enter Czechoslovakia, visa application forms, 2 passport photos (machine ones are OK but make sure it is a current likeness.), and about £14 (depending on what passport you carry) for the visa fee. If applying by post, enclose a stamped addressed reply envelope. You must enter Czechoslovakia within three months of the visa's issue date. Children under 15 who are included in their parent's passport don't need to apply for a visa. A double entry visa costs twice as much as a single entry.

The visa application form has 4 sides you must fill in. The first is in English, the others in Czech, but the questions are identical, so if there is no carbon paper, and you can't read Czech, just copy what you wrote on the first side. As far as the spaces 'Address in ČSSR (Town and street)' and 'Name of visited person—institution/hotel in ČSSR' are concerned, and you don't know where you'll be staying, you can write something like 'Prague' and 'camping'.

Unlike most countries, which give you a set duration such as one or three months for a tourist visa, Czechoslovakia gives you exactly what you ask for on the visa form. If you know how long you'll be, this is no problem. If you haven't planned how long you'll be, this is a bit of a problem. When you enter Czechoslovakia, you must change a set amount of money for each day of your visa (see 'Money'). But you can change for fewer days, and have your visa shortened accordingly. So my advice is, ask for the longest likely period you might be there. If you still don't know how long you'll be there when you arrive, change money for the shortest likely time, and apply for a visa extension if you decide to stay longer (on my last visit I did this 3 times!). If, when you apply for your visa at the embassy, you want more than one month, you'll probably be given only one month, and told you must apply for an extension of your visa once you are in Czechoslovakia.

Czechoslovak transit visas must also be applied for in advance. If you require a visa to your country of destination, get that first. With a transit visa you are supposed to travel by the shortest route to your destination. A single transit visa costs the same as a tourist visa. A double transit visa costs twice as much. A single transit visa is valid for 24 hours, and does not normally

give the right to sleep the night somewhere en route. If you wish
to spend a night, ask about this when you apply for your visa.
With a double transit visa, it is possible to sleep en route, but you
must change the compulsory minimum exchange.

Some of the Czechoslovak embassies and consulates where
you can apply for visas:

Australia	Consulate General of the Czechoslovak Socialist Republic, 169 Military Road, Dover Heights, Sydney, N.S.W.2030
Austria	Botschaft der Tschechoslowakischen Sozialistischen Republik, Penzinger Strasse 11-13, 1140, Wien
Belgium	Ambassade de la Républic Socialiste Tchécoslovaque, 152, Avenue A. Buyl, 1050 Bruxelles
Canada	Embassy of the Czechoslovak Socialist Republic, 50 Rideau Terrace, Ottawa, Ontario, K1M 2A1
Denmark	Embassy of the Czechoslovak Socialist Republic, Ryvangs Allé 14-16, 2100 Copenhagen O, (Tel. 01 29 16 64, open M-F 10-12)
Finland	Embassy of the Czechoslovak Socialist Republic, Armfeltintie 14, 00150 Helsinki 15,
France	Ambassade de la République Socialiste Tchécoslovaque, 15, Avenue Charles Floquet, 75 007 Paris
East Germany	Botschaft der Tschechoslowakischen Sozialistischen Republik, 108 Berlin, Otto Grotewohl Strasse 21
West Germany	Botschaft der Tschechoslowakischen Sozialistischen Republik, 5300 Bonn, Ferdinandstrasse 27
Greece	Czechoslovak Consulate, Rue Séféris 6, Palaio Psychico, Athénes; tel. 67 10 675.
Hungary	Ambassade de la Républic Socialiste Tchécoslovaque, Népstadion út. 22, Budapest XIV
India	Embassy of the Czechoslovak Socialist Republic, 50/M Niti Marg, Chanakyapuri, New Delhi-110021
Italy	Ambassade de la Républic Socialiste Tchécoslovaque, Via dei Colli della Farnesina, 144-Lotto VI. 00 194 Roma
Japan	Embassy of the Czechoslovak Socialist Republic, 16-14, Horoo 2-chome, Shibuya-ku, Tokyo 150
New Zealand	Embassy of the Czechoslovak Socialist Republic, 12 Anne Street, Wadestown, P.O. Box 2843, Wellington
Norway	Embassy of the Czechoslovak Socialist Republic, Thomas Heftyes Gate 32, Oslo 2,
Poland	Ambasada Czechoslowackiej Republiky Socjalistycznej, Koszykowa 18, Warszawa, Skr. poczt.00-555

UK   Embassy of the Czechoslovak Socialist Re-
                            public, 26, Kensington Palace Gardens, Lon-
                            don, W84OX (entrance from Bayswater
                            Road, open M-F 10am-1pm, with British
                            passport £14, NZ passport £5.90, normally
                            issued while you wait)
USA   Embassy of the Czechoslovak Socialist Re-
                            public, 3900 Linnean Ave N.W. Washington
                            D.C. 20008

Embassies are often open fairly limited hours only, usually in the
morning. If you apply for your visa in an eastern European country, you must pay the visa fee in western cash.

As well as receiving a stamp in your passport, you'll be given
some copies of the visa form to carry with you. You must produce
these when you leave the country, so don't lose them! While in
the country, you should keep your passport on you all the time.

Visa Extensions
It is normally possible to extend your visa. But it is not automatic,
and up to the discretion of the authorities. Some Čedok offices
will arrange a visa extension for you, or at least help you. Others
will not. In Prague or Bratislava it is possible to extend a visa so
that its total length is up to 180 days. In smaller towns, it may only
be possible to get 7 days. You can of course extend it again once
you come to Prague or Bratislava.

You extend your visa at a police station. The department you
need is called 'Pasové oddelení'. Here are the steps you need to
go through:
    1. Find out if the police will extend your visa for the time
    you require, and how much it will cost.
    2. Go to an exchange office and change your DM 30 per
    day for each day you wish to have your visa extended.
    3. Go to a 'tabák' ('tabak' in Slovak) and buy special
    stamps (not postage stamps) that you use to pay the visa
    extension fee with. (60 kcs for a shorter extension, 120 kcs
    for a longer one.) Sometimes you can buy these stamps at
    Čedok, or sometimes even from the police themselves.
    4. Return to the police and receive your visa extension.
The above performance can take some time. Both 'Pasové oddelení' and banks tend to be open fairly restricted hours, and you
may be kept waiting a long time by the police, particularly in
Prague.

Visas for Other Countries
British citizens don't require visas to cross any western European
countries. But if crossing East Germany, Poland or USSR as part
of your travels, you need a transit visa for these countries. If
visiting these countries, you need a tourist visa. Getting a tourist
visa to Poland is much the same as to Czechoslovakia. You may
be able to get a Polish visa the same day. Cost US$16. Compul-
sory minimum exchange US$15 a day, or US$7 for students. For
East Germany one must have booked accommodation in the
country before one can get a visa. If one has friends there, a
visitor's visa takes about 2 months to arrange. For USSR you must

have the complete trip booked (that is transport, hotels, etc). If in
Prague, first go to Čedok , and ask them to make arrangements
for your trip through Intourist in Moscow. This step takes 10 days.
Only after this can you apply for your visa, which takes 7 working
days. So it is best to apply before you leave home.

**Foreign Embassies in Czechoslovakia you may need for visa
applications**

East Germany, 125 39 Praha 1, Gottwaldovo nábř. 32; tel. 29 26
26.

Hungary, 125 37 Praha 6, Mičurinova 1; tel. 36 50 41.

Polish Konsulat, Václavské nám. 49, Praha. TEL : 26 44 64. Open
8.30-12.30. Consulates also in Ostrava and Bratislava.

Soviet Konsulate, Korunovačni 34, Praha 6. TEL : 37 37 97. Open
Monday, Wednesday & Friday 9.30-13.00 only.

MONEY
Czechoslovak currency consists of crowns (kčs) and hellers (h).
There are 100 hellers to one crown. It is illegal to take Czechoslovak money into or out of the country, and even if you are a
professional smuggler, definitely not worth taking out of the country, where it is worth a fraction of what you would have paid for
it! There are no restrictions on the import or export of convertible
currency.
    A condition of a Czechoslovak tourist visa is that upon entry to
Czechoslovakia you must change a minimum amount of DM 30 (or
the equivalent in any convertible currency) per day to Czechoslovak currency. This amount must be spent in Czechoslovakia. You
cannot reconvert it. If you change more than this amount, it
should be possible to change any leftover money back to a
convertible currency. The compulsory exchange is reduced to DM
15 for children between 6 and 15 years old. The following people
are exempted from having to compulsorily exchange money:
    1. Those with a credit card accepted in Czechoslovakia.
    (On condition that you spend as much as you would have
    had to under the compulsory exchange rules.)
    2. Those with evidence that they have prepaid for services
    (e.g. hotels, package tours) to at least the value of the
    compulsory exchange.
    3. Those on work camps (see relevant section).
    4. Citizens of Finland and what Czechoslovakia calls the
    'Socialist' countries (mostly eastern Europe).
    The following credit cards are accepted in Czechoslovakia:
American Express, Diners Club, ACCESS, Master Card, Eurocard,
VISA, and Carte Blanche as well as Japanese credit cards. They
can be used: to pay Čedok; in more expensive hotels and restaurants; and in some speciality shops.
    At some border crossings there is no bank, which is rather a
ridiculous situation considering that one may not bring Czechoslo-

vak currency into the country, and one is supposed to change the compulsory amount upon entry. I had this experience when crossing from Poland to Czechoslovakia at Lysa Polna by bus. I had to change buses at the border, but as I could not bring Czechoslovak money with me, and there was no bank at the border, I could not pay for the ticket! (If travelling to Poland via this crossing , there is a Polish bank at the border). If you can't change money at the border, you are supposed to go to the nearest bank and do so.

All your official money exchanges will be noted on your visa form which you must not lose. Hotels and travel agents are also supposed to write what you spend on the back of your currency form, though in practice they only do so sometimes. You'll need your passport and this page of your visa every time you change money.

The following was valid at the time of writing, and is subject to currency fluctuations:

Currency Exchanging Compulsory Exchange

	per day	Exchange Rate
Deutschmark	DM 30	DM 1 = 4 kcs
Pound Sterling	£8	£1 = 16 kcs
U.S. Dollar	$11	$1 = 11.50 kcs
Australian Dollar	$16.50	$1 = 7.50 kcs
Danish Kroner	Dkr 113	Dkr 1 = 1.10 kcs
French Franc		ff 1 = 1.30 kcs
Swiss Franc		Sfr 1 = 5 kcs
Swedish Kroner		SEK 1 = 1.35 kcs
Belgian Franc		Bfr 1 = 0.20 kcs
Italian Lire		Itl 1 = 0.006 kcs
Canadian Dollar		C$ 1 = 7.90 kcs
Dutch Guilder		Nf 1 = 3.70 kcs

The official rate is higher for travellers cheques than for cash. But have some small denominations,because if the cheques don't add up to the exact amount you have to change, you can't get change in foreign currency. If changing cash—if you're insistent enough—it is possible to get change in foreign currency. The security of travellers' cheques is negated by the fact that you have to change your full compulsory minimum exchange to Czechoslovak currency when you enter the country and so are forced to carry it all around in cash.

What you receive for your money is the official exchange rate plus a 75 per cent tourist bonus (included in the above exchange rates). If you book through a Czechoslovak travel agent, and then change more money, you get an extra 36 per cent on the extra money you change. All this doesn't really mean much, as the crown is officially valued much higher than it is really worth in a free market. If a Czechoslovak wishes to purchase foreign money from a bank to travel abroad with, they must pay the official rate plus 297 per cent! All these different exchange rates, plus the huge difference between what you receive for your foreign money and what Czechoslovaks must pay to purchase it, makes any comparison over prices meaningless. I was once talking with another traveller who was saying how cheap hotels were. I didn't agree with her. Then we discovered that she was changing money on the black market, while I was changing officially.

For budget travellers, the problem is not whether to succumb to the temptation of the black market, but in having to compulsorily exchange more than one needs or wants to spend in the first place. If camping, and eating out reasonably cheaply, you'll find the DM30 per day too much. If you want comfortable hotels, you'll be using considerably more than the DM 30 per day.

If this amount is too much for your budget, try finding something to buy that you could sell later, or buy things that you need anyway in Czechoslovakia instead of at home. This is not as simple as it may sound because: there are a lot of restrictions on what one may take out; it is not easy to buy anything; many of the things worth selling must be paid for with foreign currency. You could also take the opportunity to replace worn out clothes, but don't expect the height of fashion, and don't expect it to be easy to find what you want. If you plan to visit Czechoslovakia again, and you haven't spent all your money, it is possible to deposit the surplus at a border exchange office on the way out. You receive a receipt and can claim this money back within 3 years. During the first year you can draw it out again at any border crossing point. During the next 2 years you can draw it from Živnostenská banka. Remember that at some border crossings there is no bank! When you return you must still exchange the full compulsory amount. The money you left there is not included in that amount.

If you want money transferred to Czechoslovakia, have it sent to Československa obchodní banka. There are branches in Prague, Plzeň, Brno and Bratislava, amongst other places. Have the sender give your name and passport number, and if you have one, your address. If given an address, the bank will contact you when the money arrives. If not, the bank will hold the money, and wait for you to call.

REGISTRATION

Upon arrival in Czechoslovakia you are obliged to register with the police within 48 hours. If you stay in a hotel, camping ground, or hostel this will be taken care of for you. But if you stay with friends or people you meet along the way, then you are supposed to go to the police and register yourself. If you are in this situation, first ask your hosts if they mind if you register at their address, because many people would rather you didn't. They fear harrassment from the authorities if they have a 'westerner' staying with them. In theory you should have stamps on your visa form to account for every night you were in Czechoslovakia. But in practice, particularly if you stay in many different places, your visa form becomes such a maze of stamps, that no-one checks it properly. Many places don't even bother to stamp it. So as long as you have some stamps on your visa form, it shouldn't matter if you are not registered for some periods along the way, if registering at that particular address becomes a problem for some reason.

If you need to do something official, such as extending your visa, you must be registered in the town you are doing it in. This can land you in a bureaucratic circle in the following situation: If you try and prolong your visa on the day it is due to run out in a town you have just arrived in, the police won't prolong it until you are registered, and the place you are staying in won't register you until you have prolonged your visa!

If you plan to be in Czechoslovakia for a longer time (2 months or more), it is a good idea to contact your own embassy. Some foreign embassies in Prague:

Austria: 125 43 Praha 5, Viktora Huga 10, tel. 5465 50
Belgium: 125 24 Praha 1, Valdštejnská 6, tel. 53 40 51
Canada: 125 33 Praha 6, Mickiewiczova 6, tel. 35 69 41
Denmark: 120 21 Praha 2, U Havlíčkových sadů 1, tel. 25 47 15
Finland: 125 01 Praha 2, Dřevná 2, tel. 20 55 41
France: 125 27 Praha 1, Velkopřevorské nám. 2, tel. 53 30 42
West Germany: 118 00 Praha 1, Vlašská 19, tel. 53 23 51
Great Britain: 125 50 Praha 1, Thunovská 14, tel. 53 33 47
India: 125 28 Praha 1, Valdštejnská 6, tel. 53 62 93
Italy: 125 31 Praha 1, Nerudova 20, tel. 53 26 46
Japan: 125 32 Praha 1, Maltézské nám. 6, tel. 53 57 51
Netherlands: 125 40 Praha 1, Maltézské nám. 1, tel. 53 13 78
Norway: 125 41 Praha 2, Žitná 2, tel. 29 88 56-58
Portugal: 160 00 Praha 6, Slunná 12, tel. 32 14 22
Spain: 160 00 Praha 6, Pevnostní 9, tel. 32 71 24
Sweden: 125 52 Praha 1, Úvoz 13, tel. 53 33 44
Switzerland: 160 00 Praha 6, Pevnostní 7, tel. 32 04 06
U.S.A.: 125 48 Praha 1, Tržiště 15, tel. 53 66 41

INSURANCE

If you want any type of travel insurance, you must organize it before you arrive. No insurance can be purchased in Czechoslovakia. The only exception is if you join a ski school. People on work camps are provided with insurance cover. British citizens have the right to free first aid treatment on production of their passport. Some other countries have agreements with Czechoslovakia, or have arrangements where they repay their citizens medical expenses abroad (e.g. Denmark).

Tišnov, Moravia. 13th century monastery church

BEFORE YOU TRAVEL

TOURISM IN CZECHOSLOVAKIA

Your fellow travellers will largely come from East Germany. Czechoslovakia is the only country East Germans can freely travel to, and the only country that they can travel to without a visa. East Germans have much the same reputation as West German tourists have in the rest of Europe. Western visitors come mostly from West Germany, followed by Austria. Many Germans come because they have relatives in Czechoslovakia. The language of tourism tends to be German, especially in the west of Czechoslovakia. But although this may occasionally lead to difficulties if you don't speak German, Czechoslovaks often become very interested when they find out that you are one of the few who are not German! English speaking tourists are uncommon outside Prague and Bratislava. Because East Germans are generally not allowed to travel to the west, they are often very keen to talk with westerners.

Czechoslovakia is very much a land of package tourism, but you can also plan your own travel.Instead of being treated like a 'tourist', you are then more likely to be treated like a real person by the people you come in contact with.

INFORMATION

Information in English is hard to come by in Czechoslovakia. If you require more information than given in this book I recommend you visit or write to an office of Čedok. Czechoslovakia has no real tourist offices as such, so Čedok, the only Czechoslovak travel agent with offices abroad, is the closest you can come to one.

Čedok Offices Abroad

Austria	Čedok, Tschechoslowakisches Reisebüro GmbH, Parkring 12, A-1010 Wien 1, tel. 520199, 524372
Belgium	Čedok, Tsjechoslowaakse dienst voor toerizme, Stromstraat 19, 1000 Bruxelles, tel. 5116870 Čedok, Office du Tourisme Tchécoslovaque, Rue d'Assaut 19, 1000 Bruxelles,
Denmark	Čedok, Tjekkoslovakisk Reisebureau, Vester Farimagsgade 6, 1606 København V, tel. 01120121
France	Čedok, Office Tchécoslovaque de Tourisme, 32 Avenue de l'Opéra, 75002 Paris 2, tel. 47428773, 47423845, 47421811
East Germany	Čedok, Tschechoslowakisches Verkehrsbüro, Strausberger Platz 8/9, 1017 Berlin-Friedrichshain, tel. 4394113, 4394135,

	4394157
West Germany	Čedok Reisen GmbH, Spezialbüro Für Reisen in die Tschechoslowakei, Kaiserstr. 54, 6000 Frankfurt am Main, tel. : 232975-7
Great Britain	Čedok London Ltd., Czechoslovak Travel Bureau, 17-18 Old Bond Street, London W1X 4RB, tel. (01)629 6058
Hungary	Čedok, Csehszlovák Utazási Iroda, Kossuth Lajos tér 18, 1055 Budapest, tel. : 128233, 119855
Italy	Čedok, Ufficio per il Turismo Cecoslovacco, Via Bissolati 33, 00187 Roma, tel. 462998, 4751522
Netherlands	Čedok, Tsjechoslowaaks Reisinformatiebureau, Leidsestraat 4, 1017 PA Amsterdam C, tel. (020)220101, (020)222788
Poland	Čedok, Czechoslowackie Biuro Podrózy, ul. Nowogrodzka 31, 00-511 Warszawa, tel. 267076, 217955
Rumania	Čedok, Oficiul de Turism Cehoslovac, Str. Visarion 9A, Bucuresti, tel. 596860
Sweden	Čedok, Tjeckoslovakiska Resebyrn Information, Sveavägen 9-11, 11157 Stockholm, tel. 207290, 210790
Switzerland	Čedok, Tschechoslowakisches Verkehrsbüro, Urania- Strasse 34/2, 8025 Zürich, tel. 2114245, 2114246
USA	Čedok, Czechoslovak Travel Bureau, 10 East 40th Street, New York N. Y. 10157, tel. 212/689-9720
USSR	Čedok, Čechoslovackoe Bjuro Putešestvij, 4. Tversko-jamskaja ul., 35/39, vchod 7, kv 136, 125047 Moskva, tel. 2588932
Yugoslavia	Čedok, Čehoslovačka putnička agencija, Strahinjića bana 51/111, 110 00 Beograd, tel. 629543, 628416

Once in Czechoslovakia you could try the following for information: the hotel, camping ground or wherever you are staying; Čedok or other travel agents such as Slovakoturist or Tatratour; the travel department (odbor cestouního ruchu) of the District National Committee (Okresní Národní Výbor or ONV for short). In some centres Čedok has an office specialising in dealing with foreigners, and usually one of the staff in each of these will be able to speak English. Čedok are usually open longer hours than the other travel agents, but are open shorter hours in winter than in summer.

A lot more information is available in German than in English.

Books *Czechoslovakia* by Ctibor Rybár, published by Olympia in Prague. The same book is available from Collets in London. An alphabetical listing of places in Czechoslovakia. Good for historical background and listing of attractions. But many of the places mentioned are closed to the public, and some information is out of date (info. dates from 1981).

Another locally published book on Czechoslovakia is sometimes available. It is organized according to routes, instead of being alphabetical.

Apart from books on Europe with a little section on Czechoslovakia, there is not much available on Czechoslovakia in English. There are some books available in German.

Turen gr til Tjekkoslovakiet by Milena Poulsen, published by Politikens Forlag. A small book written in Danish for those travelling around Czechoslovakia by car. (48 Dkr).

Legends of Old Bohemia, by Alois Jirasek (a famous historian), illustrations Jiří Trnka, translated by Edith Pargeter, Paul Hamlyn, London, 1963. Fascinating book, suitable for children.

For guides to particular areas or subjects, see under the relevant section in this book.

Maps

A free map of Czechoslovakia is available from Čedok. Much more detail can be found in *Auto Atlas ČSSR*, which can be bought in bookshops in Czechoslovakia for 29 kcs. Further detail still can be found in a new series of 17 maps called simply *Automapa* (Road Map) for 13.50 kcs each. Another edition of the same maps includes information about places on the map in various languages including English. This series is called *Poznáváme Československo* (Getting to Know Czechoslovakia), and costs 24 kcs per map. Both of these series were still under production at the time of writing, so only some of the maps are available (the ones marked in red on the back of the map folder).

For hiking maps see 'Tramping'.

SEASONS & WEATHER

Czechoslovakia has a climate midway between maritime and continental, with four distinct seasons. In the mountains it can be quite cold, even in summer. Southern Slovakia is the warmest part of the country, where the temperature is often above 25°C in summer. In winter the average temperature is about -5°C, but it can be in the -20's in the mountains. Autumn starts in late August. Early autumn can be beautiful, with still clear days, and the chance of an 'Indian summer'. Late autumn tends to be foggy and cold.

The mountains have more rain and snow than the rest of the country. Bohemian mountains have more rain than Slovakian ones, because they are further west and catch the fronts from the Atlantic. The Krkonose, for example, have about 200 days a year with precipitation. This means it is wet there in summer, but good for skiing in winter, because it gets snow earlier than other areas, and the snow stays longer than elsewhere. Spring comes later to the mountains than to the lower areas, and autumn starts earlier. The climate in Slovakia is more continental and 2000 m above sea level in Slovakia corresponds to 3000 m in the Alps.

But no matter what should happen the weather in Czechoslovakia is of course just as unpredictable as anywhere in the world!

If you are the sort of person that doesn't like to plan ahead too much, it is much easier to travel in Czechoslovakia in the summer, when the camping grounds are open and you don't have to worry about finding somewhere to sleep. From the last week of August you'll suddenly find yourself alone: the Czechoslovak holidays are over but there are disadvantages: to visit such attractions as castles and caves you must be guided around in a group and there may not be enough people to make up a group (can be easier at weekends); many buses to interesting places stop running; and there is no traffic left for hitch-hiking to out of the way places. Although cold, winter can be very beautiful, and opens possiblities for winter sports. But many interesting places to visit, e.g. nearly all castles, are closed in winter. Autumn can be a nice time of year to be in the mountains. Autumn is also the grape harvest season, when burčak (SI), young wine that is still fermenting, is available for a short period in wine producing areas such as Bratislava.

LUGGAGE

What you take and how you carry it depends a lot on how you plan to travel. Here are some hints:

Pack: If not travelling in your own car, a rucksack (pack) is the most convenient way to carry your things around. A daypack (smaller rucksack) is useful if you're planning hikes, or for carrying extra clothing, camera etc. It's possible to buy very light cheap daypacks that you can stuff into your rucksack when you're not using them.

Clothes: As a general rule, take just enough so you have something to change into while you wash what you are wearing. Remember that it can be cold in the mountains, even in summer, so be prepared. It can also be almost unbearably hot at times. Czechs and particularly Slovaks and more particularly East Slovaks tend to dress up and dress conservatively. But if you are living out of a pack, it is not very practical to dress according to local norms. If camping, showers are sometimes rather filthy, so take some footwear you can wear in them (e.g. 'flip-flops', 'jandals', 'thongs', plastic sandals).

Rainwear: Bring a parka from home. Good parkas are not available in Czechoslovakia.

Toilet gear: Take just what you need. Soap, toothpaste and shampoo is easily available.

Sleeping bag: If camping you will need a sleeping bag. In hostel style accommodation bedding is provided. When deciding what type of sleeping bag to take, remember that even in summer it can be quite cool in the mountain areas.

If Camping: In summer, smaller tents can be an advantage, as camping grounds can get very full. 'Camping gaz', the blue French gas cannisters, are not available in Czechoslovakia. Neither is meths. for cookers. White spirits, benzínový čistič škurn (SI), is available in drogéria, as is solid fuel, pevný lieh (SI).

Tramping gear: It's worth having boots if you plan to hike, especially in the High Tatras. If you don't have a pair, buy them well in advance so you have time to wear them in. Puttees (to keep stones, twigs etc out of your boots) are worth having in some areas. Take a light water bottle (can't be bought in Czechoslovakia). Same goes for climbing gear, if you have plans in this direction. Have a little first aid kit with you, especially something for blisters if you are not used to boots.

Other: Writing paper: if you have friends in faraway places, air mail paper may be difficult to buy in Czechoslovakia. Insect repellant: very handy in summer and purchasable in Czechoslovakia. If travelling on to Poland, take toilet paper with you from Czechoslovakia, as it is very difficult to buy in Poland. A good pocket knife (for example a Swiss army knife) obviate the need to take scissors, bottle opener, cork screw, table knife etc.

Theft
Theft on the whole is not too much of a problem in Czechoslovakia. But watch your possessions if you are out in the evening in a big city.

Left Luggage
There is normally a left luggage service at railway stations, and sometimes at bus stations. A big problem is the frequent weight limit of 15 kg if you are carrying a pack around with tent, sleeping bag etc. This rule was brought in because it was considered the maximum women working in these places should have to lift. You can explain that you will carry it in yourself in some places, but in others (e.g. Prague, Bratislava and Žilina) this won't help—it makes no difference if it is men or women working there! Another problem is that left luggage depots can be full (e.g. Bratislava in summer). If you can leave your luggage, it costs 1 kčs per day, and it is possible to leave it there for a long time. There are lockers in many places, but they are only large enough for smaller bags.

LANGUAGE
Czechoslovakia has two official languages, Czech, spoken in Bohemia and Moravia, and Slovak, spoken in Slovakia. They are both Slav languages, and Czechs and Slovaks can understand each other. Whether they are two seperate languages, or just dialects of one another is debatable. They probably grew apart from each other because the two parts of the country had different foreign rulers for such a long time, with the two dialects becoming two different languages. They have a similar relationship to each other as Norwegian, Swedish and Danish.

Hungarian is spoken in parts of southern Slovakia. Polish is spoken in Český Těšín and a small area around it.

As far as foreign languages are concerned, German is fairly widely understood in the western part of the country, but rather less so the farther east one goes. Russian is the main foreign language in the east, particularly in East Slovakia. Russian is becoming more commonly understood amongst young people throughout Czechoslovakia, because it is a compulsory subject in school. Neither English nor French are commonly understood, particularly in the east and away from the main centres. But don't let this put you off. With a bit of ingenuity and a phrasebook, you can get by. The advent of computers seems to be causing a slight comeback for English. You might find yourself talking with East German tourists a lot, as they are more likely to have learnt English in school than Czechoslovaks. A lot of Czechs speak German, and a lot of Germans speak English, so Germans can be useful interpreters!

Most English speaking people find Czech a very difficult language. One difficulty is the strings of consonants sometimes encountered. Once you can say the following tongue-twister, you can consider youself pretty good at Czech: 'Strc prst skrz krk', which means 'Thrust finger down throat'. And this doesn't even contain the hardest letter of all for English speakers to pronounce: 'ř', which is pronounced something like 'rzh'. Slovak is more mellow than Czech. Most of the Czech you pick up can be used in Slovakia, and vice versa. You'll quickly discover what is different.

If you can get hold of it (it is available in some bookstores in England at least), I recommend you buy a copy of the English-Czech phrase-book *Say it in Czech* by Alois Krušina, published in Prague by the State Pedagogical Publishing House, in 1963 (U.K. price: £2.50). It is written for English speaking people, and has a mass of useful phrases, and a detailed pronunciation section. There should also be a book called *Basic Slovak*, but I've never been able to find it. Try asking around in Bratislava if you are interested.

Czech-English and Slovak-English dictionaries are available in Czechoslovakia: *Anglicko-Český a Česko-Anglický Kapesní Slovník (English-Czech, Czech-English Pocket Dictionary)*, by Dr. Karel Hais, Statni pedagogické nakladatelství, Praha (i.e. the same publishers as *Say it in Czech*), 1974, kčs30. *Anglicko-Slovenský Slovensko-Anglický Vreckový Slovní (English-Slovak, Slovak-English Pocket Dictionary)* published in 1984 by Slovenské pedagogické nakladatelstvo, Bratislava, kčs26.

A comprehensive Czech/English, English/Czech dictionary has been published by Hippocrene (the US distributors of this book) and is available in England through Bradt Publications.

They are useful for translating signs, menus etc., and for looking up words when trying to communicate with people but some are not quite as pocket-size as their names would suggest.

It is useful to have a phrase-book before you arrive in Czechoslovakia, so you can begin to prepare, but you might as well wait till you get there to buy dictionaries—use them to soak up a bit of the money you had to exchange (see 'Money').

Slav languages bear no resemblance to English, though the odd borrowed word is recognizable for the English-speaker. There is at least one word that English has borrowed from Czech: 'robot'. It means to work, make or do. Karel Čapek first used the word in his writing, and English borrowed it from him.

Notes on the Czech alphabet:
   'č' comes after 'c'
   'ch' comes after 'h'
   'ř' comes after 'r'
   'š' comes after 's'
   'ž' comes after 'z'
The same holds true for Slovak, except that there is no 'ř' in Slovak.

Notes on pronounciation: 'c' = ts 'č' = ch 'š' = sh 'ř' = rzh 'r' is rolled

Some words and expressions

'Ahoj'	general informal greeting in both Czech and Slovak. Comes from English!
'Dobrý den'	'How do you do' - more formal greeting. Dobrý deň in Slovak.
'Dobrý večer'	Good evening
'Dobrou noc'	Good night (on going to bed)
'Sbohem'	Good-bye. 'Zbohom' in Slovak. Literally means 'go with God'. Not used so much now.
'Na shledanou'	'See you!' as in (the French) 'au revoir'. 'Do videnia' in Slovak.
'Ahoj'	Hello! (Pronounced like the English 'Ahoy')
'Ano'	yes
'Ne'	no
'Prosím'	please
'Děkuji'	thank you
'Mluvíte anglicky?'	Do you speak English?
'Pošta'	Post Office
'Hlavní pošta' (Cz) *'Hlavná' pošta' (Sl)*	Main Post Office
'Banka'	Bank
'Směnárna' (Cz) *'Zmenáren (Sl)*	Exchange (money)
'Potraviny	Grocers
'Knihy	Books
'Nemán' (Sl.)	I have not. Common response when you ask for something in a shop!
'Hranice'	Border. Beware when you see a sign with this on it. It may mean it is a border area you are not allowed to enter. 'Hranica' in Slovak.
'Máte tu volno'	(Cz), 'Máte tu volné' (Sl) What you say if you want to ask if a seat is free in a bus, train or restaurant. It is normal practice to ask before you sit down in such situations in Czechoslovakia.
'Pitná voda'	drinking water
'Nepitná voda'	non-drinking water

Numbers

1	jeden (ms.), jedna (fm.), jedno (nt.). (Czech has 3 genders.)
2	dva (ms.), dvě (fm., nt.)
3	tři (tri in Slovak)
4	čtyři (Sl. styri)
5	pět (Sl. päť)
6	šest
7	sedm
8	osm (Sl. osem)
9	devět (Sl. devät)
10	deset (Sl. desať)
20	dvacet (Sl. dvadsať)
100	sto

For food see 'Food & Drink' section. I have mentioned other words and phrases in relevant sections of the book. I have used anglicized names where these names are in common English usage (e.g. Czechoslovakia, Bohemia, Slovakia and Prague). Otherwise I have used the correct Czech or Slovak names.

SPECIAL INTERESTS

WORK CAMPS

Each year, mostly in July and August, International Work Camps are held in Czechoslovakia. Participants work as unpaid volunteers for 2 or 3 weeks, usually for 8 hours a day for a 5 day week. There are about 20 camps organized every year. The work is of various kinds, e.g. work in forests, gardens, and helping with construction projects.

The aim of the camps is to bring young people from different countries together to work on a project of benefit to the local community, and in so doing help shape understanding and friendship between people and nations.

The number of participants varies between 15 and 25, with a restriction that there should not be more than 3 of the same nationality. Applicants should be aged between 19 and 35. English tends to be the language used for communication.

Simple accommodation and food are provided. Lectures, discussions, outings and meetings are organized for evenings and weekends.

The work camps are organized by CKM, the Czechoslovak youth and students travel bureau. Their address is CKM, Žitná 12, 121 05 Praha 2. But it is not possible to apply directly through them. You must apply through organizations in your home country. Some of these organizations are:

U.K.: International Voluntary Service, 53 Regent Road, Leicester.

U.S.A.: CIEE, 205 East 42nd Street, New York 10017.

Canada: CBIE, 141 Laurier Av. West, Suite 809, Ottawa, Ontario K1P 5JJ.

West Germany: SCI, Blücherstrasse 14, Bonn.

Denmark: Mellemfolkeligt Samvirke, Afdeling for International Ungdomsudveksling, Borgergade 14, 1300 Kobenhavn K, TEL : 01 32 62 44 (they charge a high administration fee).

New Zealand & Australia: apply through the Youth Hostel Association.

One should apply about April or May. For citizens of some countries it may be difficult to get a place (e.g. UK), while for others it isn't difficult (e.g. Denmark).

Participants must obtain a Czechoslovak visa, but may stay on in Czechoslovakia for the rest of the month, and are exempted from the compulsory exchange requirements.

TRAMPING

I am using the word 'tramping' in its New Zealand sense, not because I am a New Zealander, but because for some reason that I have not been able to discover, the word has the same meaning in New Zealand as it has in Czech! For those of you not familiar with the word, its meaning is similar to 'rambling', 'hiking', 'trekking', 'back-packing', or 'bush-walking'. Some more New Zealand-Czech terminology!: A person who tramps is called a 'tramper' (tramp in Czech). The actual trip is called a 'tramp' (same word in Czech). 'Tramping' is the activity. The verb is to 'go tramping' ('jít na tramp' in Czech).

Whatever you like to call tramping, Czechoslovakia is one of the best countries in Europe for it. The High Tatras are the highlight for many, with their highest peak towering 2655 metres above sea level. This alpine area is a national park. There are many other mountain areas, especially in Slovakia. There are also forests, areas with fantastic limestone and sandstone formations, or just pleasant walking through typical countryside.

Altogether there are about 40,000 km of marked paths, tracks and routes in Czechoslovakia. Unlike Britain, where public footpaths have a habit of disappearing in the middle of a farmer's field, or New Zealand where one needs to be an experienced route finder, tracks are (with occasional exceptions) easy to follow in Czechoslovakia. They are marked for ordinary people, by volunteers from sports clubs. The track markers are normally repainted every 3 years, or every 2 years in the mountains. This tradition of track marking goes back 80 years.

The tracks are marked in the same way throughout the country, by coloured markers on trees, walls, rocks, fences etc. The colour of the markers corresponds to the colour the track is marked on maps. Principal routes are marked in red. Others in blue, green, and the least important in yellow. The tracks are marked in 3 stripes, one the colour of the track, and a white stripe above and below it:

Some other markings you may come across are:

◪   local marking, e.g. a short round trip from a car park

◪   instructional tour

⊙   side track to water source

⚠   side track to summit or lookout point

🏰   side track to ruins or castle

◎   end of track

🏛   side track to interesting point

Good hiking maps (turistických máp) are sometimes available for some areas. They tend to be in bookshops for a few months, then disappear for a few years until the next edition is produced! So, if you see any for areas you expect to walk in, grab them! The keys are in several languages, but not always in English.

Symbols vary, but here is a guide to help you:

ϙ	viewpoint	♠	castle
🗲	ruins of castle	ᚼᛁ†	church, chapel, cross
⚄	monument	ᛩᛪ	obvious tree
	prehistoric		
◎	settlement	♯	site of fortress
	chalet with		hostel type
⌂	board	🏠	accommodation
⚲	spring	𝓛	sinkhole
⼂	gushing spring	⬭	chasm
ᛆ	cave		

There are a few long distance tracks with educational aims. For example the cesta Hrdinov SNP from Bratislava to Dukla. This is the track of the heroes of the Slovak National Uprising, and many people walk it on the anniversary of the uprising.

Long distance hikes are possible, whether or not you actually follow a track marked as a long distance track. There is a good enough network of marked routes to be able to plan your own trip, using camping grounds, hostels, or hotels to sleep in. In Slovakia there are plans to build huts which one can sleep in overnight along the way. These will be unmanned, and probably have matresses and somewhere to cook. The sites have been decided, and they should be built over the next few years.

Horska Sluzba is the mountain service for the whole of the country. It is a professional organization involved in rescue and research work.

It used to be permissable to camp out anywhere, but this is no longer permitted. People still do so, but discretely, so nobody sees! One can ask to camp on somebody's land, but in national parks, even this is forbidden. The mountain areas are generally small enough to allow you to use an official camp site as a base, and tramp on day trips. In national parks lighting fires is prohibited. Outside national parks, one may light fires if there is a place provided for that purpose. The water from mountain streams can be drunk (well, prior to Chernybol in any case!). On hot still summer days there is a strong likelihood that you will meet some of Czechoslovakia's insect life!

The most important word you need to learn for tramping in Czechoslovakia is 'Ahoj!', the commmon greeting. But when there are lots of tourists around people probably won't bother.

If you would like a tramping holiday planned for you, contact Sport-Turist, 33 Národní tř., Praha 1, (tel. 26 33 51-9 telex 122664). But they will only make arrangements for groups.

You won't find anything called Dubbin, but if you need to preserve and waterproof your boots, look for Elaskon in a plastic bottle for 4.50 kcs.

What to take?
I recommend boots, especially in the mountains.
Puttees (gaiters) are useful in some areas.
A day pack to carry things in.
Parka (remember the weather can change, and that although it may be bright and sunny in the mountains in the morning, it may snow later in the day).
Sweater
Waterbottle or thermos.
Your lunch.
Insect repellant.
Basic first aid.
Map.
Protection from the sun (hat, suncream, sunglasses).

CLIMBING

The Tatry are the best climbing area in Czechoslovakia. See 'Vysoké Tatry' section for more details. Other areas are used more for training. Good training areas are found near Bratislava, in the Slovensky Raj, and Malá Fatra. There is a guide book to smaller climbs in Slovakia, but it is available only in Slovak.

In Bohemia the climbing is in sandstone, e.g. in the Czech Paradise and České Švýcarsko (Bohemian Switzerland). Some of the climbs are very difficult.

Take your own climbing gear. It is difficult to get good gear locally. You can get ropes, karabiners and helmets, but the quality is not good.

Czechoslovak climbers have had expeditions to the Himalayas, as well as USA, Canada and South America.

CAVING

Czechoslovakia is a wonderland for caving. For the uninitiated there are many limestone caves open to the public with guided tours. These include Dobsinská Ladová Jaskyňa (Dobsiná Ice Cave) in East Slovakia, one of the most beautiful ice caves in Europe, and the Moravský Kras, north of Brno, where the attractions include a boat trip on the underground river Punkva. During the high season there are many tours, during the colder season you'll probably only be taken around if enough people turn up (try and latch on to a bus tour). In winter many caves are closed. In summer it is likely to be a lot colder underground than above ground, so take some warm clothes. Ice caves, obviously, are very cold!

If you wish to visit other caves you must be a member of a caving club, or conducting research and first need permission from the government centre for nature conservation. In Slovakia the address is Ustredie Šttnej Ochrany Prírody, 1 mája 38, Liptovský-Mikuláš. There is another office for Bohemia and Moravia. There is also a Slovak Speleological Society.

If you are interested in learning more about caves and karst landscape, a good but technical book is 'Karst', by J. N. Jennings, 1971, published by Australian National University Press, Canberra.

SKIING

Downhill skiing facilities are not up to western European standards. There are long waits, and it is difficult to hire good quality gear. But cross country skiing is good in Czechoslovakia.

The main winter sports area is Vysoké Tatry (High Tatras) here the skiing season can last from December to May—but between January and April is the best time. There is one valley in the Vysoké Tatry where skiing is possible all year: Zmrzla dolina (Frozen Valley); and another where it is possible for 10 to 11 months of the year: Studena dolina. Other important centres are the Nízke Tatry (Low Tatras) and Malá Fatra (Little Fatras). Jasná, in the Nízke Tatry has hosted interna tional skiing championships. In fact there is skiing in all the Slovakian mountains, though not so much in west Slovakia. In Bohemia Krkonoše (Giant Mountains) have a long season because they receive more snow. They also receive many day and weekend trippers from Prague. A good langlauf area is the Orlické Hory, by the Polish border, not so far from Hradec-Králové. See under the section on the various areas for more information.

It may be possible to hire gear from some hotels in main skiing centres. Both Czechoslovak and imported gear is in use.

Skiing maps are available for some of the skiing areas.

Tatra poma lifts are made under licence to the French poma company.

It is wise to have insurance cover. This should be taken out at home be fore you leave. If you join a ski school, insurance is included.

BOATING

One of the lesser known attractions of Czechoslovakia is boating: everything from white water rivers to calm peaceful lakes.

Usually it is not possible to hire boats of any sort, but one may take boats over the border. If you don't have your own boat, the only other possiblities are to make a group arrangement through Slovakoturist, or if you are travelling independently, to ask at clubs if you could borrow or hire a boat. Slovakoturist's address is Volgogradská 1, 816 15 Bratislava (telex 92321). They can arrange (for groups only) yachting at Piešťany and Senec, and rowing at Nitra, Piešťany and Púchov.

Slovakia offers the best possibilities for kayaking. Some of the most attractive Slovak rivers are in the mountain regions. They are best in spring, when the snow melt raises their level. The following are especially suitable. See map for location.

Belá: Navigable only in spring and the beginning of summer, when snow and ice are thawing in the mountains. An exacting river, with plenty of rocks in the upper reaches, and gravel shoals in the lower reaches. In favourable conditions navigable for 22 km, from Podbanské to where it enters the Váh at Liptovský Hrádok. Fabulous mountain backdrop.

Čierny Váh (The Black Váh): Navigable when water level high from Biely potok foresters' lodge for 20 km to Králova Lehota where it joins the Biely Váh (the White Váh) to form the Váh,

Slovakia's longest river. The river flows through the forests of an almost uninhabited valley. Good camping spots.

Váh: Its upper mountain reaches extend from Králova Lehota for 120 km down to Žilina, but this is broken by hydro dams.

Hron: In its upper reaches from Pohorelá to Brezno (about 35 km), the Hron is fast flowing over a gravelly river bed. Many possible camp sites.

Orava: Especially suitable for those with less experience. 60 km from the Orava dam to the Váh at Kralovany. As well as mountain scenery, the trip is interesting from a cultural and historical point of view. One passes below the fantastic Orava castle.

Poprad: Navigable from Poprad to the border with Poland (80 km). Best in April and May. A less well known river.

Dunajec: Really a Polish river, but it flows along the border for 16 km through a very interesting area. The international 'Pieniny slalom' is held here annually. Raft trips for tourists.

Hornád: One of the most beautiful and one of the fastest Slovak rivers. The most interesting stretch is the Hornád Break, starting from Hrabušice and ending 16 km downstream at Smižany. Here the river flows through a canyon only a few metres wide in places, with cliffs towering up to 150 m above the water. Best in April and May, or when flooded. Permission is needed. It is also possible to walk through here (see 'Slovensky Raj').

For non-mountain rivers try the lower reaches of the Hron, Váh or Hornád. Boating is also possible on the many dam lakes. Near Liptovský Mikuláš an artificial river has been created for kayaking. There is a windsurfing school at Liptovsk ý Mikuláš. This 7 day course can be booked through Slovakoturist, but you'll need a group of 30 in order to get an English-speaking instructor.

Then there is of course the Danube, but this is full of international shipping and not as nice a trip as it may sound. The Maly Dunaj (little Danube) is popular with people from Bratislava, because of its closeness to the city.

Outside Slovakia the Sázava is pleasant, because it is not as polluted as other rivers. It is not surrounded by factories, but has lots of castles etc along its banks. It runs from Moravia westwards to the Vltava.

Permission is not needed for kayaking, except in nature reserves (e.g. on the Hornád). Camping is only allowed in special places. If a group wants to camp outside official camp sites, permission is needed from the authorities.

In 1956 watersportsmen from Bratislava arranged a joint Czechoslovak-Hungarian trip down the Danube from Bratislava to Budapest. This was the foundations for what today is called 'TID', the 'Tour International Danubien', which now begins in Ingolstadt in West Germany and finishes in Silistra in Bulgaria. The whole trip is 2082 km, but many choose only one part of it. The trip is organized in sections: Ingolstadt (West Germany) - Linz (Austria) -

Bratislava (Czechoslovakia) - Budapest (Hungary) - Belehrad (Yugoslavia) - Vidin (Bulgaria) - Silistra (Bulgaria). To participate, contact the club at the place you would like to begin from. For Linz - Bratislava contact Österreichischer Kanu-Verband, Bergasse 16, 1060 Wien. For Bratislava to Budapest contact SÚV ČSZTV Zväz turistiky, Vajnorská 100, 832 80 Bratislava.

TID is held in summer-early autumn. Most of the participating boats are canoes and kayaks. Typically there are about 300 entries per section. It is *not* a race. For many people it is not just the trip itself that attracts them, but the camping on the riverbanks, and the companionship of people from many countries. It's said that the language barrier has been overcome by a sort of Danubian Esperanto that has developed.

For those who cannot hope to get involved in anything as ambitious or adventurous as the above, there are chances in some places for tourist trips on rivers and lakes. In season there are boat trips on the Vltava from Prague. There are raft trips for tourists on the Dunajec, not very far from the High Tatras.

HUNTING (SHOOTING) & FISHING

HUNTING (SHOOTING)

Foreigners wishing to hunt in Czechoslovakia must arrange this in advance through Čedok (for Bohemia and Moravia) or Tatratour (for Slovakia). Conditions and prices are the same with both. Either of them can also make arrangements for the whole country. Čedok in London or New York can make arrangements, or write to: Čedok, Foreign Travel Division, Department VI - Hunting, Na Příkopě 18, 111 35 Praha 1 (phone 220921 telex 121109); Tatratour - hunting office, 821 08 Bratislava, Záhradnicka 34 (phone 641 46, 683 52, telex 92147 ttpol c).

The compulsory minimum exchange is increased to 350 kčs per day for visitors who wish to hunt, and this is to be spent on day to day expenses, and doesn't include the various fees for hunting. You are not obliged to change this money at the border if you show the voucher you receive from the agency you arrange the trip through. A licence and liability insurance are compulsory and cost DM 70 for a month, or DM 147 for a year. There is an organizational fee of DM 38 per day. One must be accompanied by a guide-interpreter appointed by the travel agency. 1000 shotgun cartridges and 20 rifle cartridges can be imported duty free. Shotgun cartridges cost DM 59 per 100, and rifle cartridges DM 2 each. Then there is a whole string of charges ranging from DM 11 for shooting a duck, to charges for shots that miss, to a DM 6,850 trophy fee for a brown bear! These charges must be paid after the hunt. A whole list of charges is available from Tatratour, but in simple terms, it is expensive and not for the average tourist.

Hunting in Czechoslovakia has a long tradition. There is planned breeding and protection of game, some of which has supplementary food provided during the winter months. In Slovakia only, there are about 26,000 red deer, 1,800 fallow deer, 67,000 roebuck, 3,000 moufflon, 15,000 wild boar, 500 brown bear, 180,000 pheasant, 160,000 hare, 30,000 wild duck, as well as wolf, lynx and fox. The intention is to keep numbers at the level they are today.

Hunting of a rather less bloodthirsty kind is also possible. Bear hunters in the Oravská Magura and Beskydy mountains may photograph the protected wood-cock and wood-grouse. In April and May photographing of the mating rituals of the bustard, the largest bird in Europe, can be arranged in the shooting grounds of Žitný ostrov (Wheat Island) and the West-Slovak Lowland. Accommodation is in mountain hotels or accommodation belonging to the forestry service.

FISHING

Fishermen must have a licence. For foreigners this is only available from main Čedok offices, and must be paid for in western currency. The cost for 1 day is DM 35, 1 week DM 55, 1 month DM 85, or 1 year DM 195. Fishermen are also obliged to exchange the higher compulsory minimum exchange of 350 kčs per day. You need to bring your own gear with you, or buy gear in Czechoslovakia. Čedok or Tatratour (see 'Hunting') will organize fishing trips. Fishermen can also use forestry accommodation.

There is a wide variety of fishing in Czechoslovakia, everything from the calm of dams and lakes to gushing mountain streams and rivers. Among the fish to be caught (with closed season in brackets) are carp, tench, bream, chub, barbel (1/1-30/ 6), roach, nose-fish, pike (1/1-30/6), perch, sheetfish (1/1-30/4), eel, trout (1/9-15/4), rainbow trout (1/12-15/4), grayling (1/12-31/5), Danube salmon (rare, and suffering from pollution, 1/12-30/9) and even crayfish (1/10-30/4).

SPAS

Spa treatment used to be considered a luxury affordable only by the rich and famous. But in Czechoslovakia it has become a way of life for all the people. People recuperating from accidents or surgery are often given a stay in a spa, all expenses paid. This privilege has not been extended to foreigners, who must pay a price of between US$25 and $65 a day, depending on the standard of the accommodation. The price includes food, lodging and basic treatment. If sharing a double room it is a bit cheaper, and companions not undergoing treatment have a slightly cheaper price again. The normal length of stay is 3 weeks.

For information and bookings for spas in Bohemia and Moravia contact Balnea, Pařízská 11, 110 01 Praha 1 (tel. : 263 777, telex 0122215) and for Slovakia contact Slovakoterma, Radlinského 13, 88141 Bratislava 13 (tel.. : 572 85, telex 092238). Bookings may also be made through Cedok in your own country.

Many of the foreign visitors to spas are older people. Sixty per cent of patients come regularly. Foreigners usually ask for the older accommodation, which they find nicer and more homely. Most foreigners come from Germany and Austria, but there are also many Americans and Arabs.

There are many spas in Czechoslovakia. Some of the more famous are:

Františkovy Lázně : West Bohemia. Specialising in women's disorders. Dates back to 1707. Beautiful parks and gardens.

Karlovy Vary : West Bohemia. Founded in the 14th century. Its prominent quests have included Tsar Peter the Great, Beethoven, Chopin and Goethe. Specialising in disorders of the digestive system, metabolic disorders and disorders of the endocrine glands.

Mariánské Lázně : West Bohemia. Second largest spa in Czechoslovakia, built in Empire style and set in parks and woods. Specializes in diseases of the kidneys and urinary tract, metabolic disturbances, ailments of the skin and of the upper respiratory tract.

Nový Smokovec : High Tatras. Climatic spa. Non-specific disorders of the respiratory organs, etc.

Piešťany : Slovakia. In the warmest region of Czechoslovakia. Rheumatism, sciatica, gout, post injury conditions.

Štrbské Pleso : High Tatras. Climatic spa. Bronchial asthma and allergic colds.

Trenčianské Teplice : Slovakia. The springs were known to the Romans, but development was after 1800. Diseases of the motor organs, of the upper respiratory tract, rheumatism, post-injury conditions.

Whether you intend to have treatment or not, and whatever your views on spas are, these spas are worth a visit as tourist attractions, especially the three west Bohemian spas with their beautiful surroundings and old buildings.

FOLK TRADITION

Contrary to the tourist brochures you won't see people in traditional costumes wherever you turn, but in rural Slovakia, for example in the Spis region, you can see ladies wearing traditional wide skirts and headscarves. Folk costumes, dances and music are kept alive in annual festivals held in various parts of the country. Some of the better known festivals are at Domažlice in west Bohemia (mid August), Strážnice in south-west Moravia (June-July), Východná between the High & Low Tatras (1st weekend of July), and Terchová near Žilina (last weekend in June). In Gombasek (near Rožnava) there is a Hungarian folk festival about the last weekend in June, and in Svidník a festival of Ukranian workers about the 3rd or 4th weekend in June. Check the dates before turning up. Otherwise there are some shows arranged especially for tourists.

In some places, especially in south Moravia and in Slovakia, 'posviceni' (Cz) is celebrated. This is a festival something like 'fasnacht' in Switzerland. Its original intention was to chase the winter away and welcome the autumn. There is a parade, drinking, folk costumes are worn, and a pig is killed and roasted.

There are still villages where you can see traditional local architecture. In villages such as Ždiar in the High Tatras and Čičmany near Žilina the houses have beautifully painted exteriors.

St.John Baptist, Karlstejn Castle

ENTERING CZECHOSLOVAKIA

Czechoslovakia is easily accessible by air, rail and road. It is even possible to enter by boat on the Danube. The following is given as a guide, but bear in mind that things change, and fares tend to go up. If purchasing a ticket from Czechoslovakia to any other country, including east European countries, you must pay in western currency.

By Air
Czechoslovakia has its own national airline, ČSA, which has a network stretching west as far as North America and Cuba, and east as far as Indonesia. In some countries it is possible to buy very cheap ČSA tickets from travel agents (e.g. in Singapore). In others they are sold for full price only (e.g. Czechoslovakia itself).

From London (Heathrow) there is a direct flight to Prague with either British Airways or ČSA every day except Sunday. The flight takes about 2 hours. An ordinary one way fare costs £176, and the ticket is valid for one year. PEX (public excursion) fares are much cheaper:£161 return in the low season;£191 return from 1 July to 30 September. It is not necessary to purchase PEX tickets in advance, but availability is limited at some periods of the year. Full payment on booking is required, both dates must be booked, and reservations cannot be altered. No refund is possible. The period in Czechoslovakia must include at least one weekend, and must not be longer than 3 months. APEX fares are cheaper again. These cost from £119 to £145 return depending on the season. Available Wednesday & Thursday only. Must be purchased at least two weeks before departure, otherwise same restrictions as PEX fares. There are connections to other centres in Britain. London is one of the world's best cities to buy discounted air tickets, so you could try the back street travel agents.

From Copenhagen return air tickets are available from around Dkr 1600 and upwards (or for those under 26, Dkr 1200 and upwards).

From Oslo return tickets begin from about Nkr 1700.

An ordinary one way ticket from New York to Prague costs $793, and cheap returns range from $749 to over $1000. This means that it is much cheaper to take advantage of one of the cheap deals to London or another European city, and continue to Czechoslovakia from there.

From Montreal to Prague one way costs C$990. A winter excursion fare is C$1356 return. Other special fares vary from C$800 to C$1000 return. It could well prove cheaper to go to New York and make use of the cheap flights from there to Europe (see above).

In Singapore cheap ČSA tickets can be bought at some travel agents. For example a ticket to London, with a stopover in Prague, so that you could travel around Czechoslovakia, then fly on to Britain afterwards, costs around S$700 at Airmaster, 36-G Prinsep St, Singapore 0718.

Flying from Prague to Berlin with ČSA costs DM159. It's best to book a week ahead, but there's a possiblity of getting a seat the day before.

Rail

Czechoslovakia is connected with the international European railway system. There are frequent trains on the route Berlin-Prague-Bratislava-Budapest, but there are also regular trains from western Europe (e.g. Paris—Frankfurt am Main—Prague). From Britain you can catch a train leaving Victoria Station in London at 13.10 daily (13.00 at weekends) and arrive in Prague at 1825 the next day, having changed trains in Stuttgart. From Prague taking the 2003 train brings one to Victoria at 1905 (19.25 at weekends) the next day, via a change in Nürnberg. The Channel crossing is Dover-Oostende. For fares and other times you could contact European Rail Passenger Office, Room E211, Departure Side Offices, Paddington Station, London, W2 1FT.

Interail, Eurorail and other European train passes are not valid in Czechoslovakia. Students travelling to Czechoslovakia from another east European country can get discounted tickets with an IUS card (the eastern European international student card). These cards can be bought on production of your ISIC at a student travel office. Discount varies between about 25 per cent and 50 per cent.

Although you often won't be told this, when buying rail tickets in Czechoslovakia you can pay as far as the border in Czechoslovak currency. When leaving Czechoslovakia it can be cheaper simply to buy a ticket as far as the border, paying in Czechoslovak crowns, and then buy a ticket for the rest of the trip from the conductor.

When buying international train tickets in Czechoslovakia, there are two different price structures, one for tickets to destinations in east European countries, and one for destinations in west European countries. It is much cheaper to buy a ticket to a destination in eastern Europe, and what's more, it is cheaper *per kilometre*. So if you are travelling to the west via another east European country, the answer is to buy 2 tickets. Buy a ticket to the point you will leave eastern Europe. Then buy a ticket from there or from the conductor to where you are actually going. If you are a student, this also means you can get a student price on the first ticket (there are no student prices to the west).

International train tickets sold in Czechoslovakia are valid for 2 months. This means that you can stop as often as you like between the station you bought the ticket from and your final destination, as long as you complete your journey within 2 months.

It is possible to send baggage ahead to the west, but it is very expensive.

Road

From Britain there are a multitude of possible routes to Czechoslovakia by road. One of the simplest routes to follow is via Belgium and West Germany: take the Dover-Oostende ferry (3 3/4 hours); then follow the E 5 to Nürnberg via Bruxelles, Köln and Frankfurt; from Nürnberg the E 12 leads directly to Prague via Plzeň. London to Prague is about 1300 km (about 800 miles) by road.

From Britain the only buses to Czechoslovakia are connected with tours. There are bus services to Czechoslovakia from neighbouring countries, but many don't run very frequently, and some are seasonal. Many of them run to spas or tourist resorts in Czechoslovakia.

From West Germany there is, for example, a München-Piešťany-Trenčianske Teplice service 3 times a week from March to the end of September.

Normally there are some bus services between Poland and Czechoslovakia, but because it is no longer possible for Czechoslovaks to travel as individuals to Poland, these seem to have been suspended. For example, from Zakopane to Poprad. If this bus is not running, it is possible to get a local bus to one side of the border, walk over, then continue in another local bus. If crossing from Poland, see 'Money'.

There are many bus services between Hungary and Slovakia. Bratislava to Budapest costs between 79 kčs and 117 kčs depending on the route. In summer there are buses between Yugoslavia and Czechoslovakia.

There are various bus services between Vienna and Czechoslovakia. From Vienna to Bratislava there is a bus at 8 am and 5 pm every day for OS74. From Bratislava to Vienna the bus leaves at 7 am and 5.30 pm and costs 50 kčs. Travelling time about 2 hours. Between Vienna and Brno via Mikulov takes 3 hours, costs OS160, and is run by ČSAD and Post-u. Telegraphendirektion, Wien. ČSAD also run a service from Vienna to Piešťany (OS200) and Trenčianske Teplice (OS260) every Sunday at 15.00.

Hitch-hiking over the border is not all that easy. If hitch-hiking out of the country, make sure you don't get stuck and finish up overstaying your visa. People do try hitching the relative short hop between Vienna and Bratislava, but even that is not very easy. Even being an 'E' road or a thick line on the map won't necessarily guarantee you much traffic over the border. I've tried hitching in on the E 14 via Salzburg and Linz in Austria for example. It has less and less traffic as you near the border, and I eventually had to catch a bus to the border post at Wullowitz, to be greeted by Austrian customs officials: 'Who'd want to come all the way from New Zealand to *walk* into Czechoslovakia at a God forsaken place like this?'. Then a long walk over no man's land, past beautiful raspberries which I was too afraid to pick because I was being watched by border guards, to the Czechoslovak control. This is one possibility on this route. Otherwise catch the train before the railway and the road part company.

Boat
In summer there is a boat service between Budapest and Bratislava on the Danube. It takes about 3 1/2 hours downstream (towards Budapest) and 4 1/2 hour upstream. There is also a boat between Vienna and Bratislava, but Čedok in Vienna book it up with package tours, so the only way you can get on it as an individual is to ask the captain if he can take you when the boat is in port. It leaves Bratislava at 5 pm daily. Its not as nice a trip as it may sound, as it's a fast, closed-in boat.

Tours
Čedok has a wide range of tours by air and bus, and for those travelling in their own car. Sample tours offered by Čedok London: 2 weeks grand tour by air, coach, about 400; Prague & Karlovy Vary, 1 week, about 300; Prague & Slovakia 1 week by air, about 300; all with hotel & half board. Čedok also arrange more specialised tours, e.g. for those interested in music, castles or skiing. (See 'Information' for Čedok's addresses.)

Other companies who have tours from Britain are Cotsworld Travel (coach tour to Prague, 2 nights), Explore Worldwide (Prague & Tatras, 2 weeks), Fairways & Swinford (High Tatras, 2 weeks in hotel, botany & geology orientated, by air), Page and Moy (Prague, air), Peltours (hotel, Prague), Prospect Art Tours (Prague, air), Ramblers Holidays (1 week Prague, hotel, air), Schools Abroad (1 week skiing), Success Tours (Karlovy Vary, coach), Thomas Cook, Travelscene (Prague, air), Sovereign (British Airways) Holidays (Prague).

Other Czechoslovak travel agents are not very interested in dealing with individuals. Rekrea (Czech) and Tatratour (Slovak, and the second largest travel agent in ČSSR) are cooperatives, and deal mostly with hotels in the middle price bracket, while Čedok deal more with the higher price bracket. Sporturist (Czech) and Slovakoturist (Slovak) specialize in arranging tours for sports teams. They can organize training camps including matches with local teams if required. Sport-Turist's address is Národní 33, 112 93 Praha 1, ˙tel.   26 33 51, telex 122664. Slovakoturist's is Volgogradská 1, 816 15 Bratislava, telex 92321.

BORDER CROSSINGS
The following border crossings are open to foreigners. They are listed in clockwise order, starting from the meeting point of the West German, Austrian and Czechoslovak borders. The numbers refer to numbers on the map. The border crossings are often at small villages with names most people are unfamiliar with, so nearby larger towns or main centres are in brackets to help with orientation. These are the only crossing points open to foreign travellers. Other crossings are, for example, restricted to the use of Czechoslovaks and citizens of the neighbouring country in question, or open for freight only. All crossings are open 24 hours, unless mentioned otherwise.

Rail

With West Germany

1. Domažlice	Furth im Walde
2. Cheb	Schirnding (main line: Prague-Nürnberg)

With East Germany

3. Vojtanov	Bad Brambach
4. Děcín	Bad Schandau (main line: Prague-Berlin)
5. Hrádek nad Nisou	Zittau

With Poland

6. Lichkov	Miedzylesie
7. Petrovice u Karviné	Zebrzudowice (near Ostrava)
8. Plaveč	Muszyna

With USSR

9. Čierna nad Tisou	Čop

With Hungary

10. Slovenské Nové Mesto	Sátoraljaújhely
11. Čaňa	Hidasnémeti
12. Filakovo	Somosköújfalu
13. Štúrovo	Szob
14. Komárno	Komáron

With Austria

15. Devínska Nová Ves	Marchegg (Bratislava-Vienna)
16. Břeclav	Hohenau
17. České Velenice	Gmünd-Schiel
18. Horní Dvořiště	Summerau

Road

ČSSR control	Foreign Control	Road Number
With West Germany		
19. Strážný	Philippsreut (Passau)	4
20. Železné Ruda (Klatovy)	Bayerisch Eisenstein (München)	27
21. Folmava (Domažlice)	Furth im Walde-Schafberg	
22. Rozvadov (Plzeň, Prague)	Waidhaus (Nürnberg)	E 12
23. Pomezi nad Ohří (Cheb)	Schirnding	
With East Germany		
24. Vojtanov (Cheb)	Schönberg (Plauen)	
25. Cinovec (Teplice, Prague)	Zinnwald (Dresden, Berlin)	E 15

ČSSR control	Foreign Control	Road Number
26. Hrensko (Decín)	Schmilka (Dresden)	
27. Varnsdorf	Seifhennersdorf	

Poland

28. Harrachov(Prague)	Jakuszyce (Jelenia Góra)	E 14
29. Náchod (Prague)	Kudowa Slone (Wroclaw)	E 12
30. Bohumín (Ostrava)	Chalupki	58
31. Český Tešín (Brno)	Cieszyn (Kraków)	E 7
32. Trstená	Chyzne (Kraków)	59
33. Javorina (Poprad)	Lysa Polana (Zakopane)	67
34. Mnísek n.Popradom		
(Poprad)	Piwniczna (Nowy Sacz)	89
35. Vyšný Komárnik		
(Presov)	Barwinek	73

USSR

36. Vyžné Nemecké		
(Kosice)	Užgorod	E 85

(open April 1-Sept. 30: 8 am- 10 pm,
Oct. 1-March 31: 7 am-9 pm)

Hungary

37. Slovenské Nové		
Mesto	Sátoraljaújhely	
38. Hranicná pri		
Hornáde (Kosice)	Hidasnémeti (Miskolc)	68
39. Šiatorská		
Bukovinka	Somosköüjfalu	
40. Slovenské		
Darmoty	Balassagyarmat	
41. Šahy (Banská		
Bystrica)	Parassapuszta (Budapest)	
42. Komárno	Komárom	
43. Rusovce		
(Bratislava)	Rajka (Györ)	E 15

Austria

44. Bratislava-		
Petržalka	Berg (Vienna)	
45. Mikulov (Brno)	Drasenhofen (Vienna)	E 7
46. Hevlín	Laa an der Thaya	
47. Hate (Znojmo)	Klein Haugsdorf (Vienna)	E 84
48. Nová Bystrice		
(Jindrichův Hradec)	Grametten	

(Open April 1-Sept. 30: 7 am-11 pm
Oct. 1-March 31: 6 am-10 pm)

49. Halámky (Trebon)	Neu Nagelberg	
50. České Velenice	Gmünd-Schiel	

(Open April 1-Sept. 30: 9 am-12 am & 3 pm-7 pm
Oct. 1-March 31: 8 am-11 am & 2 pm-6 pm)

51. Dolní Dvořiště
(České Budějovice)   Wullowitz (Linz)   E 14
52. Studánkyu V.
Brodu (Vyšší Brod)   Weigetschlag (Leonfeldon)
         (Open April 1-Sept. 30: 7 am-11 pm
         Oct. 1-March 31: 8 am-8 pm)

It is possible to walk over a road crossing point, or to cross by
bicycle, except between Czechoslovakia and East Germany. It is
not permitted to enter East Germany by bicycle.

Czechoslovakia has two international airports, one in Prague
and one in Bratislava. There is also a customs post in Bratislava
for those entering Czechoslovakia by boat on the Danube.

Once inside Czechoslovakia it is best to keep away from
border areas, where you are likely to be treated with suspicion.
Near borders it is best not even to walk past no 'entry signs' on
roads.

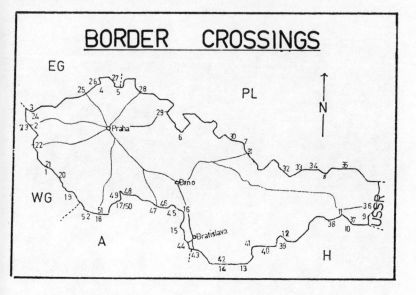

In the High Tatras

IN CZECHOSLOVAKIA

GETTING AROUND IN CZECHOSLOVAKIA

PUBLIC TRANSPORT
Czechoslovakia has a good, cheap, public transport network. The backbone is rail and bus, but there is also a domestic air service and the occasional ferry service.

Timetables are displayed at all bus stops and railway stations.It is possible to buy timetables if you want to lug them around with you. New timetables are usually issued annually, so it is possible that there have been changes but this book should be a good guide.

As a general rule trains are cheaper than buses. The exception can be with fast (rýchlik) trains, where you pay a set surcharge no matter what the distance. If your choice is between using these trains for a *short* distance or using a bus, the bus may well be cheaper.

It is normal practice to ask if a seat is free in a bus or train, before sitting down next to someone (*Máte tu volné?*).

By Train
Trains are operated by ČSD, the Czechoslovak state railways.
Train = *vlak*
Reservation = *místenka.*
Sleeper = *lúžko.*

There are ordinary trains (*osobní*) and fast trains (*rýchlik*). Another type of train that is not so common is *spešný*. These are trains to mountain areas which are faster than the normal trains. They miss some of the many stations found in these areas, and stop a shorter time at others.

Although Czechoslovakia is an 'east-west' country, the railways often tend to run in a north-south direction, reflecting the period of foreign rule during which they were built.

Train tickets are normally valid for one day. If the ticket is for more than 200km, it is valid for 3 days (the dated day is counted as the 1st day, and it is valid until midnight on the 3rd day). This means that you can stop along the way during this period of time.

Fares are very reasonable. There is a surcharge of 16 kčs for rýchlik, no matter what the distance, and of 10 kčs for spešný. First class fares are 50 per cent higher than second class. First class is not available on some trains, particularly small local ones. If you are a student, and are entering from another east European country, you can buy all your tickets there at student price. No student discount is available on domestic train tickets once you enter Czechoslovakia.

Tickets are normally bought at the station, but in the case of unmanned stations, you pay the conductor. Advance reservations are compulsory on some trains, optional on some, and not available on others. A reservation costs 4 kcs at a station, or 7 kcs at Čedok.

Sleepers are booked at Čedok, not at railway stations. They are only available on trains travelling over 300km. First class compartments cost 80 kcs per person and sleep 2, second class 50 kcs per person and sleep 3, and couchette compartments 30 kcs per person and sleep 5. If you haven't managed to get to Čedok to book a sleeper, you can try asking the staff in the sleeping cars if there is any space left, but don't be too hopeful.

By Bus
The bus service is operated by ČSAD. Bus services are generally good, but organized on a district basis, and services between districts may be sparse or non-existent, especially on country roads. For example if two neighbouring villages happen to lie in different districts, there may be no or only a very infrequent bus service between them.

Bus timetables are published in a series of books in the regions which own the buses. It is also possible to buy one book for all of the long-distance buses in Slovakia. Generally I don't feel they are worth buying and carrying around.

With buses in Czechoslovakia you cannot break your journey. Even if you have to change buses along the way, you need a new ticket.

Normally tickets are bought from the driver, but on some routes prior reservations are possible, and on some routes, particularly in peak periods, they are advisable.

Fares are calculated according to tariff zones, based on distance. You may get charged between 1 and 6 kcs extra for luggage, depending on the driver. In my experience this was the case only occasionally in Slovakia, but usually in Bohemia and Moravia.

Symbols
The following symbols are from bus timetables, and do sometimes vary. Sometimes the same symbols are used for trains.
Arrivals = Příjezd (Cz.) = Príchod (Sl.).
Departures = Odjezd (Cz.) = Odchod (Sl.)
'Workday' = Monday to Friday, and some Saturdays. 'Free time day' = Saturdays that are not working days.

(In Czechoslovakia some Saturdays are designated as working days, either for the whole country, or for a part of it. You can only find out which Saturdays are working days by asking locally.)

'Holiday' = Sundays and Public Holidays
'X' = workdays
'b' = workdays & free time
'g' = daily except free time

'a' = free time and holidays
'V' = work day before a free time day or holiday
'S' = free time
'✚' = holidays
'N' = holiday preceeding a workday
'P' = workday after holiday
'c' = schooldays
'w' = not July-August, nor Xmas-New Year period
'h' = school holidays
'y' = daily except workdays after holidays
'd' = daily except 'V'
'●' = priority to pupils
'r' = not 24/12 & 31/12
'k' = not Xmas & 30/3
'L' = summer
'Z' = winter
'A' = on work day before free time day or holiday, but not on working Saturdays
'1' = Monday; '2' = Tuesday;
'3' = Wednesday; '4' = Thursday;
'5' = Friday; '6' = Saturday;
'7' = Sunday
'R' = reservation possible
'l' instead of a time means the bus goes past that stop.
'⟨' means that the bus goes in another direction (it doesn't pass that stop).
◀ means that one can only get off at that stop.
▶ means getting on only.
'x' instead of a time means that the bus stops if signalled or requested.
'MHD' means that the stop is located in the area of mass urban transportation (i.e. local city buses etc)

Local Transport

Public transport in towns is provided by trams, buses, and in Prague the metro. Tickets normally cost 1 kčs, and cannot be purchased on the bus. They should be purchased beforehand at a PNS kiosk, and you punch them yourself as you enter the tram or bus. Once when I was checked, I was told I should have an extra ticket for my luggage. If you change you need a new ticket. Tickets from one town are only valid in that town. This is a fact that has been criticized for years, but nothing has been done about it.

By Air

Domestic air services are operated by ČSA. There are services to Prague, Bratislava, Piešťany Poprad, and Košice. Sample one way fares are: Prague-Bratislava 360 kčs; Prague-Poprad 480 kčs. Return tickets cost twice the one way fare. In winter there should not be much problem to get a seat, but in summer it's best to book 1 week in advance.

BY CAR

Red Tape

Before driving to Czechoslovakia check with your local automobile association for information. An international driving licence, an international technical certificate, and insurance are required. Insurance documents must be produced upon entry to Czechoslovakia. The licence plates of motor vehicles from the following countries are recognized as valid insurance documents along with the green card: Austria, Belgium, Denmark, Finland, West Germany, Ireland, Italy, Luxembourg, Liechtenstein, Netherlands, Norway, Sweden, Switzerland, the UK and Yugoslavia. If a driver cannot show he has 'green card' insurance for the time he will be in Czechoslovakia, he must purchase it from the folliowing address:

Česká Státní Pojišťovna (CSP), Dept Pojištění pro cizinu, Spálená 14-16 Praha 1. Tel:2148969. Approx cost 100 kčs. All damages inflicted to foreign drivers in car accidents must be notified to Kancelář zákonného pojištění motorových vozidel na území ČSSR, Praha 1, Spálená 14. Contact the same office if you require information on car insurance. No customs documents are necessary for taking a car in. International SOS cards are recognized.

Winter Driving 'Cars equipped with tyres with anti-skid spikes are not allowed to enter Czechoslovakia'. Normally all roads remain open in winter.

Road Rules   As in the rest of Europe, (apart from some strange islands out to the west!), one drives on the right-hand side in Czechoslovakia.

* Keep to the right, also on multi-lane roads, unless overtaking.
* Indicators must be used.
* Always have your driver's licence, passport and technical certificate with you when driving.
* Drink no alcoholic beverages containing more than 0.75 grams of alcohol per litre before and while driving.
* Safety belts in front seats must be used at all times, except in built-up areas.
* Lanes marked 'BUS' may not be entered, except to avoid an obstacle or to turn.
* At tram stops without a safety area, remain stationary behind the tram for as long as passengers are getting on and off.
* Speed Limits: Motorways 110 kph; normal maximum 90 kph; Built- up areas 60 kph from 5 am to 11 pm, 11 pm to 5 am 90 kph (motorbikes 80 kph).
* As well as at dusk and night, headlights must be used when visibility is reduced due to weather conditions. It is illegal to use only side lights.
* The most frequent offence committed by foreign drivers in Czechoslovakia is illegal stopping or standing. One must not stop in the following situations:

  where signs prohibit it
  before the top of gradients

within 5 metres of a pedestrian crossing
before intersections
before bus or tram stations without a safety zone
on bridges
within 15 metres of a level crossing
within 3.5 metres of tram rails (in this case you must not even
be temporarily stationary).

Fuel
Petrol costs about 10 kčs per litre. Foreigners can pay at the
pumps in Czechoslovak crowns, or buy petrol vouchers for foreign currency at Čedok (London), Živnostenská Bank in London,
certain automobile associations outside Czechoslovakia, at border crossings, most branches of Státní Banka Československá
(Czechoslovak State Bank), and some Tuzex shops. The vouchers
were supposed to be cheaper than paying in cash, but in 1985 the
price was about the same as the normal price for petrol. One is
not obliged to buy vouchers, but there have been cases of
foreigners being refused petrol if they don't have them. But diesel
fuel (called NAFTA) can be purchased only with special vouchers
obtained from any branch of Státní Banka Československá in
Czechoslovakia.
   Petrol stations are probably fewer and further between than
you are used to, and also open shorter hours than might be
expected. A list of them and the hours they are open is often
included on maps.

Breakdowns and Spare Parts
The emergency breakdown telephone number is 154 throughout
the country. On motorways only, this is a direct line. Autoturist
have a list of emergency breakdown service addresses in the
back of their magazine (if they haven't run out of them). The
European system of paying for emergency service with special
cheques operates, so you don't need to pay till you get home.
   Spare parts can be very difficult to obtain. They are sold by
Mototechna. As well as the Czechoslovak Škoda, Ford Escort
1300, Fiat 127, Fiat 125, Lada and Renault are sold in Czechoslovakia, so parts for these are sold. Other parts can be imported
if necessary, but it is a complicated procedure.

Rental Cars
There is a huge price difference between what a local pays for a
rental car and what a foreigner must pay, making renting a car in
Czechoslovakia an expensive proposition. Rental must be paid for
in hard currency or by credit card, which means it is over and
above the compulsory minimum exchange. There are connections
with western rental companies such as Avis, so it is possible to
drive their cars into Czechoslovakia and drop them off there
when you are finished. Note, however, that Hertz do not offer this
service. Cars may be rented from Pragocar in Prague, Brnocar in
Brno, and Čedok in Bratislava. (See Prague, Brno or Bratislava for
further details.) Reservations may be made through a travel agency, or through Hertz, Avis etc. throughout the world.

BY BICYCLE

Long distance cycling is not common in Czechoslovakia, but according to an experienced English cycling couple I met, Czechoslovakia is one of the best countries in Europe for cycling, because the scenery is so varied. There are hills, but according to them they are worth putting up with. If you plan a cycling and camping trip, your compulsory minimum exchange will be far more than you need.

HITCH-HIKING

Hitching in Czechoslovakia is rather erratic. I've found it good hitching in country areas in Slovakia, but I've heard of people taking 3 days to get from Prague to Bratislava! It is possibly easier to hitch on country roads than on highways, and it is definitely easier hitching into towns than out of them. Remember that public transport is cheap, and it's costing you £10 per day (the compulsory minimum exchange) just to be there anyway, so if the rides aren't forthcoming it could work out cheaper to catch a bus or train. It may be easier to get a ride if you hitch alone and with a small pack. Škodas, the all pervasive Czech car, are not all that big, and they are usually full! The working day begins very early in Czechoslovakia, so if you want to catch the morning traffic you need to be out on the road between 6 and 8 am.

The hitch-hiking sign is not a thumb, but a downward wave of the arm with your open hand facing the traffic.

Hitch-hiking is of course a good way to meet people. You are likely to get a rather better impression of the people than if the only people you meet are hotel employees etc. It's handy to have a phrase book and/or dictionary to try and communicate with—very few people speak English. From girls I have spoken with, hitching for women in Czechoslovakia doesn't carry nearly so much fear of danger as in many countries (e.g. West Germany). But as in most countries, there have been the odd case where a hitch-hiker has come to grief.

ACCOMMODATION

For every type of accommodation except YHA youth hostels there are two price categories: one for Czechoslovak citizens and the other for foreigners. Foreigners must pay the normal price plus a surcharge of between 100 and more normally 160 per cent! This brings prices up to west European levels. The surcharge can be a little less if the accommodation is booked from abroad. The prices in this book are what you pay if you haven't pre-paid from home.

Accommodation is cheaper in the less 'touristy' places. Be warned that there is often a whopping great (for foreigners) extra charge for using the shower or bath! In larger towns it is much cheaper to go to the railway station, where foreigners pay the same as Czechoslovaks. One will often have to pay for all the beds in a room or bungalow, or if camping the greatest price is for the tent, rather than the person, making it more expensive the fewer people there are.

Organized tourism is encouraged in Czechoslovakia and all types of accommodation are regularly booked up by groups or travel agents, making it difficult for individuals to get a bed. The worst time to get accommodation is during the Catholic holidays. Outside the peak season some establishments close and others in mountain areas are taken over by school groups escaping the pollution of Prague for a term. But I have always managed to come up with something in the end, even if it's a hotel receptionist moonlighting by illegally letting out rooms in her house. If you'd rather be sure, make prior reservations, or take a tent and camp.

Prior bookings can be made through Čedok (see 'Information' for addresses), a travel agent, or you can contact the establishment yourself. By telex it takes only a few hours to receive a confirmation. For summer and Christmas it is best to book 2 to 3 months in advance. It is easiest to book through Čedok. If you book and pay for hotels from abroad you are exempted from the compulsory minimum exchange of money at the border, but there may still be local tax to pay when you arrive. Once in Czechoslovakia you can also book through Čedok or other travel agencies although some may refuse to make bookings for individual foreigners.

Accommodation Guides

Various accommodation guides are available, but most of them are only in Czech or Slovak. If you have learnt a little of the language, and have a dictionary, it is possible to make some sense of some of these. But the prices are what Czechoslovaks pay, not what you pay!

Czechoslovakia Camping is one exception. It is a camping guidebook published in English, French and German in 1983 although it lists only motor camps, and not the cheaper but more primitive camp sites.

Auto Kempinky ČSSR is a camping map with some information on the back, also in English. Costs 8 kcs.

Autokempingy a verejné táboriská na Slovensku, by Vladimír Adamec, publ. Šport, Bratislava, 1983, is a complete camping guide to Slovakia, in Slovak only. 17 kcs.

Ubytování v ČSR, Olympia, Praha, 1985 is a guide to all accommodation in Bohemia and Moravia except camping. In Czech only. Price 26 kcs.

Ubytovanie na Slovensku, Šport, Bratislava, 1982. In Slovak only. A complete accommodation guide to Slovakia. Out of print at the time of writing.

Types of Accommodation

The tourist authorities will try and steer you into the more expensive hotels or motor camps. There are many other types of accommodation in Czechoslovakia, but you may have to go out and find them yourself.

Hotels
Hotels are categorized C, B, B*, A, A* or A* deluxe. You'll find the odd hotel classified under a star system in an attempt to be more international. The following prices are in kčs and are only a very rough guide.

Category	Star system	Single	Double
C	*	100	160
B	**	150	220
B*	***	170	260
A*	****	220	330
A* deluxe	*****	400	650

If a hotel costs more than the compulsory exchange, the rest must be paid in western currency at the normal exchange rate. You can pay in crowns if you can show that you have officially changed enough to cover it.

Motels
There are very few motels. Price similar to B* category hotels.

Botels
Boats moored on the Vltava in Prague used as hotels.

'Ubytovaci' hostinec' (UH)
An inn. A pub with a sleeping room. Often no bathroom. Just a place to sleep for the night. About 60 kčs.

'Turisticka' ubytovna (TU)'
Literally 'tourist accommodation'. These are hostels, with dormitories. They are the closest thing to a YHA hostel found in Czechoslovakia, though they have no connection with YHA, and tend to be a bit different from their hostels, in that there is little social interaction, being little more than just a place to sleep for the night. Normally somewhere to wash oneself, but rarely anywhere to cook. Come in two grades, depending on how many beds there are to a room. TU A about 50 kčs . TU B about 40 kčs. Often only open seasonally. There are also sometimes dormitories in hotels.

'Chatove' osady (CHO)'
Cabins, particularly found in Slovakia. One often must pay for all the beds in the cabin (typically 2 or 4 beds), making them less practical for those travelling alone. 3 grades: A* about 90 kčs per bed; A about 60 kčs per bed; and B about 45 kčs per bed.

'Horské hotely'
Mountain hotels.

'Horské chaty' (Cz), 'Turisticke' chaty' (Sl)
Mountain huts or chalets.

YHA Hostels
There are no real YHA hostels in Czechoslovakia in spite of the

fact that the International Youth Hostel Handbook lists about 2 pages of hostels in Czechoslovakia! CKM, the Czechoslovak youth and students' travel agent, have a special price of 27 kcs in their Junior Hotels for those who can show a YHA or MSS (the eastern European students association) card, both of which can be bought from CKM. Because a lot of people don't know what card is what, you may get away with using an ISIC (the western international student card). In the summer in the large cities CKM also take over student hostels and run them as summer youth hostels. (Non-YHA members pay about 70-80 kcs at these hostels.) This price of 27 kcs is not available for those who book from abroad. In this case the price leaps to £8-£9! CKM don't really cater for individuals, and although they will do their best to reply if you write to them, they may not have time in the busy season. Their address is: Klub mladých cestovatelů, CKM, Žitná ulice 12, 121 05 Praha 2 (tel. 294587, 299941-9, telex 122299CKMC).

The other 'hostels' listed in the handbook have probably never heard of the YHA, and won't know what to do with you if you turn up! These are political education centres, usually occupied by groups. If there is a group there, you may be able to stay there in exceptional circumstances. If there is a children's group there, you definitely won't be allowed to stay. If there is no group there, it will be closed! So, in theory YHA members can sleep there, but in practice they can't. If you really want to try, here is what you should do:

1. Go to CKM and reserve. But chances are CKM won't know anything about this arrangement, so tell them to phone Prague and speak to someone in their head office who does.
2. Register yourself with the police.
3. Go back to CKM and pay.
4. CKM give you a voucher, which you take with you to the 'hostel'.

'Autokempinky' (Motor Camps)
Come in 2 categories, A and B. Prices around 15 kcs to 30 kcs per tent, plus 8 kcs to 30 kcs per person, plus charges for vehicles, caravans etc. Often have some sort of food or drink to sell. No kitchens. Showers and toilets usually not terribly clean (though I noticed an improvement last time I was there), and often without hot water (whatever any camping guide you may have says to the contrary). Can be very sociable, and a good place to meet other travellers, with a couple of beers and a guitar, sitting around the campfires, which are a part of camping life in Czechoslovakia. Campfires are also the most common means of cooking. But beware if you have a nylon tent. People are not used to being too careful because a stray spark on the heavy canvas tents used in eastern Europe doesn't do much harm, but if it lands on your nylon tent it will! For details on fuel for cookers, see 'Luggage' section. Mostly open only for a short season, typically May to September.

Stanový tábor (Camping sites)

Just a site to camp, with toilets and water supply, and sometimes cold showers. Cheaper than motor camps. Often better value than autokempinky, especially the large Čedok ones. Otherwise the same as above. Many camp sites marked on maps no longer exist. You may be greeted instead with a 'No Camping' sign.

Private Accommodation

There is private accommodation available in Czechoslovakia, such as guest houses or people letting out rooms in their home, but westerners are not allowed to use it. The only exceptions are normally in large towns where there is a shortage of accommodation, but in this case one must book through Čedok (or Pragotour in Prague), and pay the usual inflated price for foreigners, putting the price up to around the same as a hotel room. In Prague, especially near Čedok's accommodation office, there are often people in the street offering private accommodation to foreigners.

Staying with friends or people you meet along the way is another story. This is fine, but you are supposed to go to the police and register if you do so. (See 'Registration'). When staying with people in this way, their hospitality can be embarrassingly overwhelming. The idea of 'crashing' with friends or people you meet along the way, and being left more or less to your own devices, is alien to most Czechoslovaks, except maybe students. But many people are very interested in meeting foreigners, helping them, and talking with them.

Postscript

After having to put up with unreliable information on accommodation while I have been in Czechoslovakia (e.g. going to a camping ground listed in the camping guide I had that didn't exist, going to a hotel listed as being open all year round, to find it is closed in winter), I have attempted to make the information in this book as reliable as possible. If anything has changed, please write and tell me.

NEWS

Foreign newspapers are not available in Czechoslovakia with the occasional exception of foreign communist party newspapers.

Radio Prague's Interprogram (on medium wave) has special programmes in English, German, French and Russian. There are news broadcasts in English at 8.45, 10.45 and 12.45 and 0.45. Concert of classical and pop music and review of cultural events on Sundays. Between midnight and 1.55 concerts of music by Czech, Slovak and world composers. Write to Interprogramme Radio Prague, Praha 2, Vinohradská 12, 120 99 Czechoslovakia for further details! It is often possible to receive foreign radio stations. I was told it is illegal to listen to 'Voice of America'.

MAIL, TELEPHONE, ETC

Mail can be sent to you c/o post offices. It should be addressed as follows: e.g.

your name,	Simon HAYMAN
'Poste Restante',	Poste Restante
post office	Hlavní posta
post code, town, post district	110 00 Praha 1
street & no.	Jindřišská 14

If you don't know the address, and want your mail to go to the main post office, write 'Posta 1' as the post office, and your mail should find you. In large towns you should have no problem, but in smaller towns you may have trouble making yourself understood when you ask for 'Poste Restante', because they don't pronounce it as in French. If you have trouble try pronouncing it as separate syllables 'Pos-te Re-stan-te'.

Some embassies may allow you to have you mail sent c/o them, but this can be less convenient than collecting mail from a post office.

In my experience letter post is fairly reliable, but sending packages is *not*. If sending something airmail, make sure it is obvious that it is airmail, and that you are sold the correct stamp for airmail—I have had postcards turning up on the other side of the world months after I have sent them! The post office by the railway station is the fastest place to send mail from (it's usually 'Posta 2').

Local telephone calls from public telephones cost 1 kčs. Calls to other countries are VERY EXPENSIVE. E.g. to Australia or New Zealand it costs 380 kčs for 3 minutes.

SHOPPING

Shopping hours: Variable, but on weekdays tend to open between 6 am and 9 am, and close at 6 pm. Small shops often closed for lunch. Some shops closed all or part of Monday. Saturday: food shops and most others open till noon, department stores open till 4 pm. Shops tend to close earlier than the specified time, or if they are still open you won't get any service in the last 1/2 hour to 1 hour because the people who work there are itching to get home! Everything is closed on Sundays and holidays.

Tuzex are a chain of shops which accept only foreign money or Tuzex vouchers. They sell export quality Czechoslovak goods and imported goods, not available from normal shops. Goods bought at Tuzex are not subject to duty.

Beautiful 'coffee table' style picture books of Czechoslovak scenery are available if you have the means to carry them. Avoid bookshops on Thursdays, which is the day new books come out, resulting in long queues. Other possiblities for shopping are Czech glass, porcelain, leather goods, embroidery, weaving, lace, classical records, the famous beers, slivovice (plum brandy), and Becher liqueur. But many of these can only be taken out of the country legally if they were bought at Tuzex. Good daypacks (rucksacks) made of canvas with leather straps are made in Czechoslovakia. Good boots are made in Czechoslovakia, but you may have trouble finding the right size. Many items purchased in Czechoslovakia, including sporting gear, but also much clothing, leather gear, antiques (which are cheap) etc, may only be taken out of the country if they are articles 'which were necessary for adequate satisfying of personal needs of the person exporting the articles in the course of the temporary stay of such a person in the Czechoslovak Socialist Republic or which are necessary for adequate satisfying of personal needs of that person during the trip from the the Czechoslovak Socialist Republic'. You should get a copy of the customs regulations if you want further information!

Chocolate is good. 'Hobby' is cooking chocolate, but it is cheaper and tastes okay. Western brands of cigarettes are available, but they are much more expensive than local ones.

In self service shops you often must have a basket to enter. If there are no baskets left you must queue. Supermarkets are not common.

PHOTOGRAPHY

Most of the film available is made in Czechoslovakia, East Germany or Soviet Union. Sometimes Agfa is available, or even Kodak. There shouldn't be any problem processing local black and white film in the west, but if buying colour make sure it can be processed in the west, as the processes used are different. East German slide film can be processed in western Europe at certain labs (see address list in film packet). To have a film processed in Czechoslovakia takes a very long time.

Don't photograph near the border, and be careful not to photograph anything which could be construed as a military target.

FOOD & DRINK

Eating out in Czechoslovakia can be cheap. Every eating and drinking establishment has a class (skupina) from I to IV. Cheapest are the class IVs, which are usually stand-up and self- service. Some class IVs are more like workers' cafetarias, with good cheap meals in the middle of the day. At class III you are more likely to be able to sit down and have service. Class II are more like a western restaurant, but the prices aren't so high. Class I are expensive. A lot of eateries are much of a muchness, so in many cases it is not worth mentioning specific places, other than those which are particularly good, or to show what is available.

Menus in restaurants usually spell out exactly what you are getting, the weight of the meat, and what accompanies it, rather than giving a name of a dish. This makes them more difficult for foreigners to read, simply because there is more to read.

Here is a little to help you. SI = Slovak, otherwise words are Czech. Some words are completely different, but usually if you know the word in one language you can recognize it in the other.

Jídelní lístek (Cz)	the menu
Jedálny lístok (SI)	
šunku s vejci	bacon and eggs
čaj	tea (pronounced as the Indian word!)

káva	coffee (*káva turecka* is Turkish coffee, with the grounds in the cup)
chléb (Cz), *chlieb (Sl)*	bread
máslo	butter
džem	jam
polévky	soup
maso	meat
hovězí	beef
roštěnka	roast beef
svíčková	sirloin of beef
pečené	roast veal
vepřové maso (Cz), *bračové mäso (Sl)*	pork
vepřová pečené	roast pork
žebírko	rib
dušené	stewed
pečené	roast
smažené	fried
vařené (Cz), *varené (Sl)*	boiled
kachna	duck
kuře	chicken
slepice	fowl
ryby	fish
omeleta	omelette
zelenina	vegetables
brambory (Cz), *zemiak (Sl)*	potatoes
okurka	cucumber
rajská jablíčka	tomatoes
zelí	sauerkraut
knedlík	dumpling
palačinky	pancakes
zmrzlina	ice-cream
ovoce	fruit
kompot	stewed fruit
nápoje	drinks
limonáda	soda water (flavoured)
pivo	beer
víno	wine
víno bílé	white wine
víno červené	red wine
studený	cold
horký	hot

A typical meal when eating out is soup followed by pork with dumpling and sauerkraut, and accompanied by beer. Another common dish is segedinský guláš, pork stew with sauerkraut (from Hungary). What one can buy when eating out is not always a good reflection of what people eat in their homes. *Bryndzové halušky*, sheep's cheese with pasta, is a national Slovak dish. Note that everything is measured by weight. Sausages may cost

'x' kčs per 100gm, but one sausage may weigh 200gm. Geese are
raised everywhere, but you won't find them on many menus. They
are fed 'šišky' to enlarge their livers prior to killing them. In
season (around August-September) piping hot fresh corn on the
cob is available, often in the street. Cakes and sweets look more
tempting than they taste, but the ice-cream (zmrzlina) is delicious,
at around 2 kčs a cone. Occasionally dumplings filled with plums
are available (*slivokové knedle* in Slovak).

Czechoslovakia produces some of the best beer in the world,
at prices one can afford. The original Pilsener beer comes from
Plzeň, and the original Budvar (Budweiser) from České
Budějovice. The most famous Slovak beer is Zlatý Bažant (Golden
Pheasant) from the little village of Hurbanovo. Beer comes in 2
strengths. A few years ago beer prices shot up. Schweik once
said that the government which puts up beer prices must fall!

Wine is also produced locally, especially in Moravia and Slovakia. In fact there are vineyards on the hills around Bratislava. Two
stronger drinks worth knowing about are slivovice, a plum brandy
most common in Moravia, and the ever- pervading *borovička* in
Slovakia. Its hard to compare *borovička* with any other drink. It is
sometimes translated as gin, but it tastes nothing like gin. Slovaks
tend to live on it and knock back the glass in one go. It's also
drunk as a beer chaser. They say that Bohemia has the best beer,
Moravia the best wine, and Slovakia the best spirits. There are
deposits on beer and soft drink bottles. Beware the trick, sometimes played on tourists, of charging for the bottle even when
they drink there, in the hope that they won't realise it.

Tea is normally tea bag tea. Coffee is usually Turkish coffee,
with the boiling water poured onto the grounds in your cup.
Expresso coffee is also available in some places. Coffee costs
upwards of 3 kčs (20p) a cup, but be warned if you are travelling
on to Poland, that it costs upwards of 100zl (50p) per cup.

Here is a rough guide to the various types of eating and
drinking establishments.

restaurace	restaurant
restaurace	
samoobsluha	cafetaria
hospoda (Cz), (Sl.	local pub (snacks such as hard-boiled
hostinec or krčma)	eggs & rolls often also available)
pivnice	beer cellar (sells food good that goes with beer)
vinárna (Cz)	
vináreň(Sl)	wine bar (sells food that goes with wine)
občerstvenie (Sl)	refreshments
cukrárna (Cz)	
cukráreň (Sl)	sell cakes and sweet things (open only in daytime)

If you enter any type of establishment within 1 hour of closing
time, you are likely to be studiously ignored by the
waiter/waitress, until you eventually grab one, by which time you
will probably be told that there is nothing left! A lot of eating
places in Czechoslovakia are non-smoking, for at least some of
the hours they are open.

A few hints if you are preparing your own food:

-There are not many supermarkets. Most food shops are not self-service. You must ask for what you want, which makes for language difficulties. But normally everything is on display, so you can point to what you want. What's not on display is on the black market! (e.g. cream).

-There are no grocery stores open on Saturday afternoon or Sunday. Many shops also have a half day on Monday.

-There are queues, especially for fresh food. If you are not too fussy about what you buy it is possible to avoid the worst queues.

-Western brand-names, such as Coca-Cola and Tang are much more expensive than the local equivalents.

-Watch that things packed in plastic and polythene are sealed properly, as they often aren't.

-It can be a problem to buy fresh fruit and vegetables, and people go to extraordinary lengths to protect their fruit with high fences and walls. In the country you can find wild berries (raspberries, blueberries). Good kompot (stewed fruit) is available everywhere in jars.

-Salami is good, and costs about 80 kčs per kilo.

-Packet soups are easily available, and handy for travelling.

-Good milk powder is available, again handy for travelling.

-Muesli is not available. But you can buy rolled oats (ovesné vločky (Cz), ovsené vločky (Sl)) sultanas (rozinka (Cz), hrozienka (Sl)) milk powder or fresh milk, kompot, and fresh fruit and berries if you can buy or find any, and make your own.

-Delicious canned peach juice.

-Bread is sold in large oval loaves. It is possible to ask for a half or quarter loaf. Be careful you are not sold stale bread. Pečivo, white rolls, are nice when fresh, but they are often not fresh!

-Sweet tooth in Slovakia? Try *arajidky v cukre*, delicious peanuts coated in sugar.

ENTERTAINMENT

Prague is famous for its classical music and opera, but be warned that seats are hard to come by, and often must be booked far in advance.

Rock and modern music is less common than in the West. Student functions and other club functions tend to be a better bet than the public nightclubs, where the staff treat you with disdain amounting at times to contempt.

A lot of foreign films are shown. Some are dubbed and some are subtitled. In Slovakia for example 'slovenská verzia' means the film is dubbed in Slovak, and 'slovenské titulky' means it is in the original language with Slovak subtitles. In summer films are shown outdoors in many places.

Late night places tend to have closed doors and hassling doormen to get past.

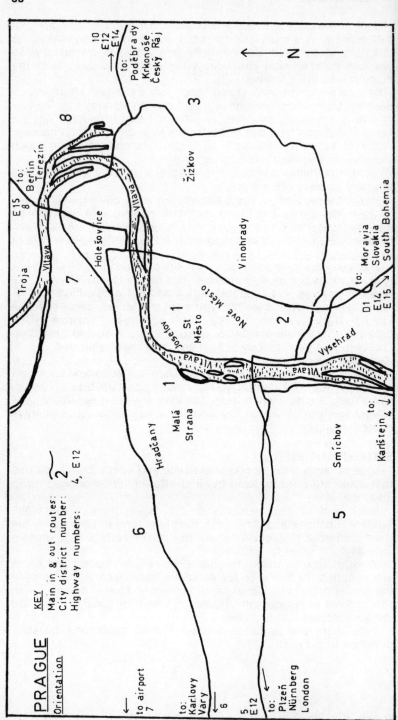

PART 2

PRAGUE

Prague for me and for many other travellers I have spoken with is the most beautiful city in Europe. The city was not bombed much during World War Two, so its Gothic and Baroque heritage was not destroyed. The newer outer suburbs are a jungle of ugly apartment blocks, but the old central city has retained its character over the centuries. A wander anywhere in the old parts of Prague is likely to uncover beautiful old churches, narrow cobbled streets and a medieval atmosphere that is very hard to find in European cities today. Words cannot describe Prague; it is a city you must see.

Prague straddles both sides of the river Vltava (Moldau in German), made famous by Smetana. Sixteen bridges connect the two sides of the river, by far the most famous and most beautiful of them being Karlův most (Charles Bridge). Hradcany, Mala Straná, Josefov, (the Jewish town), Staré Mesto (the old town) and Nové Město (the new town) were once independent towns each with their own character. Today they form the centre of a city whose suburbs spread far beyond them.

Many people say that spring is the best time to visit Prague. The blossoms are out in April and May. In summer it is warm, but crowded with tourists. In autumn it begins to get cold again, though it can be beautiful with the first snow. The average centigrade temperatures for Prague are:

	max.	min.
January	1	-4
February	3	-2
March	7	1
April	13	9
May	18	9
June	22	13
July	25	14
August	25	14
September	18	11
October	12	6
November	5	2
December	1	-1

HISTORY
The first Slav tribes settled in the area in the 5th century AD on the site of Prague Castle and at Vyšehrad, to the south on the

opposite side of the river. The vicinity of Old Town Square was a busy meeting place of long distance trading routes. Here Frankish, Byzantine, Arab and Jewish merchants bartered their goods for agricultural produce, textiles, leather goods and slaves. Prague Castle was first built in the 9th century by the Přemyslid rulers. Vyšehrad was for a time the main residence of the Přemyslids, but it was destroyed in 1420, and later developed as a fort to protect Prague from the south. The first stone bridge was built over the Vltava in the 12th century, roughly on the site of present day Charles Bridge. By the 13th century Staré Město had developed into its present form and shape and in 1257 King Přemysl Otakar II founded Mala Straná. The town of Hradčany was founded at the beginning of the 14th century.

Much of the attraction of modern day Prague can be attributed to Charles IV who became King of Bohemia in 1346. In 1349 he became Holy Roman Emperor, and Prague for a period the capital of the Holy Roman Empire. During his reign the first university north of the Alps was founded in Prague, Nové Město (the new town) was founded, the building of St. Vitus's Cathedral began as well as many other church buildings, and a new stone bridge, the present day Charles Bridge, was built across the Vltava. Charles IV is known as the founder of 'Prague Gothic'. At this time with a population of 40,000, Prague was one of the largest towns in Europe.

The preacher and founder of the Hussite movement, Jan Hus, preached in Bethlehem Chapel in the Old Town. Battles with the Hussites meant that the Renaissance came late to Prague. Baroque was at first an expression of the victory of the re-Catholicization process. The first gigantic Baroque works were Wallenstein Palace and the Klementinum. Maybe the most splendid Baroque building in Prague is the Church of St. Nicholas in Malá Strana. In the 18th century Prague Castle was extended into the complex and in 1784 the four townships were officially united.

At the turn of this century the Jewish Ghetto was sacrificed to a slum clearance project. In 1918 Prague became the capital of newly independent Czechoslovakia.

TO & FROM PRAGUE

If arriving by car try to avoid rush hours and Sunday nights, when driving in Prague's traffic can be quite an ordeal to the uninitiated.

There are many train and bus stations, so make sure you know which one you are arriving at or departing from. The main bus station is Florenc (metro line C to Sokolovska). Most international trains as well as many domestic services go to Hlavní nádraží, the main railway station. Trains for Karlštejn leave from Nádraží Praha-Smíchov on the other side of the river.

There are frequent express buses to Brno for 75 kčs. Express buses to Bratislava cost 115 kčs and take 4 hours 40 minutes, but there are not many of them. Rychlík trains to Bratislava cost 69 kčs and most of them take about 6 hours. The office for seat reservations (místenky) at the railway station is open all night. Best way to Karlovy Vary is by bus, but it is advisable to make a reservation. Trains from West Germany, Berlin, Budapest etc.

There are international air services to Prague from all over the world. See 'Travelling To and From Czechoslovakia'. Internally there are direct flights to Bratislava, Ostrava, Piešťány and Sliac near Banská Bystrica, and flights via Bratislava to Košice and Poprad. Latest check-in times at the airport: 20 minutes before domestic flights; 40 minutes European flights; 50 minutes intercontinental flights; 90 minutes Moscow, Hanoi or Havana. See 'Getting Around' below for transport between airport and city.

For hitching towards East Germany take the metro to Fučikova and the country bus from there to Zdiby for 3 kcs. Get off at the first stop in Zdiby, and walk back 50 metres from the stop to the top of a rise. For hitching towards Brno, Bratislava , Tábor or České Budějovice take the metro to Pražského povstáni. Cross nám. Hrdinů to 5. kvetna, the highway out of Prague.

GETTING AROUND
Drivers: see 'To & From Prague'.

The best time for walking around the city is at the weekend when there is not so much traffic.

There are three complementary forms of public transport in Prague: trams, buses and the fast, efficient metro. The network of trams and buses is even more confusing in recent years because of the upheaval caused by excavations for the metro. Whatever map you have is probably out of date, as the lines are constantly changing as streets are closed or reopened. But it is fun finding out, and the public transport system is excellent if you can work it out. Night trams have blue numbers. (See 'Getting Around in Czechoslovakia' for ticket system.)

The ČSA bus service to the airport runs according to a seasonal timetable, tickets 6 kčs for international flights, free for domestic flights. Downtown terminal at Revolučni 25. Otherwise take bus number 119 from the airport to Leninova metro station, from where you can take the metro into the centre.

MAPS & GUIDES
A map is a must. Three maps are available. The Praha Town Plan for 10 kčs is probably the most useful, showing the whole central area and much of the suburbs on a single sheet. If you are staying in the centre and confining yourself to this area, Praha, Plan of City Centre for 5 kčs might suffice. This is simply an enlargement of the centre part of the first map with some important landmarks drawn on. It is worth having anyhow as it is much easier to follow when sightseeing in the centre. There is also a map in book form of the whole of Prague. For trips out of Prague in south and westerly directions the map Okolí Prahy is excellent. Includes Karlštejn, Koněpruské Caves and Slapy.

A guidebook to Prague by Ctibor Rybar published by Olympia is available in French and German for 45 kčs. Strong on history and architecture. There are no plans to reprint the older English edition, which is unobtainable. There is now a guide to Prague published by Baedeker.

There is a good bookshop for maps and travel books at Staroměstske nám. 16.

SLEEPING

It is difficult to find accommodation in Prague, especially in the cheaper price bracket, and especially in the main tourist season and at New Year, Easter and the Whit holidays. Accommodation in private homes is easier to find than hotel rooms. Although accommodation in the centre is usually full, there is a quick turnover, so you may find something. On the houseboats it is a little easier as it is on the periphery of Prague.

If you know when you will be in Prague it pays to book ahead. Čedok have an accommodation service for foreign visitors at Panská 5, Praha 1; tel. 24 70 04, 22 56 57. They deal with the more expensive price bracket. They don't usually know before 10am where there are free rooms.

Pragotur, U Obecního domu 2, Praha 1, tel. 231 72 81, 231 49 24 also have an accommodation service and tend to deal with slightly cheaper accommodation than Čedok. Pragotur can book hotels, private accommodation, hostels, bungalows and camping. Their hotel rooms are in the 'C', 'B' and 'B*' classes, a 'B' class double without bath costing 244 kčs, for example. Commission 5 kčs per person per night. Hotels give them information on free rooms at about 10am and 5pm. Rooms in private houses or flats cost 108 kčs single, 154 kčs double and 195 double with an extra bed. They may be situated a *long* way out of the centre. They can book accommodation in student hostels in July and August for around 70-80 kčs per person. When booking accommodation of any sort through Pragotur, there is no need to register with the police as they do this for you.

Rekrea, Pařížská 26, tel. 232 27 51, have student accommodation available all year, but they tend to deal more with groups. These are 4 bedrooms with hot and cold water and free use of the shower in the corridor.

People often approach foreigners in the street asking if they are looking for a room.

Camping

Even camping grounds get full in Prague in the summer holiday period.

Caravan Camp Motol, A, Praha 5, Plzeňská, Post code 150 00; tel. 52 47 14. Open 15/5 to 15/9. People I have spoken with who have stayed there say it is a terrible place, and unfriendly. On the E12, the main road in from Plzeň.

Sportcamp Motol, A, Praha 5, V Podhájí, post code 150 00; tel. 52 18 02. Open 1/4 to 31/10. Tent camping & bungalows.

Troja, A, Praha 7, Trojská 171, post code 171 00; tel. 84 28 33. Open 15/6 to 15/9. Bungalows & tent camping. Full in summer. The residents on Trojská have people camping in their gardens when the camping ground is full. This must be booked through Pragotur. Not as idyllic as it sounds, as the garden is likely to be packed with tents, and there will probably be long queues to use the inadequate sanitary facilities.

Suchdol, Praha 6; tel. 34 23 05. Tents only. Perhaps the most likely camp to have some space left. Open June to September.

Arrangements for YHA members

YHA members can stay at CKM Juniorhotel, Žitná 12, 121 05 Praha 2, tel. 29 99 41, for the YHA price of 27 kcs if there happens to be a free bed, which is very rare except possibly off-season. Centrally located. Otherwise YHA members may stay in student hostels in July and August for the same price. There are 2 to 3 beds to a room, share bathroom included in price. Addresses: Spartakiádní 5, 160 00 Praha 6; Kolej VŠCHT, 140 00 Praha 4, Jizni mesto. If possible check with CKM in Žitná ul first. The hostels in use could change from year to year, and they may know where there is space. Note that you can't get this cheap YHA price if you book in advance.

Other hostels

Ubytovna TJ Spartak Karlín Dukla, TU B, 186 00 Praha 8, Malého 1; tel. 22 20 09. Open 6pm to 8am only. In daytime you must be out. By the bus station Florenc. Handy but noisy situation. Crash pad type of place, but friendly. Communal (m & f together) hot showers. Groups have priority, so you may only know from one night to the next if you can sleep there. If full and you have a sleeping bag, you may be able to sleep on the floor.

Turistická ubytovna TJ Slovan Bohnice, TU A, Praha 8, středisko Na pískovne, post code 181 05; tel. 85 52 62 8. Take metro C to Fucikova, then bus 102 to nám. Stare Bohnice (the last stop). 3 to 6 beds to a room.

TJ Dolní Mecholupy, Na paloučku 223. 65 kcs per night per person. Metro A to Želivského, then bus 229 to Mecholupy. 30 minutes from centre. Last connection 00.20. Kitchenette. Possible to use sports facilities.

Botels

To help ease the accommodation shortage Prague has some 'botels', houseboats on the river.

Botel Albatross, B*, Praha 1, nábr. L. Svobody, post code 110 00; tel. 23 13 63 4, 23 13 60 0, 23 16 99 6. Close to centre. Doubles only: 404 kcs including breakfast. Little private shower & toilet. Not worth the money! If you do stay, try and get a room on the river side of the boat, which has a nice outlook at least. Night club.

Hotels

I only list those at the top and bottom of the price range. Čedok offices have a pamphlet listing other medium range hotels.

A *****

Intercontinental, 110 15 Praha 1, nám. Curieových; tel. 28 99 or if ringing from outside Prague 2311812; telex 122681 ihc c. Near Vltava. Singles US$70 to US$90, doubles US$100 to US$125. Must be paid in foreign currency.

Esplanade, 110 00 Praha 1, Washingtonova 19; tel. 22 25 52-4,

22 60 56-9; telex 011067. US$65 single, US$110 double. Very
flash. Near main railway station. 110 00 Praha 1, Rybná 8; tel. 23
19 284, 23 14 240. Central, close to Powder Gate. Some rooms
with bath or shower. See Botels.

B

Erko, 197 00 Praha 9, Kbely, Luštěnická 723; tel. 89 21 05. 40
minutes by tram and bus. Double only, extra beds available.
Hybernia, 115 44 Praha 1, Hybernská 24; tel. 22 04 31. Very
central, can walk to the bus & train stations.
Juniorhotel, 120 00 Praha 2, Žitná 12; tel. 29 99 41. 2 to 3 bed
rooms with private facilities. From 110 kčs (15 if booked from
abroad). Usually full. YHA members see above.
Juventus, 120 00 Praha 2, Blanická 10; tel. 25 51 51. Small
student hotel. Singles & doubles. Metro to nám. Miru.
Modra hvězda, 190 00 Praha 9, Jandova 3; tel. 83 02 91-2.
Doubles only with extra beds available. Half hour by tram 19 or
15.
Solidarita, 100 00 Praha 10 - Strašnice, Soudružská 1; tel. 77 84
41-5, reception 77 71 45. Large modern type hotel. Singles &
doubles, extra beds available. Tram 29 or 11.
Union128 00 Praha 2, Jaromírova 1; tel. 43 78 58-9. Singles &
doubles. Tram 18 or 24.

C

Balkán, 150 00 Praha 5, Svornosti 28/218; tel. 54 07 77. In
Smichov. Tram 15 to Lidicka stop.
Moravan, 170 00 Praha 7, Dimitrovovo nám. 22; tel. 80 29 05, 80
24 49. 2 & 3 bed rooms. Tram 12 to U Uranie stop.

ADDRESSES & PRACTICAL INFORMATION

Prague Information Service, Praha 1, Na příkopě 20; tel. 54 44 44.
A rarity in Czechoslovakia: a real tourist office! Information on
Prague. Open Monday to Friday 8am to 8pm in summer, or to 7pm
in winter, Saturday 8am to 12 noon, Sunday closed.
Čedok, Praha 1, Na příkopě 18; tel. 22 42 51. Large Čedok
office for foreign tourists. Here you can exchange money, book
flights and trains, book tours, and find someone who speaks
English to help you with other problems. Čedok's accommodation
service is at Panská 5.
Pragotur. See 'Sleeping'.
Rekrea, Praha 1, Pařízská 26, tel. 232 27 51, is the Rekrea
travel agency office for foreigners.
Sport-Turist, Národní 33, 112 93 Praha 1; tel. 26 33 51, telex
122664. Make arrangements for groups only, mostly sports groups,
but also others. Can accommodate in dorms etc, so could be
cheaper than Čedok.
Autoturist. Opposite Hlavní nádraží. At Opletalova 29, (tel. 22
35 44-9), travel agency office for motorists. Won't make accommodation bookings for individuals. At Opletalova 21, emergency
breakdown service (tel. 22 49 06).
CKM, Žitná 9, Praha 1, tel. 29 85 87. The youth and student

travel bureau. For international student identity cards (both the western and eastern varieties) go to their office at Jindřišská 28 on Tuesday or Thursday between 2pm and 4pm only. ISIC cards cost 40 kčs, MSS 15 kčs and YHA 40 kčs.

Balnea (for spas), Pařízská 11, Praha 1, tel. 232 19 30. Open Monday to Friday 8am to 3pm, Tuesdays to 6pm.

Hlavní pošta (main post office), 110 00 Praha 1, Jindřišská14. Has pens and desks to write your letters. Open 24 hours, but poste restante is closed outside normal hours. When poste restante is closed, someone from a nearby counter will sometimes oblige and check your mail for you. Telephone and telegram office in same building.

Changing money: At the airport, banks, Čedok, the more expensive hotels.

Sending money to ČSSR: send to Československá obchodní banka, Na příkope 14, 115 20 Praha. Swift-telex: CEKO CS PP.

Police (for registering & visa extensions), Olsanska 2. Open Monday to Friday 8.00 to 12.00, 12.30 to 15.30, except Wednesday when it is closed in the afternoon. If you want a visa extension, change your DM30 per day for the number of days you want before you go to the police station.

Left luggage. At Florenc bus station. Must be under 15kg. Closed 11pm to 4am. At Hlavní nádrazí (the main railway station), 15kg maximum, maximum 45 days. Also lockers, which people have trouble working out how to use. You choose your own combination and set the interior combination to the one you chose, put in 1 kčs and close the door. Remember the combination and the locker number or the number you set on the outside. Open 24 hours. Also left luggage at the ČSA terminal.

ČSA, Praha 1, Revolucní 1; tel. 2146. By Kotva. ČSA Terminal is on Revolucní near the Vltava.

British Airways, Praha 1, Štepánská 63; tel. 24 08 47.

Medical. There is a medical & dental clinic for foreigners at the Poliklinika, Karlovo nám., 3rd floor. First aid for UK citizens is free. Otherwise you must pay in western currency.

American Embassy: has a library open to the public, and shows videos of US news in the afternoon. Address: Trziste 15, 125 48 Praha 1. Tel. 53 66 41.

Rental Cars: Pragocar, Praha 1, Štepánská 42, tel. 24 84 85, 24 00 89, telex 122 641. Also at the airport (tel. 36 78 07, telex 122 729) and Hotel Intercontinental (tel. 231 9595, telex 121 353). Rates from US$23 to US$30 per day, US $137 to US$180 per week, plus 21c to 28c per kilometre. Unlimited mileage rates US$61 to US$97 per day, US$270 to US$350 per week. 15 per cent tax is added to all these rates. Petrol US$0.65 per litre. Insurance: driver pays first US$120 in case of damage to vehicle. This can be waived on payment of an extra US$5 per day or US$30 per week. Passenger insurance US$2 per day. Delivery fee US$0.20 per kilometre. One way rentals: up to 200 km free, 201 to 500 km US$50, 501 to 1000 km US$80, over 1000km US$150. If between Pragocar stations, no extra charge. Tie ups with international rental car companies, so cars may be taken out of Czechoslovakia or vice versa. Caravans can also be rented. Small caravans cost US$8 per day and sleep 2 adults and 1 child. Larger caravans cost US$11 per day, and sleep 2 adults and 2 children. Plus 15 per cent tax again. Mostly Czechs rent caravans.

If seeking visas for onward travel, see under 'Visas' in the introductory part of this book for addresses of embassies.

If you wish to contact your own embassy, see 'Registration', (also in the introductory part of this book) for addresses.

TO SEE

Staré Město (the Old Town)

Staré Město, the Old Town, centres on **Staroměstské náměstí**, the Old Town Square. A beautiful place by day, and a haunting place by night, Staroměstské nám.'s most famous tourist attraction is the **astronomical clock** on the Old Town Hall. First built in 1410, it has undergone modifications through the centuries. Damaged by the Nazis in 1945, it was operational again by 1948. Every hour the skeleton, the symbol of death, rings the bell, nodding his head at the Turk, the miser and the figurine representing vanity. But the others nod their heads back, showing that they are not ready to die. As the bell strikes, two windows in the top of the clock open, and the twelve apostles parade between them. The performance is completed by a crowing rooster.

The **Old Town Hall** itself is a complex of several buildings erected between the 14th and 19th centuries. A large part of it was destroyed in World War Two. It is open daily from 8am to 6pm from March to October, and 8am to 5pm during the rest of the year.

In 1621 Staroměstské nám. saw the execution of 27 of the leaders of the uprising of the Czech nobility against the Hapsburgs, after the Hapsburgs defeated them at the Battle of White Mountain. The square was a meeting place during the Hussite period, and has a **monument to Jan Hus** which was unveiled in 1915 on the 500th anniversary of his burning at the stake. The large Gothic church with its two steeples just back off the square is the **Church of Our Lady of Týn**. Begun in 1380 and completed in 1511, it was the main church of the town, and the seat of the archbishop, during the Hussite period. The towers are said to represent Adam and Eve. Presently under reconstruction.

The narrow little streets around Staroměstské nám., with their quaint old buildings, date from medieval times.

The **Powder Tower (Prašna brána)** at the north-east end of Na příkopě is one of Prague's landmarks. This Gothic tower dates back to 1475 and it was used for a time as a magazine for gunpowder; hence its name. Open Saturday, Sunday & public holidays. May to September 10am to 6pm, May & October 10am to 5pm, November to March closed. Museum and view. Near the Powder Tower, at nám. Republiky 5, is **Obecní dům**, a beautiful building in art nouveau style, dating from 1910. It houses the Smetana Concert Hall.

The **Karolinum** (Železná 9) is the oldest building of Charles University, dating from the 14th century. Baroque adaptation 1718.

The **Klementinum** was originally a Jesuit college. Baroque from 17th century. The second largest building complex (after the

castle) in Prague. The Klementinim was a centre of the counter-
Reformation. Father Koniás burnt 30,000 'heretical' Czech books
here. Today it houses the State Library, Slav Library and the
University Library, which includes a collection of rare manuscripts
starting from the 14th century.

The original **Bethlehem Chapel (Betlémská kaple)** was built in
Gothic style in 1391. The Czech reformer Jan Hus taught and
preached here in the Czech language (which was not allowed)
from 1402 to 1412. In the late 18th century the chapel was
demolished, but part of the walls survived and it was reconstructed from 1949 to 1954, but worth finding a guide to explain
the history to you. Open daily April to September 9am to 6pm,
October 9am to 5pm, rest of year closed.

Just before Karlův most there is a fantastic Baroque church on
the right, founded by the Order of the Knights of the Cross in the
17th century. Its patron saint is St Frances of Assisi. In the square
outside it is a statue of Charles IV.

Prague's Bridges

Karlův most (Charles Bridge) is one of the main attractions of
Prague. Named after Charles IV, this beautiful bridge is open to
pedestrians only. At both ends are towers, and the bridge is lined
with statues. From it you can gaze up at Prague Castle and St
Vitus's Cathedral. The bridge itself and the tower at the Staré
Mesto end of the bridge were built in the 14th century. The tower
at the Malá Strana end of the bridge was added in the 15th
century. The other smaller Malá Strana tower is Romanesque,
being the only relic of the 12th century Judith Bridge, which was
destroyed by a flood in 1342. At that time Judith Bridge and the
stone bridge at Regensburg were the only stone bridges in
Europe. (There were earlier wooden bridges spanning the Vltava).

There is a legend that Charles Bridge was to be the strongest
bridge in the world, so the builder used mortar mixed with eggs
and wine. As there were not enough eggs in Prague, all towns in
Bohemia were ordered to contribute. But the citizens of Velvary,
not understanding properly, were afraid the eggs would break, so
they hard-boiled them first. The citizens of Unhost wanted to help
even more, so they sent curd and cheese as well.

Charles Bridge was originally called Stone Bridge, or simply
Prague Bridge. Its name was changed last century. Until 1841 it
was the only bridge in Prague. Today's statues were added at
various times between the 17th and 19th centuries. The tower at
the Malá Strana end was restored in 1969-70, and you can climb it
from April to October inclusive from 10am to 5pm (2 kcs, 1 kcs
children & students).

The next bridge to be built was a chain bridge named after
Frantisek I. Built in the first half of the 19th century, tram passengers had to alight and walk across, continuing their tram trip
from the other side. The second oldest bridge still in use is the
railway bridge linking Holesovice and Karlín. It was designed by
Alois Negrelli, the designer of the Suez Canal. Opened in 1849,
parts of the bridge are still original and unrepaired. The shortest

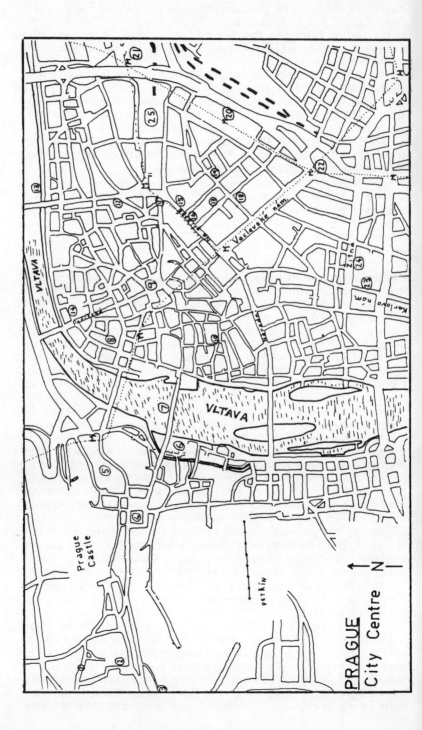

PRAGUE
City Centre

KEY TO PRAGUE MAP

1 Nový Svet
2 Loretto
3 Strahovský Klášťer
4 St Nicholas Church
5 Wallenstein Palace
6 Kampa
7 Karlův Most
8 Old Jewish Cemetery
9 Staroměstské Náměstí
10 Bethlehem Chapel
11 Powder Tower
12 ČSA Office
13 Botel Albatross
14 Hotel Intercontinental
15 Prague Information Service

16 Čedok
17 Čedok Accommodation Service
18 Hlavní Pošta
19 CKM (for student and
    youth hostels)
20 Hlavní nádraží
21 Florenc bus station
22 National Museum
23 Poliklinika
24 CKM Juniorhotel
25. žel. st. Praha střed

Metro (with station) ----M---
Railway - - - -
Cable car •-•-•-•-•

of the bridges is Svatopluk Čech Bridge, an iron bridge named after the Czech writer. Built early this century in art nouveau style, its original road surface was the Australian timber, jarrah, which lasted up to 1961.

Malá Strana
Malá Strana developed as a noblemen's suburb. The nobility and church wanted to be close to the castle. After the Battle of White Mountain, whole blocks of houses, streets and gardens disappeared to make room for palaces for the nobility. When the political administration moved to Vienna, there was a decline in the importance of Malá Strana. The dominant feature of the suburb is the dome and bell-tower of St Nicholas Church. Today Malá Strana is still a 'posh' suburb, with many fo reign embassies.

Steps off Karlův most to the left take you to **Kampa**, a nice island with an embankment, and an old watermill at Čertovka. At the end of the bridge, there is an interesting herb and spice shop 'U Salvatora'. Continuing straight ahead up Mostecká leads you to Malostranské nám. In the centre of this square stands **St Nicholas Church**, the culmination of Bohemian Baroque. It was built from 1704 to 1755 and the architects included K.I. Dienzenhofer. The ceiling paintings have recently undergone a thorough restoration. Open daily November to February 9am to 4pm, March & April 9am to 5pm, May to September 9am to 6pm, and October 10am to 5pm.

Wallenstein Palace (Valdštejnský palác), the first monumental building of Prague Baroque, was built between 1623 and 1630. To clear the site, 23 houses, a brick kiln, and 3 gardens were demolished. Today the palace houses a government ministry, but the gardens, which are surrounded by an enormous wall, are open to the public between May and September from 9am to 7pm.

Powder Tower and Obecní dum, Prague

In the gardens are copies of the original statues by Adrian de Vries (1626-7) which were carried off as war bounty by the Swedes in 1648. A stroll around Malá Strana will uncover many other palaces and churches.

In the southern part of Malá Strana is the hill **Petrín**. A cable car operates between 5am and midnight, or you can walk up one of the many paths. On top is a 60m lookout tower, built in 1891 as a miniature Eiffel Tower. The tower has been closed for some time. There is a diorama painting of Prague's citizens fighting the Swedes on Charles Bridge, and a mirror maze, the latter being open April to September 9am to 6pm, October 9am to 5pm. The wall by the tower is the so-called Hunger Wall, built by Charles IV as part of MaláStrana's fortifications. Legend has it that during a period of drought Emperor Charles IV had a large crowd of poor people assembled in the castle courtyard. He fed them well, and then gave them the task of building a long wall from the castle fortifications over Petr Hill and down to the river. They worked for two years, unpaid, but were provided with clothing and food for themselves and their families, which saw them over the worst of the drought. Pleasant area to walk, with nice views.

Hradčany

One of Prague's dominating landmarks is **Pražský hrad (Prague Castle)** which you can walk up to from Malá Strana. Today's castle is an incredible mixture of architectural styles. Now 1100 years old, the castle has undergone constant transformation. Inside the complex is the amazingly intricate structure of **St Vitus' Cathedral (Katedrála sv. Víta)**. The castle was founded in the 9th century as a fortress, rebuilt as a Romanesque palace in the 12th century, extended in Gothic style by Charles IV, and extended and adapted at various times later. On the 23rd May, 1618, a large group of noblemen demanded an audience with the two Habsburg vice regents. The noblemen became so het up, that the meeting ended with the two ministers and their secretary being thrown out of the window. Their lives were saved by the large heap of sweepings which had accumulated under the same window through the years. This is known as the second Prague Defenestration. In the 18th century Maria Theresa had the unfinished parts of the castle completed. From the 9th century until 1918 Prague Castle was the official seat and place of coronation of Czech sovereigns. Now it is the seat of the president of Czechoslovakia.

St Vitus' Cathedral replaced a Romanesque basilica, which itself replaced a rotunda built in the 10th century. Construction of the cathedral began under the rule of Charles IV in 1344 and was finally completed in 1929! The most important chapel is that of St Wenceslas, built by Peter Parler in the 14th century, decorated with frescoes and semi-precious stones. Czech kings were crowned here. The coronation jewels are kept in a special chamber, and only on special occasions moved for exhibition purposes.

St Georges Church (Bazilika sv. Jiri) is a beautiful Romanesque basilica founded in 920 A.D. and completed in the 12th century, without later additions. The adjoining nunnery was adapted between 1963 and 1974 to house the **Old Czech Art Collection of the National Gallery**. Open daily except Monday, 10am to 6pm.

At the end of the 16th century, and especially in the 17th century, Prague Castle became a place of refuge for those wishing to evade the jurisdiction of the Prague authorities, which reached only to the castle ramparts. So many, especially tradesmen and artisans, who for various reasons wished to elude the authorities, built parasite dwellings in all sorts of places around the castle. Because of the numerous improvised fireplaces the fire risk was high, so in the 18th century the parasite dwellings were demolished. For some reason **Zlatá ulička (Golden Lane)** was overlooked and here remain tiny little dwellings built into the castle wall. At the end of the street stands **Daliborka**, a prison used mainly for debtors.

In the 1960s the castle stables were converted into a gallery **(Obrazárna Pražského hradu)** housing paintings of Prague Castle. Open daily except Monday 10am to 6pm.

Tours of the castle and cathedral are not conducted in English, but you can hire an English speaking guide if you would like to learn more. Best to book in advance at the tour office at the castle. The whole complex is open all year. The castle is open daily except Monday, November to March 9am to 4pm, April to October 9am to 5pm.

Hradčany was the third of the Prague towns to be founded. It arose around the castle in about 1320. Charles IV extended and fortified the town. Hradčanské nám., just outside the castle, is surrounded by palaces. From the square there is access to **Štern berk Palace** (Baroque, 1698-1730), which today houses a **Collection of European art**. A must for art lovers, it is one of the collections of the **National Gallery**, and open 10am to 6pm, closed Mondays. In the **Schwarzenberg Palace** on the south side of the square is a **military museum.**

Following up Loretánská from Hradčanské nám. brings one to Loretánské Náměstí and the **Loretto**. The Loretto are **pilgrimage** churches built as copies of the original Santa Casa, in the Italian town of Loretto, which was supposed to be the dwelling of the Virgin of Nazareth, conveyed by angels from Palestine to Italy in the 13th century. The Czech Loretto was built as part of the re-Catholicization process after the victory of the Habsburgs at White Mountain; as Catholic propoganda to win back the Czechs. The Loretto Church was built during the Thirty Years War. The Loretto itself was built from 1626-31 and stands in the yard. It may be 'Closed at the present time for technical reasons', but the outside is very beautiful.

Nový Svět (which means 'New World') was formerly the quarter of the poor. Despite later alterations the area still retains something of its atmosphere of simple little houses.

Strahovský klášter (Strahov Monastery) was founded in 1140, but rebuilt many times in different styles. It now houses a **museum of Czech literature**. One of the halls has rich wall paintings by Anton F. Maulbertsch. Traces of the original Romanesque structure can be seen in places. In the richly decorated Church of the

Virgin Mary, Mozart played the organ. Closed Mondays. From here there is access to Petřín.

Josefov (the Jewish Quarter)
On the other side of the river again from Hradčany is the Jewish quarter. Jews have lived in Prague for 1000 years. But in 1896 the whole quarter except the synagogues, cemetery and town hall was demolished in a large scale urban renewal project.

From the mid 15th century the main Jewish cemetery which lay outside the bounds of the Jewish town was closed for burials, and the **Old Jewish Cemetery** arose. This cramped area was not big enough, so the old graves were covered over and new ones laid above them. The last burial here was in 1787. The oldest preserved tombstone is dated 25 April, 1439. The reliefs on the tombstones often symbolise the name of the deceased (e.g. stag, cock) and his profession (e.g. doctor's instruments, tailor's scissors).

In the former ceremonial hall, the building at the entrance to the cemetery, are haunting reminders of the Nazi occupation in the form of a display of drawings by children in the concentration camp of Terezín. (Unfortunately not respected enough to be untainted by propoganda.)

The **Staronová (Old-New) Synagogue** is one of the oldest synagogues in Europe still in use. Dating from about 1270, it was one of the first Gothic buildings in Prague. The Klausen Synagogue was built in Baroque style at the end of the 17th century. The Maisel Synagogue was built in Renaissance in the 1590s, and rebuilt in Baroque after the great fire in the Jewish town in 1689. The High Synagogue was built in Renaissance style in 1568 as a part of the Town Hall, and separated from the Town Hall in the 19th century. Now houses a collection of tapestries, ornaments etc.

The cemetery, the collection of drawings, Staronová Synagogue, and the other synagogues which house various collections of Jewish significance comprise together the State Jewish Museum. Many of the exhibits were collected under   orders from Hitler so that he could set up a museum of 'decadent Jewish culture'. Open daily except Saturday, from 9am to 5pm (or 4.30pm out of season), a ticket from any one of the museums etc. gives access to all of the others. The Staronová Synagogue closes to the public at 3pm on Fridays. There are services here on Saturdays, and daily at dawn and dusk.

Nové Město (the New Town)
Once a Hussite stronghold, Nové Město fared badly during the religious wars. Today it forms the commercial centre of Prague. At its heart lies **Václavské Náměstí (Wenceslas Square)**, which has been a site of protests since Hussite times. A long wide street lined with elegant hotels and shops, it is dominated by the **National Museum**, which was built 1885-90. Unless you have a particular interest in any of its subjects (geology, palaeontology, zoology, mineralogy, pre-history) you may not find the museum very interesting - open 9am to 4pm Monday & Friday, 9am to 5pm

Wednesday & Thursday, closed Tuesday.
The old part of the **main railway station** is in art nouveau style, and worth a look.The **New Town Hall (Novoměst. radnice)** is on Karlovo nám. Presently under reconstruction.

Vyšehrad
Vyšehrad is the former seat of the Přemyslid princes. Situated high on a bluff overlooking the Vltava. The Church of St Peter & St Paul, the Romanesque rotunda of St Martin, the deanery, and gardens and cemetry are there today.

Žižkov
Národní památník na Žižkově (Žižkov National Monument) stands on the hill where the Hussite army defeated the 'crusaders' in 1420. The remains of leading members of the Czechoslovak Communist Party lie here, and there is a memorial to the Soviet army.

Troja
In the northern suburb of Troja is Prague's **zoo** (bus 112 from Fujikova metro station).

Roztoky
Castle with very nice garden in the northern suburbs of Prague. Bus from Leninovo metro station, or train from Praha Střed.

Out of Prague
One of the main attractions in the vicinity of Prague is **Karlštejn Castle**. Charles IV had Karlštejn built in the 14th century to house the royal jewels. The foundation stone was laid in 1348 and the castle was finished in record time , Charles IV taking possession in 1355. The present appearance of the castle reflects two major periods of reconstruction: from 1575 to 1597, and from 1887 to 1897. In 1420 the treasures were removed from the castle. In 1422 Karlštejn was under seige by the Hussites for 7 months. In 1648 the castle was badly damaged by Swedish attacks, and from then on lost its political importance. The restoration work commenced in 1887 was intended to restore its Gothic appearance.
The exterior of the castle is perhaps more impressive than the interior. The exterior walls are 6 metres thick, and the interior 2 metres. The tower which dominates the castle houses the Chapel of the Holy Rood, which is decorated with precious stones.
From Prague, Karlštejn is 28 km by car. Take Highway 4 towards Zbraslav, Dobřichovice. Trains leave from Praha Smichov station, and take about 40 minutes—pleasant trip. The village of Karlštejn itself is also nice, and the castle looks quite imposing above it. Open 9am to 4pm, May to September 8am to 6pm, may be closed in January & February. Closed Mondays. Tours Czech and German, but good displayed multilingual information. Attractive walks in the area (see map 'Okolí Prahy').
Near Karlštejn, but a bit difficult to get to without a car, are the **Koněprusy Caves**. There have been many archeological finds from Palaeolithic times here. 15th century coin counterfeiting

centre. Stalactites. Open April to October Monday to Sunday 8am to 3pm.

In the summer **Slapy Dam**, on the Vltava south of Prague, is a popular destination, accessible by boat (3 hours) or bus.

Konopiště is a chateau with a wonderful big park, 44km southeast of Prague near Benešov. Once owned by the Austrian Crown Prince Ferdinand d'Este, who was assassinated at Sarajevo in 1914. Open May to August 8am to 12, 1pm to 4pm; April, September & October 9am to 3pm; closed Mondays. Train to Benešov, then local bus to Konopiště. Nice motel & restaurant.

Lidice was razed to the ground by the Nazis after the assassination of Reinhard Heydrich by Czech patriots who were parachuted into Czechoslovakia. Hitler said that one Czech town must be 'wiped off the face of the Earth', Lidice was chosen. The men of the village were shot, and the women and children taken to concentration camps. Lidice was left as it was, and a new village built a little north of the old. Lidice was a mining village. British miners from Birmingham decided that 'Lidice shall live'. A movement was started with contributions from all over the world. A large rose garden was planted on the sight of the village, and many other villages were renamed 'Lidice'.

A film was taken by the Nazis of the destruction of the village. The memorial ground is open daily throughout the year. The museum Oct. to March 8am to 4pm, April to Sept. 8am to 5pm. 22km north-west from Prague. Driving, take highway 7 towards Kladno. Public transport: metro to Leninova, then take the Kladno ČSAD bus (Lidice is before Kladno).

Between Prague and Plzeň there are a lot of woods. Nice hiking in Brdy.

To the north and east of Prague, around the Elbe, is fruit and vegetable growing. Mělník is a historic town and a wine growing area.

BOATING ON THE VLTAVA
In summer there are boat trips on the Vltava if the water level is high enough. One trip is around central Prague, another north to Roztoky, and another south to Slapy (see above). Also only in summer you may be able to hire small boats by the National Theatre or House of Artists.

SIGHTSEEING TOURS
Čedok sightseeing tours leave from Praha 1, Bílkova 6 (opposite Hotel Intercontinental) at the time stated, or from Panorama Hotel 30 minutes earlier. Book at Cedok.

Historical Prague. 3 hour guided tour beginning 10am daily all year, and also 1.30pm from 1 April to 30 September. Possibly more frequently in summer. Bus tour of main sights & visit to Prague Castle. US$8.

Prague at Night. 4 hours. 1 hour sightseeing tour followed by folklore show 'Prague Party' and dinner in a Slovak 'koliba' restaurant. May 15 to October 15 Wednesday & Friday 7pm. US$23.

Excursions from Prague

Karlovy Vary - Lidice, whole day. (For details on these places see the relevant section in this book.) May 15 to October 15, Monday, Wed., & Fri., 8.30am. US$22.

Bohemian Castles & Chateaux. Karlštejn, Slapy Dam lake and Konopiste. Whole day. May 15 to Oct. 15, Tue., Thurs., Sat., & Sun., 8.30am. US$17.

Attractions of Southern Bohemia. Tábor & Hluboká Palace. (See Tábor & České Budějovice sections for details on these places). Whole day. 15 May to 15 October, Wed., Fri., & Sun., 8.30am. US$23.

Slapy - Konopiste. Half day. July 1 to August 31, Sundays, 8.30am. Visits town of Zbraslav, Slapy dam lake & Konopiste Chateau. US$18.

Discovering Bohemian Wine. Tour to Mělník, sightseeing, visit to vineyards, wine-tasting. May 15 to Oct. 15, Saturday, 2pm. Half day. US$13.

Czech Garnets & Costume Jewellery. Museum of costume jewellery in Jablovec nad Nisou. Museum in Turnov with collection of semi-precious stones & Czech garnets. Also visit to Sychrov Chateau with its memorial hall dedicated to Antonín Dvořák. 15 May to 15 Oct., Tuesdays only, 8.30am, whole day. US$20.

Tours of Czechoslovakia

There are one week and two week tours of Czechoslovakia leaving Prague every couple of weeks during the summer. 1 week US$400-500, 2 week US$700-800. Much cheaper to travel on your own, but if time is more important than money, and you have suddenly discovered you would like a glimpse of some more of this country, one of these tours may be the answer.

EVENTS

Mostly in May, but running a bit into June, an International Spring Music Festival is held in Prague.

EATING

Prague eateries can get crowded, and it can be very hard to find a seat somewhere. If you're not too fussy about what you want, your best bet may be to go to one of the large 'bufet' around Václavské náměstí and choose the shortest queue. If there are two of you, one can queue for the drinks while the other queues for the food! Try bramborák, the potato pancakes you can often buy on the street.

The Old Town & Jewish Quarter

In Malé Naměstí, behind the town hall, is a busy crowded sk. III restaurant called U Radnici with better than average food.

In the Jewish Quarter at Maislova 18 is a kosher restaurant (košer jídelna rest.) open 11.30 to 13.30 only.

Next to the old synagogue, but on Pařízská, is the restaurant U Staré Synagogy. Better than average sk. III in its surroundings and food. Open 9am to 10pm.

In Obecní dům, the nice building by the Powder Tower, Plzeňská Restaurace is a nice uncrowded sk. III restaurant in the cellar. Because tourists don't come here you get treated a lot better than in other places. Find it by going right through the entrance hall and inside the building, then downstairs to the right past the 'vratna'. Open 12.00 to 23.00, but come for lunch, as in the evening it becomes a disco. In the same building on ground floor level there is a nice sk. II restaurant to the right of the entrance hall, and a nice sk. II kava'rna to the left.

Václavské náměsti & nearby streets

At the bottom of Václavské náměstí, on the corner with Na příkopě, is Automat Koruna. This is a huge, cheap stand up place with many counters offering different types of food, and long queues.

Dům Potravin at the top of Václavské nám. is a very fine restaurant, and one can normally find a seat.

On Štěpánská, just off Václavské náměstí, is the Indian restaurant 'Mayur'. Sk. II. About 50 kcs. Usually need reservation. Don't eat the cashews or whatever is put on the table unless you want to pay for them.

Bistro na Můstku on Na můstku at the bottom of Václavské náměstie has palačinky (pancakes) and the famous but hard to come by švestkové knedlíky (plum dumplings). Also spaghetti and pizza. Open Monday to Saturday 9am to 8pm, Sunday 10am to 5pm.

U Šuteru vinárna at Palackého 4 is Moravian. Not bad, usually not full. Sk. III. Open 11am to midnight, Saturday 4pm to midnight, closed Sunday.

Others on same side of Vltava

At Hlavní nádraží there are bufets, a sk. III restaurant with terrible service and a sk. II restaurant.

I would recommend avoiding the restaurant (sk. II*) in the new national theatre, as the food etc is not up to standard.

Opposite CKM in Žitná is a sk. III restaurant with quite okay food, nice wooden tables, and filthy toilets. Can usually get a seat.

If shopping for your own groceries in the potraviny underground at Kotva you can buy all sorts of things that you can't find elsewhere. Open Monday 6am to 7pm, Tuesday to Friday 6am to 9pm, and Saturday 7am to 6pm.

Malá Strana

U Mecenáše on Malostranské nám. is a very good sk. II* restaurant, but it has recently become expensive. Open 5pm to 1am, closed Saturdays. Booking advisable.

Vinárna U Kolovrata (sk. II) is small, nice and rather different with good food. Popular with diplomatic staff. The waiters speak English. Best to reserve. Open 10am to 7pm, closed Sunday & Monday. At Valdštejnská 18, just off Valdste jnská nám. in Malá Strana. Cheaper than U Mecenáše.

Liquid refreshments

Obtainable of course in any of the above, but the following are more specialist.

For those coffee addicts among us, on the Týn Church side of Staroměstské nám. is a sk. II snack bar with a wide variety of coffee.

On Karlova, near the bridge, is the pivnice 'U Malvaze', with a barrel over the door. Here you can taste black beer from 10am to 9pm. Sk. III. Small, lively place, with good atmosphere, but smokey. Black beer also at railway station.

EVENINGS
To find out what's on in Prague visit the Prague Information Service. Best cultural season, spring.

Pubs
Personally I avoid the well-known tourist spots of Prague, but here are a couple if you would like to try them for yourself:

U Kalicha at Na Bojišti 12 was Švejk's pub. This is a tourist attraction; few Prague people come here. Difficult to get in, as full of German package tourists who are shuffled in, then kicked out again to make room for the next bus load, almost before they have time to drink anything.

U Fleků, Praha 1, Křemencova 11. Famous for its dark beer (which is often watered down!). International clientele, but unfriendly staff who rip you off. Nice building and large courtyard.

U. sv. Tomáše at Letenska 12 in Malá Strana is also popular with tourists, but has a much nicer atmosphere than the above two. Sk. II. Open 11am to 3pm, 4pm to 11pm. Good beer, but I wouldn't recommend the food.

Some of the establishments mentioned above under eating are also suitable for an evening drink. Otherwise just head out and find yourself a pivnice or vinárna.

Discos, night clubs etc
The Plzeňská Restaurant in Obecní Dům becomes a disco on Tuesday, Thursday, Friday & Saturday evenings from 7pm to 10pm. 10 kčs entry.

Video Discotek Zlata Husa, Václavsk náměstí. 30 kčs entry. Come early on Saturday night or you won't get in.

Barbara's at Jungmannovo Nám 14 near the bottom of Václavské náměstí is a small bar with disco and dancing open till 4am.

Jalta Club, in Jalta Hotel at Václavské Nám. 45. Live music, disco, show. Expensive. Open 9pm to 4am, closed Tuesday. Tel. 26 55 40-9.

Alhambra: variety show in Ambassador Hotel, Václavské náměstí 5. 50 kčs.

Theatre, Music, etc
It is a major problem to get tickets in Prague. Try asking your hotel, Prague Information Service or Čedok for help, or try the booking office in Alfa Arcade, Václavské náměstí 28. Apart from classical concerts, the best entertainment available in Prague is possibly traditional jazz. Rock music is not common as in the west; keep your eyes open for posters about what is on in

workers' and students' clubs etc, but there could well be only rock videos.

Prague is famous for its Laterna Magika, a sort of blending of cinema, theatre, pantomine and music. Nightly except Monday. Book well in advance, but chance of tickets same day. Národní 40; tel. 26 00 33.

In summer there are outdoor events in courtyards around the city. Mime is especially good, and no knowledge of Czech is required to understand it.

Jazz & folk at Malostranská Beseda, Malostranské nám. Open 8pm. Best to book a table. Bookings tel. 53 04 82 from 7pm.

Reduta on Národní Třida has good jazz, beat & theatre.

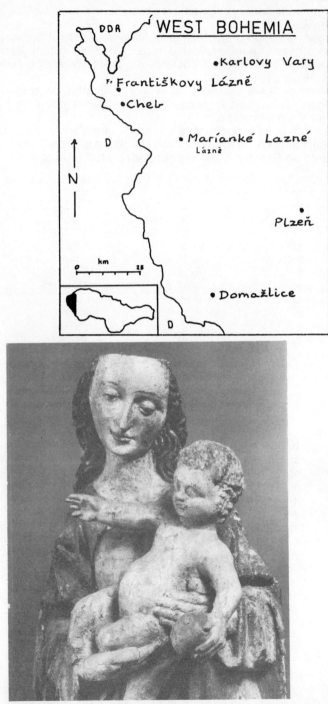

Madonna and Child, Cheb museum

WEST BOHEMIA

CHEB
The centre of Cheb has recently been restored—or at least the front of the buildings that the tourists see. On the main square is a group of restored Gothic merchants' houses known as Špalíček. Behind Špalíček is the building where Albert Wallenstein, the Thirty Years War military commander, was murdered. It now houses a museum (open Tues. to Fri. 8am to 12, 1pm to 4pm; weekend 9am to 12, 1pm to 3pm; closed Monday). The former New Town Hall on the square was built in the 18th century, and now houses an art gallery (open 9am to 12, 1pm to 5pm; closed Mon.; 4 kčs, 2 kčs child, student).

The Church of St Nicholas below the square is a huge forbidding rectangular building from the outside. It was built in the 13th century, and has original Romanesque features. The Church of St Bartholomew has a group of Gothic statues, and during reconstruction after 1945 frescoes were discovered here.

Cheb Castle was built by Emperor Friedrich Barbarossa in the 12th century on the site of a Slav fort. The tower was added in the 13th century, and from 1665 to 1700 the castle's Baroque fortifications were built. The castle features in Schiller's work 'Wallenstein'. Open April to October only, closed Mon.

There are other churches of historical interest, as well as old houses from various ages.

Cheb is small enough to walk around.

NEAR CHEB
Komorn'í hůrka, is the youngest extinct volcano in Czechoslovakia. Last century tunnels were dug into the hill to ascertain its origin. The entrance to one of these has been preserved on the southern slopes. Between Cheb and Františkov y Lázně. Accessible only by car or foot.

Soos is a thermal area with springs and mud pools. Nothing on New Zealand or Icelandic standards, but an interesting area. Some of the plants, normally only found by the sea, grow here due to the salt in the ground from the springs. Entry 1k in season. From Cheb take the Luby train and get off at the 3rd stop, Nový Drahov (1 kčs). The only convenient trains leave at 13.22, 16.00 and 18.50, returning at 14.56, 17.34 and 20.26. There are a few more trains from Trsnice. Walking to Soos from Cheb is 16km via Komorní hůrka (short detour) and Františkovy Lázně (red markers).

Recreational areas on the **Skalka** and **Jesenice** dam lakes.

TO & FROM CHEB
Train connections with West Germany. Trains and buses to Karlovy Vary, but trains are quicker (train about 1 hour, bus 1 hour 40 minutes). Trains and buses to Mariánské Lázně; both take 3/4

hour. Trains & buses to Prague; both take about 4 1/2 hours.
Trains and buses to Frantiskovy Lázne; train much less often but
quicker; regular buses cost 2 kcs, ticket from special automat or
driver. Train fares (osobní): Karlovy Vary 8 kcs; Mariánské Lázne
4 kcs; Prague 32 kcs (48 rychlík), Decín via Chomutov 32 kcs, via
Prague 48 kcs; Frantiskovy Lázne 1 kcs (17 kcs rychlík!). The bus
and railway stations are beside each other. There is also a bus
stand nearer the centre.

INFORMATION & ORIENTATION
Money can be changed at the railway station, but the exchange
office is not always open at the time international trains depart
and arrive. Walking straight ahead from the railway station (the
route veers slightly to the right) brings you to the centre of town.
On the way you pass Cedok at 1. máje 31; tel. 339 51. Money can
be changed at Cedok and Hotel Hvezda on the square.
   'Orientacní Plán Mesta Chebu' is a useful little free map of the
town with addresses in Czech and information in English on the
back. Detailed map of the surrounding area: 'Západoceské
Lázne' (8 kcs).

SLEEPING
It is difficult to get accommodation all year round. Book through
Cedok, Cheb.

Hotels
   Hotel Hvezda, B*, nám. Krále Jiriho 4-6. tel. 225 49. On the
square.
   Hotel Slavie, B, ul. Cs.-sovetského prátelství 32; tel. 332 16.
Near Cedok.
   Hotel Chebský Dvur is not normally available for travellers, as
it is usually full of workers, Vietnamese when I was there.

Private A little private accommodation is available.

Camping At Drenice on Jesenice lake. Open 15/5 to 15/9.

EATING
Restaurant (open 9am to 10pm) and stand-up bufet (6am to 6pm)
at the railway station, both sk. III. Hotel Slavie has a restaurant
open 7am to 11pm, and a vinárna open from about 8pm to 2am
(closed Sun. & Mon.), both sk. II. Hotel Hvezda has a nice sk. II
restaurant open 7am to 11pm; also a sk. IV jidelna, good value,
good variety, sit-down, for workers, get in before they begin to
run out of things. Fortuna, sk. II vinárna & cukrárna on the square.

FRANTISKOVY LÁZNE
One of the three famous West Bohemian spa towns, Frantiskovy
Lázne, with its peaceful atmosphere, large parks, and elegant
white buildings, is a lovely place to stroll around. The spa was
founded last century—named after the Austrian Emperor Franz
I—with buildings in Empire style. Many famous people have visited here, including Beethoven and Goethe. The Spa is known for

treatment of gynaecological diseases (particulary sterility), heart diseases and rheumatism.

Komorní hurka (see 'Cheb') is a 3.5km walk from Františkovy Lázně, red markers.

Although closer to Františkovy Lázně, by public transport Soos (see 'Cheb') is more easily accessible from Cheb. From Františkovy Lázně you must change trains at Tršnice, with the likelihood of a long wait, or take the bus to Cheb and the train from there. By car to Soos, drive to Háek via NovýDrahov. Walking to Soos is 7.5km on the red marked route. Hitching is useless.

The train from here to Karlovy Vary costs 8 kčs, change at Tršnice. Regular buses to Cheb, 2 kčs.

Town map 'Františkovy Lázně', 5.5 kčs.

SLEEPING

Hotel Slovan, Národní třída 5, 351 01 Františkovy Lázně, tel. 94 28 41, opposite Čedok on the main street. Sometimes possible to stay in pensions. Book through Čedok, Františkovy Lázně. Good camp and bungalows at Amerika, 1.5km from the centre. Tel. 94 25 18. Open 1/5 to 30/9.

KARLOVY VARY

Karlovy Vary is the best known of the many spas towns in Czechoslovakia. The resort is tucked in the valley of the River Tepla, and surrounded by forest covered hills. It was founded in the 14th century by the Bohemian king and Holy Roman emperor Karl IV, who bestowed his name on the town. Other famous visitors include Tsar Peter I, Empress Maria Theresa, Goethe, Schiller, Beethoven, Chopin, Brahms, Bismarck and Marx. The Karlovy Vary of today still preserves an air of Victorian grandeur.

Here your ears ring to the sound of German, and your eyes goggle at the expensive clothes, unaffordable in Czechoslovakia, that people are wearing. This is the West Germans' resort. East Germans complain that they can't afford the hotels. The shops are stocked with things that are difficult to buy elsewhere in Czechoslovakia - especially in the food and drink line.

Karlovy Vary could be dubbed a giant sized pick-up joint! Czechoslovaks usually go on spa cures without their husband or wife, and many find a 'spa husband/wife' for the time they are here.

GETTING THERE AND AWAY AGAIN

The quickest and most convenient means of transport between Karlovy Vary and Prague is bus. These buses run frequently, but it is wise to book in advance, especially in peak season. There are some trains.

International services include a bus service between Karlovy Vary and Vienna (269 kčs or 380 ÖS one way), and one train a day to Berlin at 7.40 am (compulsory seat reservation). To/from West Germany, Paris and Britain, change trains at Cheb.

Trains to Cheb run roughly hourly. Rychlík take just under an hour, and osobní just over an hour. The only direct service to Děčín is the train to Liberec which leaves at 11.12 am (rychlík).

There are two railway stations in Karlovy Vary, horní nádraží, the main station where the above services leave from, and dolní nádraží, which is the terminal for the service to Mariánské Lázně, which takes 1 3/4 to 2 hours.

GETTING AROUND
From the main railway station one can cross the road and catch a bus one stop to the local bus station, or walk down the hill and across the bridge. The middle part of the valley is closed to traffic. The main way of getting around is walking, and it's a lovely area to walk in. There are buses to the upper part of the valley from the bus station. They climb along the hill on the east side of the valley, before dropping down higher up and doubling back to Leninovo náměstí.

SLEEPING
It is difficult to get accommodation in Karlovy Vary in the summertime. In winter it is okay, except at New Year.

Camping & Motel
Camping is at a Čedok A category camp in Břczová, a few kilometres up the valley from Karlovy Vary. Phone 252 21-5. This is also an A* category motel. Open from about May to September.

Youth Hostel
CKM's Junior Hotel Alice has a separate building used as a hostel. The price is 27 kcs for those with YHA, ISIC or MSS cards. If booked from abroad, same price as hotel. There are 2 dorms with 13 beds in each. Linen is provided. Shower included. No kitchen. In the summer it's usually full. Junior Hotel is located up the valley in Březová. Local bus no. 7 runs up there about once an hour, or there is an occasional ČSAD bus. Restaurant in hotel open 8 am to 8 pm. Ph. 248 48- 9.

Turistické ubytovny
Best try Junior Hotel (above) first, if you have the right type of ID card. Here are some others you could try:
   Ubytovna TJ Slavia, TU B, Lidická 12, ph. 252 35. 25 beds in 2 to 6 bed rooms. Food from Hotel Slavia, 50 metres away.
   Ubytovna TJ Slovoj, TU B, Školní 21, ph. 252 35. 50 beds. 1 or 2 beds to a room. Open 1/5 to 31/8.

Hotels
   Grandhotel Moskva 4 & 5 star . Mírové nám. 2, ph. 221 21-5, telex 156220. THE hotel in town! Founded in 1701, 300 metres above Čedok, it is one of the oldest extant hotels in the world. Singles from US$25 to US$50 depending on season and whether the room has a private bath or shower. Doubles US$40 to US$80.
   Atlantic Hotel**, Tržiště 23, ph. 247 15 is in the same building as Čedok. Singles 125 kcs, doubles 178 kcs, without bath.
   Juniorhotel Alice. Double rooms with shower: 234 kcs; with an extra bed: 291 kcs. Booked up in the summer. If booked from U.K. price is £12.20 per person full board, £9.90 half board. Showers

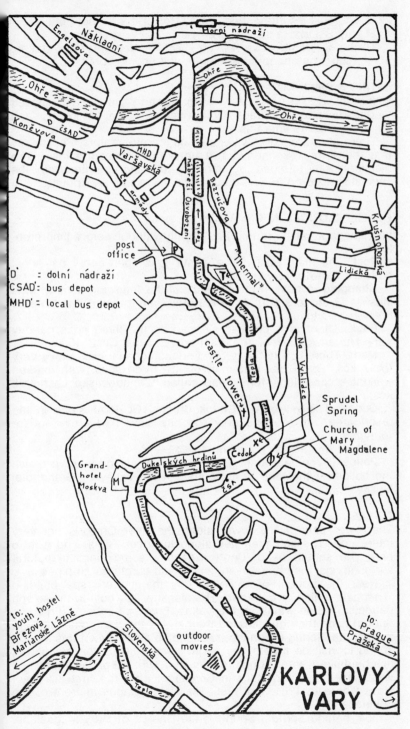

D` : dolní nádraží
CSAD`: bus depot
MHD`: local bus depot

extra and cost a fortune. See 'Youth Hostel' for further details.

Slavia, B, Lidická 12, ph. 272 71-3.

Turist, C, Dimitrovova 18, ph. 268 37. Near the bus station. Something a bit cheaper. Nothing to write home about.

EATING & DRINKING

In the castle tower is a sk I vinárna. Open 7 pm to 2 am. Closed Wednesdays & Thursdays. Otherwise there are the hotels, and plenty of other restaurants etc.

There are 12 mineral water springs in Karlovy Vary. People say that the 13th is Becherovka, a herb liquor from the town. The distillery was founded by Jan Becher, and the liquor in the special shaped bottle is reputed to be made from 123 plants.

OTHER PRACTICAL INFORMATION

Left Luggage: at horní nádraží, usually without weight limit problems.

Post: The main post office, pošta 1, is open every day. Post code for Karlovy Vary is 360 00.

Changing Money: at the bank, or at the following: Grand Hotel Moskva (7 am to 9 pm); Atlantic Hotel(7 am to 7 pm); the Motel at Březová (anytime).

Book: There is a book in German on the three spas Karlovy Vary, Mariánské Lázně, and Františkovy Lázně. Costs 18 kčs.

Maps: There is a not very good orientation map of Karlovy Vary for 7 kčs. For a detailed map of the three spas, with marked walking routes, look for a map called 'Západočeské Lázně' (8 kčs).

Čedok: There are two Čedok offices. Go to the one in the resort area, not the one near the bus station which is not for foreigners.

ČSA: Office across river from Čedok.

Police: If you need to register yourself or extend your visa, visit the police up the lane at the corner of the valley by Grandhotel Moskva.

TO SEE

The lower part of the town, along the river Ohře, is not very interesting. The spa area lies along the river Tepla, and it is to here you should head. Don't expect to see springs in natural surroundings; they have been tamed, and gurgle out of pipes.

Near the bottom of the valley is the modern spa building 'Thermal', which I would dub 'The Monstrosity', built to house spa patients. As one walks up the valley, Pramen Svobody (Freedom Spring) is on the right. Around the bend in the river, one comes to the Sprudel Spring Colonade, shooting up as a geyser. It is a good spring to visit on a cold day, as it is warm inside the building, a much-admired steel structure, finished with Bulgarian marble. It was named the Yuri Gagarin Colonade, after the first astronaut stayed here in 1961 and 1966. His statue stands in front of the colonade.

Just behind Sprudel Spring is the Church of Mary Magdalene, designed by K I Dienzenhofer and built in Baroque style between

1732 and 1736. On the other side of the spring is the castle tower, built in 1608 in place of an older hunting lodge which belonged to Charles IV. In the 18th century it was reconstructed in Baroque form. Now a vinárna. There are many old buildings in Karlovy Vary. Just walk around and you'll find them as you soak in the spirit of the place. A lot of the sanatoria are under reconstruction.

There are many paths in the woods around the valley, most of which are not marked on the town map. If you want to do more than stroll, there are signposts marking longer distance routes outside Čedok and outside the main post office.

CULTURE & ENTERTAINMENT
Karlovy Vary has a reputation for an active cultural life. There is an International Film Festival held in about July every second year or even numbered year. (1988, 1990).

Higher up the valley there are open air movies in the summer.

The place to go at night is the Disco at the Grand Hotel Moskva. Open every night. Entry 20 kcs.

MARIÁNSKÉ LÁZNĚ
Mariánské Lázně is the second most famous of Czechoslovakia's spas. Founded last century with buildings in Empire style. Mariánské Lázně's famous visitors included Gogol, Kafka, Ibsen and Goethe, whose 'Marianbader Elegie' was about the love he felt for Ulrika von Levetzow here. (Marienbad is the German name for Mariánské Lázně). There are 140 springs in the area, 39 of which are used for therapeutical purposes. Worth seeing, the colonade housing Křízový and Rudolph Springs.

The Municipal Museum (Městské Muzeum) at náměstí Klementa Gottwalda 11 has exhibitions on the history of the town and spa, Goethe and West Bohemia. Goethe stayed in this house, one of the oldest in Mariánské Lázně, in 1823. Chopin was in Mariánské Lázně in 1836, in the house called Bílé Labuté. There is a Chopin Museum (Památník Fryderyka Chopina) at Dům Chopin, Tř. Odborářů 47, open Tues. to Thurs. 10am to 12, 2pm to 4pm. Every year in about August-September a Chopin Music Festival is held in Mariánské Lázně

Pravoslavný kostel sv. Vladimira (St. Vladimir Orthodox Church) was built in 1901 and has noteworthy icons.

Golf course in summer. In winter it is used for skiing. At the lake Lido-koupaliště (take bus 17 to the last stop) there is swimming, rowing boats and a restaurant.

EXCURSIONS FROM MARIANSKE LAZNĚ
All of the following are accessible by car or by walking routes. **Kladsky zamek** is a small wooden hunting castle. **Lázně Kynžvart** is a small spa for children. The chateau there is closed. In **Teplá** is a monastery founded in 1193. Mariánské Lázně lies on the edge of Slavkovský les, a large area of woods offering numerous hiking possiblities.

ORGANISED TOURS
A walking tour of Mariánské Lázně leaves from the Čedok office

at 1.30pm every Wed. 3 hours, US$3, refreshments included.
A whole day tour of Karlovy Vary, Františkovy Lázně and Cheb leaves from Cristal Hotel at 8am on Tuesdays. US$8.
Both tours operate from May 15 to Sept. 15. only.

TO & FROM MARIANSKE LAZNĚ

International trains from Frankfurt & Nürnberg to Prague pass through Mariánské Lázně. Most trains to Prague are rychlík. Also buses to Prague. Both via Plzeň. Many trains and some buses to Plzen & Cheb.

One bus a day to Karlovy Vary (not in Xmas-New Year period), leaving Mariánské Lázně 12.30, and leaving Karlovy Vary at 17.00. 20 kčs return, 13 kčs one way. Otherwise several trains a day, but they are much slower than the bus.

One bus a day to České Budějovice, two a day to Domažlice.
Buses leave from outside the railway station.

GETTING AROUND

There are parking places at the north and south ends of town. Local bus service. Route 2, 5, & 6 are trolley buses which operate from 3am to about 0.30am. Cost 1 kčs. Other buses operate from about 6am to about 22.30. Cost 2 kčs. On all buses you must have the exact change.

SLEEPING

For accommodation during the season you should reserve 2 months in advance. All the following have post code 353 01 Mariánské Lázně unless mentioned otherwise.

Camping at 'Autokemp Luxor', 354 71 Velká Hleďsebe, open 1/5 to 15/9. Bungalows or private tents. 5km from Mariánské Lázně. Trolley bus no. 6, then walk 1km south on highway 21. Tel. 3504.

'Autokemp Start', Plzeňská ul., tel. 2062 (camping, bungalows & motel). Open 1/5 to 30/9. 20 bungalows sleeping 2, 2 sleeping 4; 47 kčs per person. Tent camping, 5 sites only, tent 21 kčs, car 21 kčs, adult 10.50 kčs, child 5 kčs. Kitchen. Camping is by a noisy road. Motel, 45 beds, 2 beds to a room, 2 rooms to a bathroom, 91 kčs per person. Noisy on the street side of building. Restaurant (sk. III). Parking. The manager can read English.

'Ubytovna TJ Lokomotiva', TU, Plzenská 9, tel. 39 17. Dorms all year, and bungalows 1/5 to 31/10. No tent camping.

'Juniorhotel Krakonoš', tel. 26 24-5. Two hotels, B & a B* dependence. YHA hostel on the top floor 27 kčs for members. Booked from abroad £10 to £14, half or full board. Bus no. 12, which runs roughly hourly between 5am & 11pm.

The following hotels can be booked through Čedok. 'Corso', B, Odborářů 61, tel. 30 991. Central. 'Excelsior', B*, Odborářů 121, tel. 27 05-6. Central. 'Esplanade', ***, Karlovarská 438, tel. 21 62-4. Towards the golf course. 'Hotel Golf', A* de luxe, 353 00 Mariánské Lázně, tel. 26 51-5. Outskirts of town by golf course. Flashiest hotel in Mariánské Lázně.

INFORMATION

Čedok is in Hotel Excelsior. A map of the town is available for 9 kčs. For the surrounding area use the map 'Západočeské Lázně'.

EATING & EVENINGS
Sk. II & III restaurants at railway station.
The following have been recommended to me. Grill at Hotel Slunce, Vrchlivkého 30. Koliba on Dusíkova. The best restaurant in town is Hotel Golf's, sk.I, expensive. Lunapark: restaurant (with music) in daytime, disco at night when it becomes a young peoples' hangout, out of town to the north, get there by car, taxi or walk. Good disco (sk. I) at Hotel Corso. Lil Club, U Sokolova 336, sk. I nightclub, open all night.

PLZEŇ
Everyone has heard of Plsener lager. Plzeň is its original home. In 1295 King Václav II gave the town the right to brew beer and 25 breweries were built. In 1839 the inhabitants got together and built a large modern brewery, since when 'Pilsener Urquell' (Plzeňský prazdroj) has been exported all over the world. Plzeň is also well-known for its Škoda works.

It is a problem to build here as the rivers keep moving. The old town was not on the same site and no one is certain when the first settlement developed

Today with a population of 170,000 Plzeň is the 6th largest town in Czechoslovakia, and the capital of West Bohemia. Easily accessible from Germany, in the weekends it is full of German groups.

TO SEE
Individuals may not tour the brewery. But if there is a group going on a tour you may be able to tag on (weekdays only).

In the main square, nám. Republiky, is the 15th century Gothic St Bartholomew's Church. It has a very high ceiling, and nice glass windows and other decor. Its 103 metre steeple is the highest in Bohemia. There are angels on the iron gate of the church facing Supraphon. Only one is clean; the others are black. If you hold the clean angel and make a wish it will come true. Students come here before exams and the spot is a popular meeting place. While in the square, take a look at the frontage of the radnice (town hall).

In Masné krámy, the old butcher shop on Pražska the Západočeská galerie holds temporary art exhibitions. The main gallery is at Kopeckého sady 2. Opposite Masné krámy the old watertower is being restored.

Around the corner on Perlova' is the entrance to a network of passages under the town (Plzeňské Historické Podzemí). They were opened to the public in 1985. Open all year Wed. to Sun. 9.30am to 5pm. Entry 5 kčs. No children under 6 years old. The underground passages were used to store food, wine and beer. Later they were used by the brewery to store beer in 1000 litre barrels.

Nearby is the Pivovarské muzeum at Veleslavinova 6, a museum of beer brewing. You must go around with a guide.

Other museums are the Západočeské (West Bohemian) mu-

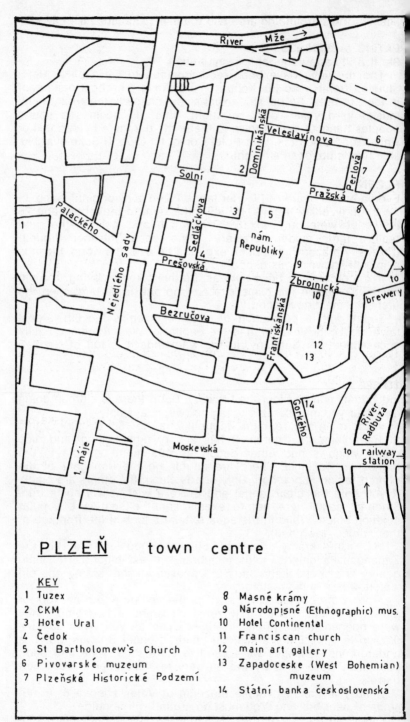

PLZEŇ town centre

KEY
1 Tuzex
2 CKM
3 Hotel Ural
4 Čedok
5 St Bartholomew's Church
6 Pivovarské muzeum
7 Plzeňská Historické Podzemí

8 Masné krámy
9 Národopisné (Ethnographic) mus.
10 Hotel Continental
11 Franciscan church
12 main art gallery
13 Zapadoceske (West Bohemian) muzeum
14 Státní banka československá

seum next to the main art gallery, and the Národopisné (Ethnographic) museum at nám. Republiky 13.

On Františkánská is the Františkánský (Franciscan) church. It has good acoustics, and its organ is the oldest in Plzeň. There are sometimes organ concerts here. There was also a monastery here, now partly destroyed.

The suburb of Bílá Hora has lakes and woods and is the nicest part of town.

Outside Plzeň
Kozel is a nice castle and park near Štáhlavy. Get there by train (České Budějovice line), then walk a couple of kilometres or so.

EVENTS
Every year in about the first week of July a festival of folk and tramping songs called PORTA is held in Plzeň.

TO & FROM PLZEŇ
Plzeň lies on the E 12 between Prague and Nürnberg. International trains pass through here. Direct trains to Prague, Cheb via Mariánské Lázně, Domažlice, Železné Rudy and České Budějovice (osobní & rychlík)

INFORMATION
Čedok and CKM are both just off the square. Čedok are at Prešovská 10, on the corner with Sedláckova (tel. 37216, 36776, post code 303 21). CKM are at Dominikánská 1 (tel. 37585, post code 305 36).

Autoturist emergency breakdown service, 1. maje 61, tel. 276000.

Státní banka Československá, Gorkého 1. Československá obchodní banka, Tomanova 5, open Mon. to Fri. 8am to 1pm, Wed. also 3pm to 5pm. Use the second bank if you want to have money transferred to Czechoslovakia.

Tuzex are at Kollárova 1.

There is a town map in book form with information in Czech.

SLEEPING
Camping
Intercamp Bílá Hora, ul. 28. října, 301 62 Plzeň-Bílá Hora; tel. 628 50. Tent camping and 4 bedded chalets. Bus no. 20 from nám. Republiky. Open 1/5 to 30/9.

Autokemp Ostende, tel. 377 24. Tent camping & 2, 3, & 4 bed chalets. Bus no 13 A, 1km walk from the last stop at Bolevec. Open May to September.

Turistická ubytovna
Ubytovna TJ Lokomotiva, TU A, Úslavdká 75, 301 59 Plzeň; tel. 480 41. 2 to 6 to a room. Tram 2, towards Světovar.

Hotels
Ural, A*, Nám. Repuliky 33, 305 31 Plzeň; tel. 326 85-8. Right on the square. Parking for guests on square. Posh sk. II restaurant.

Škoda, B* (***), nám. Českých bratří 10; tel. 275 840. Short way
out of centre.

EVENINGS
Svazáček, tř. 1. máje 125. Tram 1 or 4. Pub downstairs. Dancing
upstairs (different entrance).
Two pubs with black beer: U Žumbery, Bezručova 14; Na
Rychté near the south railway station.
In the same building as CKM is Kavarna Dominik, popular when
there is something good on.
Moravská vinárna, Bezručova 2, open 10am to 10pm, go early,
wine in carafe brought in bulk from Moravia.
Jadran vinárna, Bezručova 9.
U námořnika, with sailing decorations, near bus station.
Dancing at Hotel Continental (Zbrojnická 8), Slávie (nám. Re-
publiky 28), Ural, Beseda (centre of town), Sport (near ice skating
rink), Svazaček (see above) and Sputnik (U Borského parku 20).

DOMAŽLICE
A south-west Bohemian town, not far from the West German
border, Domažlice is the centre of the Chod region. The Chods
are an ethnic group of unknown origin who were given special
privileges by the Přemyslids and the Luxemburgs in return for
guarding the western borders. No-one knows if they were brought
here for the task or if they are indigenous to the area. Their
culture has survived, and in August the Chodsko Region Folklore
Festival is held in Domažlice.
Domažlice is one of the nicest towns in Bohemia. It was
founded in 1262 on the site of an older settlement. At the end of
the 13th century a royal castle was built. You can climb to the top
of the round castle tower which has been preserved in its 13th
century form. There is a Chod museum, which, when I visited,
had information sheets one could borrow in English out the back
gathering dust. A really nice town to wander in.
Hotels and turistická ubytovna. Camping at Babylon, a few
kilometres towards the border. The nearby Folmava-Furth im
Wald-Schafberg road border crossing is open 24 hours.

Karlovy Vary

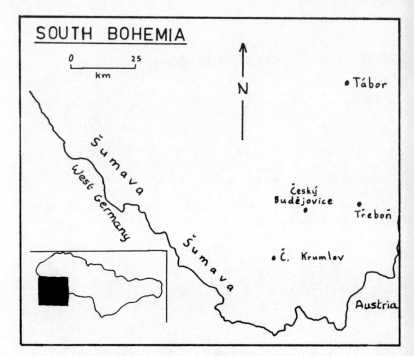

Cesky Krumlov, South Bohemia

SOUTH BOHEMIA

SUMAVA

The Šumava are low forested mountains stretching along the Czechoslovak-West German border in south-western Bohemia. They include glacial lakes, and lots of peat bogs, some of which are completely closed nature reserves. With their beautiful tranquil nature the Šumava are a popular holiday area for Czechs. From the Czech side the Šumava don't seem as high as they are, because they incline gradually into the interior. Human settlement is sparse. The area includes Lipno hydro lake. For the last 10 years there have been plans to make the area a national park, but a problem is the industry already in the area.

Only half of the area is open to the public, as the rest is a closed border area with the military taking over more and more of it. The far side of Lipno Lake is now closed, and the road to Ovesná, Černý Kříž, Stožec and Nové Údolí has been closed. The only access to this is by train and marked track. Nové Údolí is completely closed. The whole central part of Šumava is a closed military area, making access between the northern and southern Šumava difficult. Sometimes other tracks may be closed by the military. I recommend that you ask for up to date information before walking on tracks anywhere near the border. You can often *hear* the military!

ACCOMMODATION (General)

Accommodation is difficult to get, even in the off season when there are many children's groups and workers on company paid breaks. All dormitory accommodation etc. is full in summer. Campsites could possibly be used even when closed.

EATING (General)

If there is no pub in the village, chalets owned by factories etc. will have some hours when they are open to the public.

MAPS

The two maps which cover the Šumava area are occasionally available. Most of what I describe below is on the map 'Šumava Prachaticko'.

PRACHATICE

Prachatice is one of the Šumava towns worth visiting. Founded in the early 14th century as a trading post for Bavaria and Bohemia. Wencesles IV gave Prachatice a monopoly on the supply of salt at the end of the 14th century, resulting in prosperity for the town. Some of the fortifications built in 1323 survive. The oldest and best preserved building is St. James Church, with its striking roof timbers and beautifully carved wooden decoration. The exteriors of both the new and the old town halls on the square are worth seeing. They are decorated with biblical and legendary scenes.

Personally I found Prachatice a very pleasant place, and the people friendly and helpful, even if no one spoke English.

HUSINEC
Nearby Husinec was the birthplace of Jan Hus. In the house on the square where he was born is a museum devoted to his life and work. One can see the lime tree under which he preached. He preached under lime trees in other villages too. There is a baker's school in Husinec, explaining why the area has such good bread.

Information
Information on Šumava from odbri cestovníhr ruchu (travel dept.) of Okresní Národní Výbor (Distric National Committee) on the square.

Sleeping
There are two hotels, both on the main square. Národní dům, (B); tel. 35 61, 25 64. Doubles 120 kčs without bath, 180 with bath. Doubles only. Individuals must pay for two beds. Zlatá stezka, (B); tel. 38 41. Newly renovated.

There is no dormitory accommodation for tourists, but you could try asking if you could sleep at the workers' hostel Ubytovna OSP (20 kčs).

Eating
Prachatice's nice local bread is baked in big round loaves. The restaurant opposite the town halls is a rather ordinary smoky place, but I found the waitress friendly and the cooking better than normal.

Tramping
From Prachatice you can climb Libín (1086m) on the red marked track heading south. The 6km walk takes about 1 1/2 hours. The track is good, but is sometimes blocked by felling. On top is a tall lookout tower, open all the time. From Libín one can drop down to the Prachatice-Volary road at Libínské Sedlo (1/2 hour, 2km), from where one can follow the green marked track back to Prachatice, or walk, hitch, or hope for a bus on the road. One can also continue to Volary (22km from Prachatice).

Following the red marked track in a northerly direction from Prachatice brings you after a 6km walk to Husinec.

KŘIŠTANOVICKÝ RYBNÍK
A nice lake off the Prachatice-Volary road, 8km from Prachatice, and 1 1/2 km walk from the nearest bus stop. You can see it from Libín, from where it is a 6km walk. Camp site open June to August.

VOLARY
A useful centre for the Šumava, with houses in alpine style.

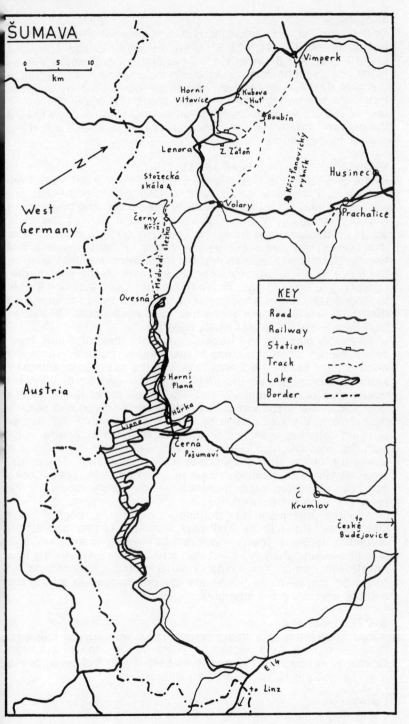

ŠUMAVA

0   5   10
km

N

Vimperk

Horní Vltavice

Kubova Huť

Boubín

Lenora

Z. Zátoň

Křišťanovický rybník

Husinec

West Germany

Stožecká skála ▲

Volary

Prachatice

Černý Kříž

Medvědí stezka

Ovesná

KEY

Road

Railway

Station

Track

Lake

Border

Austria

Horní Planá

Hůrka

Lipno

Černá v Pošumaví

Č Krumlov

to České Budějovice

E 14

to Linz

Sleeping

Difficult to get accommodation at any time of the year. Both hotels, Bobík (B*, tel. 923 51-4, on the square), and Turistická chata (B, tel. 922 60, near the railway station) are usually full, as is the ubytovací hostinec Sport, down a side road near the station (tel. 923 12). Turistická chata is usually booked up by schools. Your best bet may be the Turistická chata (TU A, tel. 921 67) in one of the old wooden buildings on the right if you head toward the square from the station. Open all year (but when I was there closed for painting!).

MEDVĚDI STEZKA (THE BEAR TRAIL)

Medvědi stezka (the Bear Trail) is the yellow marked track from Ovesná at the top of Lipno Lake to Černy Kříž. Both ends are accessible only by train. The walk is 15km long, and takes about 6 hours including time to sightsee. The first part of the route winds up through large intriguing boulders, good to shelter under if it rains. There shouldn't be any bears to disturb, as the last bear in the Šumava was shot at the monument you pass later on the trip. Now there are bears only in Slovakia. At the sign 'kaple' (chapel) you can get right inside the rocks. If you look uphill from the sign to the top of a rock, you might be forgiven for imagining that the builders of Stonehenge had been here. About 100 metres past here is Vik Ian, a rocky balancing trick.

From the boulders the track drops to the beautiful little lake, Jelení jezírko. Then you come to the village of Jeleni, where the ditch coming out of the tunnel is part of the 44km Švarcenberský kanál which connected the Vltava with the Danube to transport timber. It was built from 1789 to 1822 and part of it was in use until 1962. The section at Jeleni is the only part you can see, as the rest is in the area closed by the military. Roughly 2km further on from Jeleni is a short side track to Medvědí kámen, a stone with the inscription in German 'Bären Stein' marking the place where the last bear in the Šumava was killed in 1856. The actual bear is in the hunting museum in Hluboka (see 'České Budějovice'). From here the track winds slowly down to the railway station at Černy Kříž.

Although this track was definitely open to the public, I was stopped by the military just past Medvědí kámen and told I shouldn't be there. Then I was tailed all the way to the train. This was in autumn, when there were no other walkers. Maybe it's less hassle in summer. You could turn back at the lake instead of going on to Jeleni, as the locals are encouraged to inform the military when they see strangers.

STOŽECKA SKALA

A two hour return trip from Černy Kříž railway station following the blue marked track westwards. From the top one can see West Germany. Although this was open in 1985, I wouldn't be surprised if you encounter hassles with the military.

LIPNO

Lipno Hydro Lake (726m.a.s.l.) on the upper reaches of the river Vltava is about 43km long, with many resorts on its shores.

Popular for boating and fishing. The causeway at Černá v Posumaví is particularly popular with fishermen (men only), especially around the bridge. In season rowing boats can be hired by the south end of the causeway. Look for the sign 'Půjčovna Lodí'. Note that Černá v Posumaví railway station lies on the other side of the causeway at Hůrka.

The blue marked track on the east side of the lake is not very interesting, and the other side of the lake has been closed by the military.

Sleeping

At Hurka there's Turisticka ubytovna (A) opposite Cerna v Posumavi railway station. On the Hurka side of the causeway is a campsite open in season only.

In Cerna v Posumaví itself there is autocamping near the causeway, and there are 3 campsites on the road to Jestřábí. All open seasonally only. Not far along this road is Hotel Racek (B, tel. 961 03) where you are unlikely to be able to get a bed.

SOUMARSKÝ MOST

5km from Volary towards Lenora. Popular with canoeists who use the Vltava above Lipno lake. Campsite by the station open mid June to mid September.

LENORA

Lenora is the last of the former glassmaking places in the area. Accessible by bus or train. Sleeping: Ubytovací Hostinec U Hynků, 384 42 Lenora; tel. 988 43.

HORNI VLTAVICE

Horni Vltavice has the best camping ground in the Šumava, as well as a good pub. Tent camping and cabins. Open summer only. From here one can make a roundtrip over Boubín (see below). Horni Vltavice Railway Station is up above the village. Trains stop here in summer only. From Horni Vltavice it is 13km to the Strázný-Philippsreut road border crossing, open 24 hours. Winter sports at Strážný.

BOUBÍN

There is some interesting walking in the area of Boubín. The following is described as a one way walk from Kubova Hut to z. Záton (railway station), but as a longer walk you could make it a round trip from Horni Vltavice. Horni Vltavice to Kubova Hut is a 4km walk. From Kubova Hut it is 5.5km on the blue marked track to Boubín, at 1362m, the highest point in the publicly accessible part of the Šumava. This part of the trip is neither very interesting nor very steep, taking 1 1/4 hours up through the forest. There is not much view from the top, as it is covered in trees. The monument Johnův Kámen and the monument on top of Boubín have the altitude written in feet!

Following the blue markers again brings one to a deer park. In the park you must walk on the marked paths only. The park is closed to the public in the months of June, September and October. From here the blue markers lead down to Boubínský prales, a small area of virgin forest. You can't enter it, but you can walk around its perimeter. There is a little lake at the bottom, Boubínské Jezírko, with refreshments for sale in season. From here it is 3km following the green markers to z. Záton. On the way you pass a campsite, accessible by road, and open from mid May to mid September. The entire trip from Kubova hut to z. Záton is 14.5km and takes 4 hours with stops, if you neither enter the deer park nor circumnavigate Boubínský prales. To Horni Vltavice, instead of following the green markers from the lake, continue following the blue markers to the village of Záton, then the green markers to Horni Vltavice.

VIMPERK
Vimperk was a German town before the war. It still has a German flavour. It has a not very interesting old castle. One can also climb Boubín from here, but it is a much longer walk than from Kubova Hut.

CHURAŇOV
A good winter sports area. Access by bus from Vimperk. Hotels only; no dormitories or camping.

ANTIGL
Another pleasant area.

ŽELEZNA RUDA
Železná Ruda and nearby Špičák are winter sports resorts. There are two pretty glacial lakes nearby, Černé (Black) jez. and Čertovo (Devil's) jez. 2km away is the Železná Ruda - Bayer. Eisenstein road border crossing (open 24 hours). Hojsova Stráž, 12km north of here, is another winter resort.

PUBLIC TRANSPORT
The main means of getting to and getting around Šumava is by train. The bus service is bad. Volary is the transport hub of southern Šumava, where various different train routes have their terminuses. Most of these run about once every 3 hours.

One of them runs to České Budějovice (3 1/2 hours) via Lipno and Český Krumlov. Use this train for Lipno, Medvědi stezka & Stozecká skála. From Volary be careful that you get in the right carriage, as most trains split at Cerný Kříž with one part going on to Nové Údolí (the public may travel only as far as Stozec). But some trains run via Stozec anyway.

Another train runs to Čicenice on the České Budějovice—Plzeň line via Prachatice. There are also buses between Volary and Prachatice, but the train runs more frequently.

A third line is from Volary to Strakonice, also on the České Budějovice - Plzeň line, via Vimperk. Use this train for Soumarský most, Lenora, Záton, Horni Vltavice & Kubova Hut.

There is a bus once a day between České Budějovice and Volary, leaving České Budějovice at 13.30.

Bus is the best way between České Budějovice and Prachatice.

From Volary to Plzeň take the train to Strakonice or Čicenice.

CESKÝ KRUMLOV

Český Krumlov is one of the most picturesque towns in Czechoslovakia. A medieval town on the banks of the Vltava, with cobbled streets, little back lanes, and arch covered footpaths, Český Krumlov is overlooked by what is considered to be the second most outstanding castle in the country.

The old town covers a large area. Entering it via Horní, you cross a very high bridge, and can see that the Vltava almost cuts off the old town as an island here. Many old houses are falling down, but an effort is underway to reconstruct them .

GETTING THERE

There are buses roughly once an hour from České Budějovice on working days, but the service is slack at the weekend. Český Krumlov is within easy daytripping distance of České Budějovice.

PRACTICAL INFORMATION

Čedok is on the square at Gottwaldovo náměstí 15, phone 3444. There is a bank on the square.

SLEEPING

Camping

There is a camp site 2 km upstream from the centre of Český Krumlov: **Veřejné Tábořiště Nové Spol'i** It is a site only, not a fully fledged camping ground. Open 1/5 to 31/10.

Hostels

Turistická ubytovna Panská ulice, A & B class, tel. 44 01. 91 beds, 3 to 14 beds to a room. Open summer season only, from 6 pm. In the old centre, 50 m from the square. Partly permanently booked by Čedok Český Krumlov.

Turistická ubytovna Slavoj I & II, A class, Chvalšinská silnice, tel. 22 11. 135 beds altogether, mostly 3 bed rooms, one 12 bed room. Most beds in No. II. Open 1/5 to 30/9.

Hotels

It is difficult to get a hotel room in the summer. Best to reserve before you come to Czechoslovakia!

Hotel Růže, B*, tel. 22 45. Nice hotel in the old centre. Reception open 3 pm to 8 am only. Snack bar open evenings only in hotel. Otherwise restaurant 200 m away in the town square. Double rooms only. Extra beds available.

Interhotel Krumlov, B*, Gottwaldovo nám. 13, tel. 20 40. On the square in the centre of the old town. Not as nice as Růže. Prices (half board) booked from abroad through Čedok: single with shower US$13 to 17, without shower US$12 to 16; double with bath US$12 to 16 per person, with shower US$11 to 15, without shower US$10 to 15. Variation in price depends on season. Price if you walk in off the street: double 210 kcs with bath, 150 kcs without bath, single 120 kcs with shower, 100 kcs without shower. A few 'B' class rooms without bath: double 120 kcs, single 80 kcs.

From June to September you need a reservation. The rest of the year is not so bad. Reception open day & night.

Hotel Vyšehrad, B*, tel. 23 11, 23 51 or 30 70. In the newer part of town to the north.

There are no other hotels in Český Krumlov.

EATING & DRINKING

Restaurant U hroznu, class III, on the square. Class II vinárna (open 8 pm to 2 am) in the same building. **Pub of Peter of Rosenberg**. The Czech family, Rosenberg, possessed Southern Bohemia. The 5 leaf rose symbolises the 5 families of Rosenberg. Restaurant **U mešta Vidné** ('at the town of Vienna'), sk. III, okay.

TO SEE

The whole old town is worth seeing, just stroll around. Sv. Vít kostel, the main church of the town, is magnificent, even under restoration! The back alleys can also be worth exploring. For example from Radniční, just before the bridge, walk back towards Horní bridge along the lane near the river. Go under the arch at the end of the lane. To the right is Horní bridge. To the left is an old mill. If the river is low enough go down to the river and rock hop to the left and you can see the remains of the waterwheel etc. If you head directly towards the castle viaduct from the square, there is another old mill before the little footbridge.

The museum is on Horní, opposite Hotel Růse. Open Tuesday to Saturday 9 am to 12 noon, 12.30 pm to 4 pm (to 6 pm on Wednesday). Sunday 9 am to 12 noon only.

The castle is situated on a hill on the opposite side of the river to the old town centre. The lower castle was built in the 13th century, and the upper castle in the first half of the 14th century. The entire complex was rebuilt in Renaissance style by Italian architects in the 16th century. There were once bears in the moat. From May to August it is open to the public from 8 am to 5 pm, and in April, September and October from 9 am to 4 pm. Closed during the rest of the year, on Mondays, and between 12 noon and 1 pm. When the castle is closed it is still possible, and worth while, to walk up through the courtyards. Up the hill above the castle are the gardens (open until 7 pm) in which is an open air theatre where the audience's seats move to follow the actors. Plays during summer holidays only. There is also a Baroque theatre from the 18th century, presently under reconstruction.

On the same side of the river as the castle is the monastery. It was rebuilt in Baroque style in the 17th century, but the cloister with the Stations of the Cross is Gothic, dating from 1491. The monastery is not open, but one can walk around the outside.

NEAR ČESKÝ KRUMLOV
Klet

Klet (1008 m.a.s.l.) is the highest peak in the area. On top is a TV tower, a lookout tower and a pub (Horská chata Klet, 382 03 Křemže, tel. 32 89) with dorm accommodation for 14. In good weather you can see the Alps from here, but usually only in autumn or winter. There is a green marked track up Klet from the castle in Český Krumlov. The 8 km climb takes 2 to 3 hours. There is also a chairlift up from Krasetín, 2.5 km from Holubov, which is on the Český Krumlov - České Budějovice railway line. Bus to Krasetín. The chairlift operates all year, except Mondays, but may be closed in October and November for maintenance. One can also walk up from Holubov (green marked track).

Zlatá Koruna
At Zlatá Koruna is a former Cistercian monastery founded in 1263. Built in Gothic style, there was major reconstruction in the 18th century, and restoration after the Second World War. The library of theological literature is open to the public from 1 April to 31 October from 9 am to 4 pm, closed Mondays. There are buses to Zlatá Koruna from Český Krumlov. The railway station is up the hill 1.5 km out of the town, and there are not many trains. Klet can also be climbed from here by the red marked route which leads up past the railway station.

Dívčí Kámen
Dívčí Kamen was a Celtic settlement. The name means 'maidens rock'. Today one can see fantastic extensive ruins of a castle overlooking the Vltava. The nearest village is Třísov, 1 1/2 km walk away (red markers). Buses and trains in this area are infrequent. Hitch-hiking may be possible, but there is little traffic. From the railway station in Holubov, Dívčí Kámen is 3 km along the yellow marked track, or from Zlatá Koruna, 7 km on the red marked track (opposite direction to Klet). One can also walk the 12 km along the red marked route beside the Vltava to Dívčí Kámen from Boršov n. Vltava on the main České Budějovice - Český Krumlov road. Unfortunately the Vltava stinks here of pollution. A lot of the problem comes from a pulp mill above Český Krumlov. The effluent is piped to an outlet below the town so you don't smell it in Český Krumlov itself.

ČESKÉ BUDĚJOVICE
České Budějovice is the capital of the picturesque South Bohemian region. It was founded in 1265 by King Přemysl Otakar II, as a fortress protecting the Crown's interests in the south cof Bohemia. The town grew through trading salt and wine from Austria. During the Renaissance České Budejovice owned silver mines in the area but the town was impoverished during the Thirty Years War. In 1641 České Budějovice was almost completely destroyed by fire, resulting in a lot of Baroque reconstruction. The population was half Czech and half German before the Second World War. The inhabitants usually spoke both languages, and got on well together.

The first horse-drawn railway in continental Europe ran from České Budějovice to Linz in Austria last century. Goods trains had the right of way over passenger trains. Giving way consisted of going back to the nearest station, or if that was too far, the drivers jacked the carriages off the tracks! In the heyday of the horse-drawn railway, around 1868, the railway company owned

662 horses, 1092 goods wagons, and 65 passenger wagons. Some remnants can be seen from today's railway, which by and large follows the same route.

The highlight of the town is its magnificent square, one of the largest in Europe. The houses surrounding it have Renaissance gables and arcades. In its centre stands the Baroque Samson's Fountain, designed by Josef Dietrich in 1727. The town hall on the south-west side of the square is also Baroque, replacing an earlier Gothic town hall in 1731. At one corner of the square is the 16th century Black Tower. At 72 metres high it used to provide a good view, but now it is under reconstruction and consequently closed to the public. Adjoining it is St Nicholas Cathedral, founded in the 13th century, but rebuilt many times. Its present style dates from restoration work undertaken in the middle of the 17th century. During the Thirty Years War, one of its chapels was converted into a strongroom to house the coronation jewels. One of the oldest buildings in České Budějovice is the early Gothic Dominican monastery, dating from 1265. What remains of the town walls dates from the 15th century. A couple of the more interesting streets to stroll along are Česká and Knežská. Museum of South Bohemian history.

The other highlight of České Budějovice is Budvar beer, better known to some by its German name, Budweiser. České Budějovice is the home of the original Budvar beer, which to my palate is the best in Czechoslovakia. Unfortunately the brewery is not open to the public, but you can buy its product around the town.

There is a local bus service in České Budějovice. There is also a night bus service which consists of one bus running once an hour to all parts of the town via a complicated route.

HLUBOKA NAD VLTAVOU

A small replica of Windsor Castle set in a magnificent park on a steep hill above the Vltava. Founded by King Přemysl Otakar II, it was originally built in Gothic style in the 13th century. Hluboka was at this time considered a strategic point. During its life-time it has been owned by various noble families, and has undergone reconstruction at various times. One of its prior owners, Záviš of Falknstejn, was executed in 1290 below the castle in Execution Meadow, as a result of court intrigue and politics. During the Hussite period the castle was a stronghold of the Catholics. After the Battle of White Mountain, the castle was confiscated by the Emperor and sold to the Spanish general Balthasar Marradas, in recognition of the services he rendered to the Hapsburgs in the suppression of the revolt. In 1661 the castle came into the ownership of the Schwarzenberg family. Between 1840 and 1871 the Schwarzenbergs had it rebuilt in neo- Gothic style and it became the centre of the Schwarzenberger domains, the largest private property in Bohemia. In 1945 the entire Schwarzenberger holdings were nationalized.

The castle is open to the public from April to October from 9 am to 12 noon, and 1 pm to 5 pm. Closes 1 hour earlier in April, September & October, and always closed Mondays. The last entry is 1 hour before closing time. A tour in English is unlikely, but maybe you could find someone on the tour who could translate for you. The castle contains various collections, e.g. Bohemian and Venetian glass, works of art, hunting trophies. The riding school houses the Aleš Art Gallery, named after the popular Czech painter Mikuláš Aleš. It contains works of South Bohemian Gothic, and 17th century Dutch and Flemish art. Open same hours as castle.

At Ohrada, 2 km south of Hluboká, in an old hunting mansion, is an interesting museum of hunting, milling and fishing. The last bear killed in the Šumava is exhibited here. Open the same time as Hluboká Castle. Some labelling of exhibits is in English. There is also a little zoo at Ohrada.

There are fishing lakes everywhere in the area. Pleasant walks can be made among the lakes and forests.

There are buses from České Budějovice to Hluboká nad Vltavou, but the service is slack at weekends. There are two Hluboká railway stations, one on the České Budějovice—Plzeň line, and one on the České Budějovice—Tábor line, but both are out of town, especially the one on the Plzeň line. Fare 1 kčs, takes 10 minutes. From Hluboká to Ohrada is a pleasant 2 km walk among trees and lakes (follow the yellow markers). One can also drive. From Ohrada one can walk back to the main road, or walk in the opposite direction to the railway station on the Plzeň line (ask for directions).

GETTING THERE & AWAY AGAIN There is still a rail service to Linz, but the horses are gone. České Budějovice is the first main town on the E 14 after it enters Czechoslovakia from Linz. The E 14 is the main route from Salzburg to Prague. There is a bus service to the border (you might have to change buses in Kaplice).

The bus station is beside the train station in České Budějovice. Both have a left luggage service, although the bus station's is only open limited hours. Both have a 15 kg weight limit. The road opposite the railway, but a bit to the right, Maršála Malinovského, later becoming Kanovnická, leads to the square.

INFORMATION
Čedok, Norb. Frýda 31.
CKM, tř. Osvobození 14, 370 21 České Budějovice, tel. 36 138.
Šport Turist, Štitného (near station). Only change money for people from socialist countries.
Autoturist, Kanovnická 11 (near the square).

SLEEPING
Camping
Autokemping Dlouhá louka, A class, tel. 383 08. Bungalows & tent camping. Čedok camp. Dirty & primitive, but lot of friendly East Germans. Restaurant & bar. Bus no. 6.
Autokempink Stromovka, B, tel. 288 77. Open 1/4 to 31/10. Bus 6. Largely booked up by Autoturist for their package holidays for Czechs.
Camping also near Hluboká.

Student Hostels
In the summer holidays one can stay in student hostels by booking through CKM. But they are nearly always full!

Hotels
Gomel, ****, tř. Míru, tel. 289 41, 279 49. Skyscraper 10 minutes walk north of the square towards Prague, with a 'G' on top. 469 beds, mostly in double rooms.
Hotel Zvon, A* & B, Žižkovo nám. 28, tel. 353 61-62. On the square. With bath singles 312 kčs, doubles 351 kcs. Without bath singles 104 kčs, doubles 156 kcs, plus 21 kcs every time you want to use the communal shower. Breakfast is available in your room, or from 6 am in the restaurant. Full in the summer; at other times of year should be able to get a room.
Malše, B, Nádražní 31, tel. 276 31, opposite the railway station.
Interhotel Slunce, B, Žižkovo nám. 37, 370 42 České Budějovice, tel. 367 55, 387 61, telex 144325. On the square. Singles without bath US$12 to 16; doubles without bath US$11 to 13 per person, with bath US$13 to 17, prices varying with season. Exchange office.
Parkhotel, B class Čedok hotel in Hluboká nad Vltavou. Tel. 96 52 81, 96 53 41. Similar prices to Slunce.

EATING & DRINKING
Slunce seems to be popular with the locals. Smoky, and a little sleezy. Restaurant. Kavárna. Vinárna (not a nice one).
Masné Krámy('Butcher Shop'), 23 Trida 5 Kvetna. Sk. III restaurant with large alcoves. More a pub, but has food as well. Good place to taste the local suds. Women a distinct minority!

TŘEBOŇ
Třeboň epitomizes a certain type of South Bohemian landscape, with its forest, meadows, peatbogs and fish lakes. This peaceful South Bohemian town and spa is the centre of a large area of fish lakes, created centuries ago for breeding fish and connected by an ingenious system of canals created in the 16th century. The lakes are surrounded by centuries old oak and linden trees and the whole district is a major sanctuary for water birds. The town is famed for carp breeding with the fish harvested in autumn.
Třeboň was founded in 1220. Many Late Gothic, Renaissance and Baroque buildings remain today. Today's castle buildings were erected on the site of the original 13th castle from the 16th to 18th century. The Town Hall and remnants of the town walls, ramparts and gates date from the 16th century. There are many old houses, and a Baroque brewery from the 18th century.
One of the fish lakes is right by the town, attractive with its trees and boats. Walking around it to the left brings one to the imposing neo-Gothic mausoleum of the Schwarzenberk family (1874-77).
For walking in this area, buy the map 'Táborsko', which includes Třeboň.

GETTING THERE

Třeboň lies on the Vienna-Prague express train route. Bus service from České Budějovice and Brno. The bus station is a little out of the centre of town towards České Budejovice. The road frontier crossing to Austria, Halámky-Neu Nagelberg, is 30 km away, and open around the clock.

TÁBOR

A Celtic settlement may have existed on the site of Tábor as early as the 1st century BC In the 13th century a community called Hradiste existed here and a castle was built in the 14th century. Tábor is best known as one of the focal points of the Hussite movement. In 1420 a Hussite town was founded here, and given the name Hradiste Hory Tábor (Castle of Mt Tábor) after the biblical mountain Tábor. The streets were purposely made crooked, to help the town withstand enemy attacks. The military commander of the Hussites, Jan Žizka, was one of the chief leaders. He died in 1424, and the head on the 20 kc note comes from a statue of him. The community was formed on the basis of everything being communally owned. Whenever fire destroyed the town, most of the new houses respected the original plan of the town. The castle was later converted into a brewery, but today only the castle tower, Kotnov, remains. In 1903 the first electric railway in what was then Austro-Hungary was constructed between Tábor and Bechyne.

Construction of the Town Hall began about 1440 and was completed in 1521. Its concert chamber is the 2nd largest in Czechoslovakia and in summer, concerts of medieval music are held in it. Today the Town Hall is a museum and open from April to October from 8.30 am to 5 pm. It shows the history of the Hussite movement. Historians are not sure when Jan Hus was born. He was important for Czech nationalism as well as the religious Hussite movement and he became an important symbol because he died as a martyr. After his death people gave up thinking they could change things through the power of words, and took to arms. Sigismund, the Czech king and Roman Emperor, didn't like the Hussites but 452 Czech and Moravian nobility presented a petition to Sigismund complaining about Hus's death. A copy of it is in the museum; the original is in Edinburgh. The 3 bells were made in the 16th century in memory of Hus.

From the Town Hall access is gained to the 12 to 15 km of underground passages built in the 1430s as protection, the temperature is ideal for storing beer and food. Only 650 metres are open to the public today and most of the network has been destroyed because of lack of money for reconstruction. The tunnels must be visited with a guide.

Both the Town Hall and the church are on the main square, Žižkovo náměstí. The church was originally built of wood, and is called The Church of the Transfiguration of Our Lord on Mount Tábor. The Renaissance fountain in the square with a warrior in armour dates from 1567.

A couple of bastions, and one gate, Bechyně, remain. Some of the houses are well worth seeing. The setting of the old town is in itself beautiful, high above the river Lužnice. Jordan Pond on the River Tismenice was created in 1402 by the oldest dam in Czechoslovakia to supply the town with water.

In my experience the people working in shops, hotels, etc in Tábor all seemed more friendly and helpful than normal in Czechoslovakia.

Near Tábor are Chýnovská Jeskyně, limestone caves with several small lakes. They have been open to the public since the end of the last century. Open 1 May to 30 September, 8 am to 5 pm.

PRACTICAL INFORMATION

There is a Čedok office next door to Hotel Palcát.

Information in English on Tábor and a map of the old town is found in the series 'Getting to Know Czechoslovakia' No. 10, 'Česko-Moravská Vrchovina'. (24 kčs).

For a detailed map of the area, but not the town, see 'Táborsko' (8 kčs).

Change money at Státní banka Československá or Hotel Palcát.

The railway station and bus station are together. They are a little way out from the old town, but within walking distance, via the area the hotels, shops etc. of today are situated.

Emergency breakdown service for E14, tel. 8428.

GETTING THERE & AWAY AGAIN

Brno: By bus 45 kčs. One direct train a day takes 4 hours, otherwise must change trains.

České Budějovice: Trains. Rychlík 1 hour 48 kčs, osobní 2 hours 32 kčs. Reasonably regular.

Vienna: Trains twice a day, at 2.42 and 17.08.

Left luggage at the railway station. They don't seem to complain about weights of packs.

SLEEPING & EATING
Hotels

The best hotel in town is **Hotel Palcát**, ***. It has a nice interior, class II restaurant, kavárna with a band playing sometimes, and night club called 'P Club' (closed Sunday & Monday). It is in the centre of the new town, at tr. 9 května, tel. 229 01-5.

Second best hotel is by the railway station. **Hotel Slávia**, **, Valdenská 591, tel. 235 74. About 75 beds. Difficult to get a room in the summer. With bathroom: doubles 150 kčs, singles 100 kčs. Without bathroom: doubles 120 kčs , single (there is only one) 80 kčs, plus 20 kčs if you want to take a bath.

Hotel Jordán, B & C, ul. Ant. Zápotockého, tel. 235 74 is cheaper. In the B class rooms on the 1st & 2nd floors single cost 80 kčs, doubles 120 kčs, 30 kčs extra for an extra bed. The C class rooms are on the 3rd floor, and cost 60 kčs single, 100 kčs double, and 150 kčs for a 3 bed room. No private bathrooms. Sk. II restaurant. Sk. IV bufet with hot meals, sausages, sweets, and drinks, open 7 am to 7 pm, closed Sundays. Sk III pivnice: local,

smoky, boozy hangout.
Hotel Slovan is B class, in the main street, noisy, and not very nice.

Hostel
Turistická ubytovna, TU B, Pinkova ul. 21 01, tel. 241 26. Good but primitive. Out of town by the river. 2.5 km from the railway station on the red marked track west, or take bus no. 3 or 4. Restaurant Harachovka 1 km away.

Camping & Cabins
Autokemp Knížecí rybník, Tábor 4-Zárybnična Lhota, PSČ 391 54, tel. 224 80. Camping, accommodation in cabins (both A & B class), plus pub with rooms. 6 km from centre. Driving take highway 19 towards Jihlava. 700 m walk from Smyslov railway station. Bus no. 3. Pub open all year. Cabins only from 15/5 to 15/9.

Autokemp Maý Jordán, Tábor-Náchod, tel. 321 03. Camping & class B cabins. North of Tábor. 2.5 km walk on the red marked track northwards from Tábor railway station. Driving: north on the E 14. Bus no. 2. Open 15/6 to 15/6.

There may still be a camp site down the river, U Harachovky, open 15/6 to 15/9.

There are eateries around the square in the old town.

Zvíkov Castle

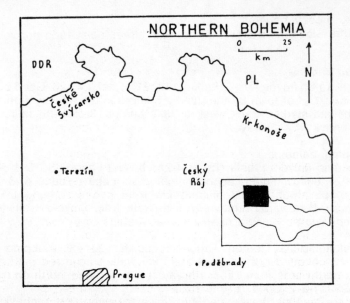

Krkonose

NORTHERN BOHEMIA

TEREZÍN
The fortress and town of Terezín was founded in 1780 by Joseph II. In the 19th century the fortress was a political prison. In 1942 the Nazis converted the town of Terezín, known to many by its German name Theresienstadt, into a ghetto, a concentration camp where 150,000 Jews were sent from various countries in Europe. The so called 'Small Fortress', the best fortified section, became a prison of the Prague Gestapo. Over 35,000 people lost their lives in Terezín during the Second World War, and 84,000 died in the concentration camps they were taken to from Terezín.

Today there is a cemetry as a memorial. The Small Fortress is open to the public all year, its underground passages having been converted to a museum of the resistance against fascism.

Terezín lies on the E 15, the main road to Berlin from Prague. There is a map of the town on the back of the map 'Severní Čechy' in the 'Poznáváme Československo' series, which also includes information on Terezín in English.

SLEEPING
The following have post code 411 55 Terezín, and are on Litoměřice telephone exchange (416). Parkhotel, C, Máchova 1, tel. 922 60, doubles and trebles only. Sokolovna, TU A, U hřiště 4, tel. 9924 73. Autokemp Terezín, A, tel. 922 78, open 1/4 to 31/10.

ČESKÉ SVÝCARSKO (Bohemian Switzerland)
České Švýcarsko (Bohemian Switzerland) is an amazing area of extraordinary sandstone rock formations, described as forgotten by God and mankind, and fit only for thieves and robbing knights in 1717. In 1726 two Swiss painters were so overawed by the beauty of the countryside, they decided not to return home, saying they had discovered Switzerland here. Hence the name. Also known as Českosaské Švýcarsko (Czech-Saxon Switzerland), Labské Pískovce (Elbe Sandstones) and Děčínské stěny (the Děčín Rocks).

České Švýcarsko is mostly forested, and is lovely in autumn when the leaves are changing colour. In spring and summer there are beautiful flowers around Tisa. I noticed lots of birds, which seem to be lacking in some parts of Czechoslovakia.

The area lies on the border with GDR and you may be checked, so have your passport with you. When I took the bus back to Děčín the driver tooted his horn outside the police station in Hřensko to signal that he had a foreigner on board!

Some of the most interesting places to visit are Pravčická brána, the Kamenice River canyons and Tisa.

DĚČÍN

The main centre of the area is the town of Děčín, situated on the Elbe. The main railway station and the bus station are both across the river (3 stops by bus) from the centre of town. Be careful that people understand you when you ask for directions in Děčín, as seeing that you are a foreigner with luggage, they might assume that you are homeward bound to GDR, and will send you to the railway station or the road to Dresden!

There are two chateaux in Děčín. The one to the true right of the river is an impressive complex developed from the original castle built in 1128. Chopin was a guest here in 1835. But it is now definitely not open to the public, as it has been taken over by the Russian army. On the other side of the river is a small chateau perched on top of a high bluff directly above the river. You can walk up on the red marked track by the bridge, or an elevator (výtah) operates up inside the hill from 10am to 7pm in season, afternoons only off season. Costs 2 local bus tickets each way; buy them in advance; vending machine at entrance. Large gardens.

There is a 28°C thermal pool at the camping ground.

The drive along the road from Děčín to Hřensko follows the Elbe and is beautiful. One can also walk all the way to Hřensko via bluffs and woods along the red marked route which starts in Děčín.

Getting There & Away Again Děčín lies on the main Prague-Berlin railway and is the customs post on the Czech side.

Between Děčín and Karlovy Vary and Cheb there is one direct train a day. Leaves Děčín at 7.46am. Rychlík. 48 kcs to Cheb (valid 2 days).

Bus service to Krkonoše.

In the summer there is a regular boat service on the Elbe between Děčín and Hřensko. There is also a service between Děčín and Dresden in GDR (must have a visa first).

To hitch to GDR or Hřensko walk to the edge of town to find a good spot.

Getting Around The local buses are same as normal, except that you can't use the front door which is reserved for the driver.

Sleeping
Hotels:
Grand Hotel, B, Děčín IV, Zbrojnická 18, tel. 22414, 224 16, opposite the railway station.
Sport, B, Děčín IV, Teplická 44, expected to open 1987- 88.
Pastýřská stěna, C, at the chateau, expected to open 1987-88.

Other:
Hotel Pošta, TU B, Děčín I, Leninovo nám. 82, tel. 228 31. On the main square. A run down old hotel now used as TU. 32 kčs per person per night. 10 kčs per hot shower, otherwise cold water only. Various number of beds to a room, including some singles. Reception open 2pm to 6am only. Best to book by letter one month in advance. Write the dates and number of people in a way that a non-English speaker can understand. Some chance of a bed if you just turn up out of season.
Ubytovna TJ Spartak TU B, Děčín II, Riegrova 8, tel. 235 85. Kitchen. Central. U Kaple, TU B & CHO B, Decín VI, U kaple 554, tel. 235 41. Open 1/4 to 31/10. Ubytovna TJ Sokol
Bělá, TU B, Děčín X-Balá, Tělocvičná 9, tel. 238 35.
U koupaliště, A-kemp & TU A, Děčín I, tel. 227 55. Centrally located camping ground, open 1/5 to 30/9.

Eating On Leninovo nám: Hotel Pošta has a sk. III restaurant, closed Wed. Koruna rest. just along from Pošta, sk. II, nothing to write home about. Sk IV cheap restaurant open daytime only (till 7pm).
Kavarna in the chateau.

Evenings The best rages are probably not in the hotels, but those organized by trade unions and the socialist youth movement etc. ROH (trade union) sometimes have something on at Labská 691/23, especially at weekends. (From the town square head towards GD R in a straight line and you'll walk into it.)
Kavárna in the Grand Hotel.
Národní Kavárna on the main square by the pedestrian underpass. 10 kčs cover. Open Mon. to Sat. 8pm to 2am.

HŘENSKO
Hřensko is a beautiful village, nestled under cliffs where the Kamenice River meets the Elbe. At 116 metres above sea level, it is the lowest village in Bohemia. The inhabitants were fishermen and forestry workers. In 1567 a customs post was established here.
The tourist boom began last century.

PRAVČICKA BRANA
Pravčická brána is the largest natural bridge in Europe. At 30

metres long and 21 metres high, only two natural bridges (both in USA) can compete with it. It is truly a fantastic site. The whole area (2 kcs entry in season, otherwise free) around the bridge consists of amazing sandstone rock bluffs, cliffs, towers etc. There is an incredible view from behind and above the restaurant built in the 18th century.

The path to Pravčická brána leaves the road at Tři prameny. Parking. There are not many buses from Děčín to Tři prameny, so check the times. In winter the first 3 run at 5.30, 9.30 and 12.50 daily from the bus station (3 minutes later from the ČSAD stop on the town side of the bridge). In summer there is another bus at 8.40. If you can't get a bus or hitch up to Tři prameny, it is a nice 3km walk up the road from Hřensko. Pravcická brána is a 2km walk from Tři prameny. You must keep to the track—in any case the GDR border is very close. The detour path leads to a cave.

From Pravčická brána the track continues below bluffs, then descends to Mezní Louka, a lot of it with sandstone or sand underfoot. The entire walk from Tři prameny to Mezní Louka, including sightseeing, takes about 4 hours or from Hřensko 5.

At Mezná Louka is a B class hotel open all year, and chalets open 1/4 to 31/10. Sk. II and III restaurants—you may be the only customer in the off season. Infrequent bus service to Děčín, Mezná, & Vysoké Lipa.

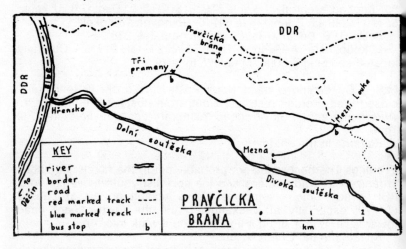

DOLNI SOUTĚSKA & DIVOKA SOUTĚSKA

These two popular sections of the Kamenice River are accessible only by boat from May to the end of August .

Access to Dolní soutěska from Mezná, and to Divoká soutěska from Mezná Louka (blue markers, after 15 minutes walk turn to the right) or from a bus stop further up the road to Vysoké Lipa.

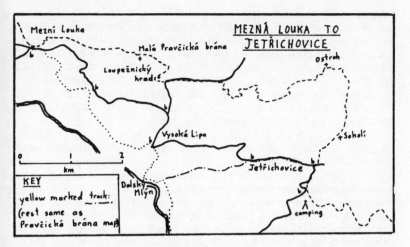

MEZNA LOUKA TO JETŘICHOVICE

A 14km tramp following the red marked track, but one can break the journey at Vysoké Lipa. This is more difficult going than the Pravcická brána path, but okay. After 45 minutes through birch and evergreens the track follows a roadway for 5 minutes, then turns sharp right and climbs up to **Malá Pravčická brána**, a much smaller natural bridge (3km from Mezná Louka). Good view if you climb up the sandstone steps to the top of it.

A scramble down, then more level with bluffs above and below, and you come to the site of **Loupežnický hrad** (4km from Mezná Louka). The diagram shows how it was. The amazing access way is via clefts in the rock. If the gate is open, it is really worth clambering up to the top. Just before the top, you can go two different ways. Try the lower of the two, right to the very end, and you will be surprised. From the road below, you can continue following the red markers through bluffy hills and past the ruins of Sokoli castle to Jetřichovice, or follow the road to the right to Vysoké Lipa. Mezná Louka to Vysoké Lipa, with stops, 1 3/4 hours.

Another route from Mezná Louka to Jetřichovice is via Dolský Mlýn (14km). This route is not so spectacular, but still a nice walk. From Mezná Louka follow the blue markers. After 1 hour there is a short side track to a lookout point, marked with triangular blue markers. From here the view encompasses the hill Růzovský (which has a track to the top) and the Kamenice gorge below. After 5km (1 1/2 hour with stops) you come to Vysoké Lipa. There are traditional style houses as you enter this sleepy little village. General store.

Continue following the blue markers down a steep ravine to Dolský Mlýn, the ruins of an old mill. Nice spot. Some hairy little bridges around here, that the elderly might have problems crossing. Trout in the clear rivers. Now follow the blue and yellow markers until they divide (muddy here). From here the blue markers lead to the outskirts of Srbská Kamenice (3km) and on to Česká Kamenice (10.5km). To Jetřichovice follow the yellow markers (3km). Soon after you come in sight of the first house, the remains of a little log hut can be seen covered in earth on your right. Opposite the house are doors into the cliff! The sign on the swimming pool says 'No Swimming'! Jetřichovice has nice old traditional houses. Camp site 1km the other side of town, 5.50 kčs per person, 7 kčs per car, 7 kčs per tent. Nice spot. Access roadway crosses a ford, or park before the ford for 3 kčs (motorbike 2 kčs). Swimming baths next to camp, open 10am to 7pm, 2 kčs, 1 kcs child. Refreshment stall.

Other walks from the camp: Česká Kamenice, green, 6.5km; Studený, red, 4 1/2km; turnoff to Studenec, a 736m peak with lookout tower, red, 9km.

Buses Vysoká Lipa marks the dividing point for bus services. There is no through service here. In one direction buses run to Děčín via MezniLouka & Hřensko, and in the other to Nový Bor via Jetřichovice & Česká Kamenice. From a different stop in Jetřichovice buses run to Děčín. From Studený there is a practically non-existent bus service to Česká Kamenice, and no buses in the other direction.

KAMENICKÝ ŠENOV - PRACHEŇ
At Kamenický Šenov—Prácheň is a natural rock organ and lake. On highway 13 east of Děčín just before Nový Bor.

BENEŠOV
Museum of porcelain and china in the castle. Historical buildings. 14km south-east of Děčín. Train or bus from Děčín. Near Benesov are the ruins of Ostrý Castle.

TISKÉ STĚNY
A 'rock town'. Natural rock formation at Tisá. Infrequent bus service from Děčín bus station to Tisá takes 3/4 hour. If you are staying on the town side of the bridge, you can catch the bus from the ČSAD bus stop across the bridge and a few metres along to the right. Hitching is not bad. Another way to get there is to take the bus or train to Libouchec, and walk or change to a bus to Tisá there (these run more often than those from Děčín). Or you can walk the 18.5km from Děčín on the red marked track starting by the bridge. The rocks are 500 metres up from the town of Tisá. 2 kčs entry in season, otherwise free. Marked route leads around, over and under the rocks. Begins with a circular route to the left, then out to the road east of Tisá via the rocks to the right. You can return to Tisá via the red marked track which cuts back over the top of the rocks giving a good view. Allow about 2 hours to explore.

Campsite just west of the rocks, and turistická ubytovna with kitchen. Tel. Ústí nad Labem 902 47. Open all year. Where the route around the rocks exits to the road, there is a turistická chata (Ve skalách), with rooms and dorms and a restaurant. Tel. 902 75. Open Mon. noon to 5pm, Tues. 10am to 8pm, Friday & Sat. 10am to 10pm, Sun. 9am to 4.30pm. Closed Wed. & Thurs. You can't start seeing the rocks from this end. The track is not marked in that direction.

SNĚŽNÍK
Buses to Tisá from Děčín stop here. At the crossroads is Hraničrní bouda, with a nice little sk. III restaurant open 7am to 7pm, and TU B accommodation in season. Tel. Děčín 933 49.

From Sněžník you can walk up Děčínský Sněžník (726m), also known as Vysoký Sněžník, a strange mountain with bluffs all around and a big plateau on top (2km, 1/2 hour). The road up is closed. Lookout tower. The chata on top was wrecked in 1985. Nice area of dwarfed forest on top, but acid rain has just about finished it off.

SNĚŽNÍK TO DĚČÍN
Apart from returning to Sněžník village 3 other possible ways of continuing to Děčín are as follows. One is to follow the green markers down to Jílové (6km) and catch the train from there. Another is to follow the red marked track back to Děčín (9.5km). The third is to follow the red markers until the junction with the green marked track to the left (40 minutes). Then follow the green markers 13km to Děčín. After the village of Maxičky this route drops down to the Elbe valley at Čertova Voda and follows it upstream past holiday cottages and houses. A shorter alternative from Maxicky is to follow the yellow markers to the right to Děčín (5.5km). An alternative from Čertova Voda is to follow the yellow markers downstream 3km to Dolní Žleb, where there is a car ferry across the Elbe.

OTHER PRACTICAL INFORMATION

Map: 'Českosaské Švýcarsko', published by Kartografie, n.p., Praha & Veb Tourist Verlag, East Berlin. Detailed map with walking tracks. Sometimes not very accurate, but a good guide.

Accommodation: A lot of the accommodation in the area is controlled by Centrálni ubytovaci sluzba Grand Děčín.

Hitch-hiking: Generally not so easy. No traffic. Possibly easier in season.

Bus Timetables: The timetables at the bus stops are often illegible or out of date.

PODĚBRADY
Poděbrady is a nice relaxed spa town, specialising in the treatment of cardio-vascular diseases. In the castle here Jiříz Poděbrad (George of Poděbrady), known as the Hussites' king, was born in 1420. After the country had been ruled by foreign monarchs, King George mounted the throne in 1458 as the first Czech king since 1306. He envisaged the establishment of an alliance of European states, partly in the cause of peace, partly to ward off the Turks, and partly to weaken the influence of the church on European politics. In the 16th century the castle was converted into a Renaissance mansion, and used as a hunting

lodge by Ferdinand I, Rudolph II and Maria Theresa. Parts of the castle are open to the public from May to October (closed Monday). Behind the castle you can watch the barges on the Elbe. The rail and bus station are next door to each other. Poděbrady is on the bus routes Prague—Špindlerův Mlýn and Prague—Pec pod Snežkou, both in Krkonoše. Across the road from the station is a Bohemian glass exhibition with cut crystal glass. From opposite the station a nice constitutional walkway leads to the town square. You may find music being played for the spa's patients along the way.

Two B* hotels in the middle of the town. Turistická ubytovna. Camping open May to September.

ČESKÝ RÁJ (BOHEMIAN PARADISE)

Český Ráj is a region of castles, towering rock outcrops and bizarre rock formations, created by the erosion of soft sandstone, lying between Turnov, Jičín and Mnichovo Hradiště. Some of the best places to see are as follows. The Hrubá Skála rock formations which resemble a ghost city. Many of the over 200 rocks can be climbed. Valdštejn, where there is a castle where many films have been made. Trosty, with the ruins of Trosty Castle perched upon two adjoining hills, and affording a beautiful view over Český Ráj. Prachovské skaly. All of these are easiest accessible from Turnov, except Prachovské skaly which is easiest from Jičín. One can walk from Turnov to Jičín: 30km and a long day.

Camping in the area, or other forms of accommodation in the towns.

Mnichovo Hradiště and Turnov are on the E 14, north-east of Prague.

KRKONOŠE

The Krkonoše (Giant Mountains) lie along the Polish border in northern Bohemia. The highest peak, Snežka (1602 m.), is the highest mountain in Bohemia. The Krkonoše are typically shaped as rolling hills with rounded tops, but there can be near vertical dropoffs into the valleys. Typical for the mountains are the dwarf pines which grow on the slopes above 1300 metres. The source of the Elbe (Labe in Czech) lies in the Krkonoše. The largest resort, Špindlerův Mlýn, lies on the Elbe.

Because of their proximity to Prague, which lies 139km away, the Krkonoše can be very crowded, especially on Sundays. The main centre of the region is Vrchlabí. It lies outside the mountains, but is a centre for transport and accommodation booking. The main centres in the mountains are Harrachov, Špindlerův Mlýn and Pec pod Snežkou.

The Krkonoše are famed for their weather. There is some form of precipitation on 200 days of the year. This means good snow conditions in winter, but can lead to many cancelled or miserable trips in summer. The Krkonoše are deceptively low. Lying about 800 km north of the Alps, you can expect the same weather at 1000m here as you would receive at a height of 1800 to 2000m in the Alps. The average temperature around Špindlerův Mlýn is 4°C and at the top of Snežka 1.1°C.

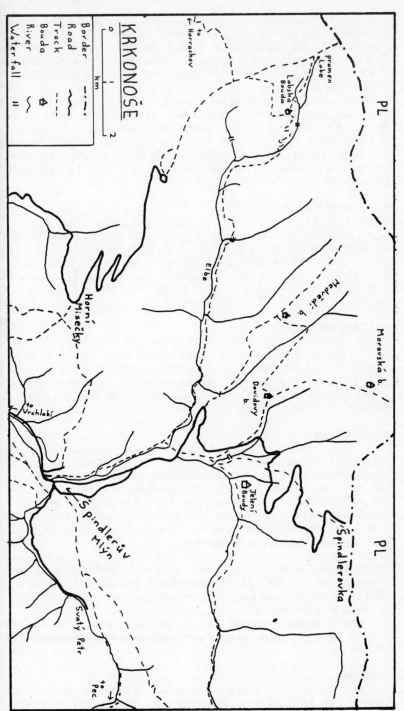

Krkonoše was declared a national park in 1963. But the trees are dying since it is one of the areas in Europe worst hit by acid rain. Over 10,000 ha of mainly pine forests are slowly losing all their needles as insects are attacking the weakened trees. There is a lot of milling, in an attempt to stop these insects spreading to the more healthy trees.

Goats and cows have grazed the mountain meadows through the years. The herdsmen built wooden huts called 'boudas' to protect themselves from the weather. The original huts developed into farmsteads, and later into chalets where visitors could spend the night. Today the name 'bouda' has been preserved, but a bouda may be anything from a simple hut to a big hotel. The term bouda is known only in the Krkonoše.

TO & FROM KRKONOŠE

Direct buses from Prague to Vrchlabi, Špindlerův Mlýn, Janské Lázne, etc. Trains from Prague to Vrchlabi or Svoboda nad Úpou. To Děcín take the Ustí n. L. bus from Vrchlabi, which runs 3 times a day, takes about 4 hours to Děcín, and costs 39 kčs. Crossing to the Polish side by road from Harrachov only. Of course you must first have a Polish visa, and you cannot return to Czechoslovakia again without another Czechoslovak visa.

GETTING AROUND

There are many buses between Vrchlabi and Špindlerův Mlýn (5 kčs, 1 kčs for luggage). There are buses between the various resorts in summer only. Otherwise travelling between resorts by bus requires many changes. Buses as far as the Polish border above Špindlerův Mlýn. This road is open only to buses in winter. Buses to Vítkovice-Krkonoš above Horní Misecky in summer only.

INFORMATION

In Vrchlabí there is a national park centre in the palace on the square. At the top end of Špindlerův Mlýn, on the Špindlerovka road is a National Park Information Office. No one speaks English, but they are very helpful, and it is amazing how much you can communicate with your hands and a map and a few words of Czech and English. Open 7 days a week from April to September inclusive, rest of year Monday to Friday. At the top of the road above Horní Misecky there may be an information office open in season.

The main Čedok office for the area is in Vrchlabí. Address: Leninova ul. 148, 543 01 Vrchlabí; tel. 3180, 3181, 3182. Telex 194431. There are also Čedok offices in Špindlerův Mlýn, Pec pod Snežkou and Janské Lázne.

There is a good walking map 'Krkonoše' costing 8.50 kčs. It may be difficult to find, so grab it in another part of the country if you see it.

SLEEPING

It is difficult to get accommodation in the Krkonoše. In season it is booked out, and out of season most accommodation is closed! Čedok have a near monopoly on accommodation in the area. Čedok Vrchlabi make bookings for the whole Krkonoše . The local office at Špindlerův Mlýn can't make bookings directly. So if you have planned ahead, you can book by contacting Čedok Vrchlabi yourself, or by booking through Čedok in Prague or your home country, or booking through a travel agent in your home country. Čedok prefer bookings by the week, but it may be possible to make a shorter booking. It is difficult to get bookings if you want to walk from bouda to bouda, as Čedok don't like this, but it is possible. Otherwise you could use one bouda as a base instead.

Neither Sport-hotels nor camping can be booked through Čedok. Except in Pec pod Sněžkou Čedok don't book private accommodation. As far as staying in mountain bouda is concerned, you'll be lucky to get in anywhere except Labská Bouda without prior reservation.

Many of the hotels are small cosy wooden buildings.

Harrachov
Accommodation open in season only. Hotels in B*, B and C grades, hostels (turisticka' ubytovna) in TU A and TU B grades. Camping ground (B) open 1 May to 15 October.

Horní Misečky
C class hotel and good cheap hostel (TU A) accommodation. There is one reception for all the hotels and hostels. With 220 beds here it shouldn't be difficult to get a bed. Open all year except May and November.

Labská Bouda
The mountain hut to end all mountain huts! A huge modern looking place. B class hotel. Access by foot or ski only (the roadway is not open to the public). The shortest way in summer to walk in is the 2.5km trip from the top of the road above Horní Misečky. Buses run to the top of this road in summer only. In winter the shortest way in is the 5.5km trip from Horní Misecky. Open all year except May & November. A reservation should not be necessary. Doubles 273 kcs, and a few singles at 182 kcs. Pleasant sk. III restaurant, but a little expensive. Sk. IV bufet in season. Tel. Špindlerův Mlýn 932 21.

Špindlerův Mlýn
A wide range of accommodation here, from camping to an A* hotel, but it still is not easy to find somewhere to stay.

Camping. Autokemping B next door to the National Park Information Office at the top end of Špindlerův Mlýn. Open in season for tents and caravans. 21 kcs per tent, 21 kcs per car, 10.50 kcs per person, 2 kcs tax per person per nig ht. Some refreshments available. Just below here on the other side of the road on-site 2 man tents are available from about June to September. Everything is provided.

Hotel & Hostel Accommodation. Most owned by Čedok: book through Čedok Vrchlabi.

Montana, A*, modern, large, sk I restaurant, tel. 935 51.

Hotel Savoy, B*, opened in 1891, recently renovated, nice looking, 300m up from bus stop & parking area, don't cross the river.

Praha, B, nice old building, central, tel. 933 15.

Hotel Hvĕzda, hotel C & TU B, central by the bridge, tel. 934 59.

Hotel Start, hotel C & TU A, sk II* restaurant, old building, open 8am to 2pm & 6pm to 10pm, closed Thursday. Lomnice, TU A, nice building, tel. 932 20.
Nearly everything is open only in season. Some private accommodation, which can't be booked through Čedok. If nothing else, just turn up and ask around.

Vrchlabi
Private accommodation through the town, not Čedok. Two campsites owned by the town.

Pec pod
Snĕžkou Hotel Horizont , B*, a huge hotel which is anything but horizontal! tel. 963 13, 963 78.

Hotel Hořec, B, hotel on a more human scale, tel. 962 04. Both open in season only, and owned by Čedok, who will also book private accommodation here.

Janské Lázně
All accommodation owned by Čedok. B & C class hotels, and hostel accommodation.

TO SEE (WITHOUT TRAMPING OR SKIING TO IT)
The road from Špindlerův Mlýn to Špindlerovka on the Polish border is open to foreigners, but foreigners may not walk along the border track. In summer open to cars, but in winter open to buses only.
In Vrchlabi is the Krkonoše Museum.
The drive through Jizerský důl is very nice. Janské Lázně is a holiday and spa resort. The springs are said to have been found by one, Jan, who was sent to find the hideout of robbers. Hence the name 'Janské'. The majority of today's spa buildings were built in 1868.

LIFTS
Most lifts are open for both summer and winter seasons, but closed in October, November and May.
There is a chairlift up Snĕžka from 1 1/2 km north of Pec pod Snĕžkou. The 4km long trip has a mid-station at Růzová hora. It is an open lift, which some find a bit frightening at first—and remember warm clothing. There is a hospoda at the top open while the lift is operating, but one cannot sleep there.
The Špindlerův Mlýn-Mĕdvedín lift leaves almost opposite the camp at Špindlerův Mlýn. But the bridge across the river here is

private, so to reach it walk up the blue marked track on the west side of the river from the town.

There is a cableway up Čierná Hora (1300m) from Janské Lázne.

TRAMPING

The Krkonoše seem deceivingly safe. Sudden weather changes can occur at any time of year, so it is wise to take precautions. Don't be on the tops in fog or during storms. Tell someone where you are going and when you expect to return. Avoid areas where there is avalanche danger.

Foreigners may walk to the border, but not along the track along the border. In winter one may walk in the valleys only; one may not walk on the mountain tops. Many tracks have been closed, either temporarily or permanently, to give nature a chance to recover, as the Krkonoše are overutilized. So even if you have a map, check what tracks are open before planning your trip.

Walking Times from Harrachov

Vosecká bouda, red markers, 2 1/4 hours.
Dvoracky, green markers, 2 1/4 hours.
Labská Bouda, 3 hours.
Špindlerův Mlýn via Dvoracky, 4 hours.

From Špindlerův Mlýn

The oldest part of Špindlerův Mlýn is the mining village of Sv. Petr, a 20 minute walk from Špindlerův Mlýn.

Walking up the Elbe from Špindlerův Mlýn is a nice trip. From Špindlerův Mlýn the 9.5km to Labská Bouda takes 2 3/4 hours. It is a good track, but rough—best to have boots. It is a long but pleasant walk up the valley. In the upper reaches there are big bluffs above you. At the top of the valley, the track zig-zags up beside the first Elbe waterfalls to Labská Bouda. It is not hard going, though you climb a long way up. The tops around Labská Bouda are open and flat, and it can be *cold*. From Labská Bouda it is only a short 1 km walk to Pramen Labe, the source of the Elbe. The spot is nothing fantastic. There are coats of arms of the towns down the Elbe, all the way to Hamburg. From Labská Bouda it is a further 10.5km following the blue markers to Harrachov. A possible round-trip from Špindlerův Mlýn is to follow the Elbe up as described, then return via Horní Misecky. This whole round trip, including a visit to Pramen Labe, other stops and lunch takes about 7 1/2 hours. From Pramen Labe the way leads over open tops, past army pill boxes to Vrbatova bouda. Don't follow the poles if they are up—they mark ski tracks, not walking tracks.

Other Walks from Špindlerův Mlýn Post Office:

Špindlerovka, 8.5km, 2 hours.
Horní Misecky, red markers, 4km.
Pec pod Snězkou, green markers, 12km, 3 1/2 hours.
Vrchlabi, 15.5km.
Lucní bouda, red markers, 2 1/2 hours.
Davidovy bouda, yellow markers, 4 1/2 km. A new Davidovy bouda is under construction. From here it is a further 2km to

Moravská bouda, or 1 1/2 km to Medvedí boudy (blue).

From Pec pod Sněžkou:
Remember that the track along the border may not be used by foreigners, so you cannot use it to climb Sněžka.
Špindlerův Mlýn via Výrovka, green markers, 3 1/2 hours.
Luciny, 1 hour.
Černý důl, blue markers, 2 1/2 hours.
Růžová hora, 1 hour.

SKIING
The Krkonoše gets a lot of snow, being the first and last mountains in Czechoslovakia to receive snow, and so having the longest season. There is snow on the ground from about November to April. The ski season is from about the end of December to the end of March. It is a good area for cross country skiing, but it is very crowded. Facilities are not up to west European standards. There are long waits for lifts (e.g. 1 to 2 hours at the weekend). Ski gear can be hired in Špindler ův Mlýn, but it is difficult to hire good quality gear. Cross country skiers must follow the marked routes. For example there are marked routes from Horní Miescky, and an 8km long route along Labský důl. Ski tracks on the tops are marked with poles. As well as the main resorts, there is a ski centre at Janské Lázně.

CLIMBING
The Krkonoše is not a good area for climbing. The climbing season is winter, and permission is needed from the park office.

DISCOS
Disco Labužník, just up from Savoy Hotel. Open 8pm to 3am, closed Tuesday. Sk II*. 15 kčs entry. 'Entry in formal attire only'.
In season there is another disco at Vinárna Bernardýn up the valley opposite the campsite in Špindlerův Mlýn. Closed Thursday.

Bohemian Paradise

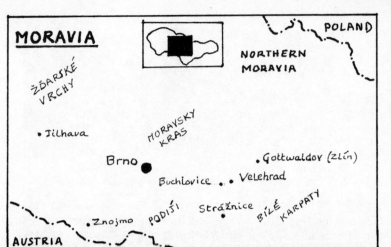

Cross country skiing

MORAVIA

BRNO

Brno, with a population of 372,000, is the third largest city in Czechoslovakia, and was the ancient capital of Moravia. It was the home of Mendel, and the modern composer Leos Janáček (1854-1928). Today Brno is an important industrial centre, particularly for the machine industry. It is also an important university town, and the student influence is strong.

TO SEE

Overlooking Brno is its castle, Špilberk. Built in the second half of the 13th century, as an early Gothic stronghold, it was later rebuilt as a Baroque fortress. Špilberk successfully resisted assaults by the Mongols, Hussites, Swedes, Turks and the Prussian King Frederick, but Napoleon succeeded in capturing it. Under the Hapsburgs the castle became a notorious prison, and the horrors of this were revived during the Nazi occupation, when an estimated 80,000 prisoners suffered here .

From 1984 to 1994 Špilberk is under reconstruction. But parts of it are open to the public. There is a lookout over the town in the tower. The dungeons used as a prison are open to the public. 'The Spielberg Castle', a leaflet available in English gives a history of the castle, and detailed information about the dungeons, including who was imprisoned here. There is a gallery of modern art open 9am to 5.30pm. Both prison and gallery are open all year, but are closed Mondays.

Between the castle and the railway station is Petrov Hill. Brno's original castle stood here. Premysl II recognized the strategic importance of Špilberk Hill, and moved his residence there. Today St Peter & Paul's Cathedral stands on Petrov Hill, on the site of a former Romanesque baslica. The cathedral is huge, and its two towers with their distinctive spires are a Brno landmark, especially noticeable if you enter Brno by train. The cathedral suffered severe damage during the siege of Brno by the Swedes from 1643-45. Late last century and early this century it was 're-Gothicized'. It has recently been restored. Worth a look inside if you find it open.

Connected with the cathedral is the story of the bell-toller who saved Brno from the Swedes. On Ascension Day, 1645, General Tortensson decided to launch the last attack, declaring that if the town did not surrender by midday he would raise the siege. The bell-ringer could see that Brno was on the point of yielding, when, moved by a sudden inspiration, he rung the bells of the cathedral, announcing midday, while it was in fact only 11 o'clock in the morning. The general halted the attack, and the Swedish troops withdrew. Since that time midday has been rung from the bells of the cathedral at 11 o'clock.

The railway station itself has a nice exterior. It has been under reconstruction for some years now. Today's town centre lies north of the station and east of Špilberk. Here you will find the Old Town Hall (Stará radnice) with the Brno Dragon hanging from the roof inside the entrance and the Brno Wheel. The foundations of the Old Town Hall date from the 13th century, while its present Gothic appearance date from the beginning of the 16th century. The 'dragon' is actually a crocodile received by Archduke Matthias as a gift from the Turks in 1608. Matthias presented it to the town of Brno. There are many legends attached to the Brno Dragon. The Brno Wheel is said to have been made by the Lednice cartwright Jiří Birk in 1636. He made a bet that he could fell a tree, make a cartwheel from it, and roll it to Brno, all before the evening bells (that is within 12 hours). He won the bet even though Lednice is 33 miles south of Brno. But people began to suspect him of being in league with the devil, and orders for his work dwindled, leaving him to die in poverty. Another legend concerns the Portal with the Crooked Pinnacle which you can see on the front of the Old Town Hall. The Aldermen promised much for the work of Master Pilgram, but gave little. So Master Pilgram incurred the City Fathers wrath by carving a crooked pinnacle over the statue of justice as a symbol of their breach of promise. A new straight pinnacle was fixed there by another master sulpture, but it curved by itself overnight! The tower of the Old Town Hall is open from April to September from 9am to 5pm, closed Mondays.

The New Town Hall (Nová Radnice) on Naměstí Družby Národů is today the seat of the Municipal National Committee. It has a nice courtyard, open from 8am to 5pm, 9am to 3pm Sundays and holidays. Only the courtyard is open to the public. On the same square is the Gothic St. Michael's Church founded in the 1330's. It was the church of the Dominican Monastery. In the second half of the 17th century it was reconstructed in Baroque style. Carved figures of saints.

Náměstí 25. Unora (Square of the 25th February) was the vegetable market, commonly known as 'Zelný trh' (Vegetable or Cabbage Market), which was its name up until the communists changed it. The old fountain, designed as a cave of immense unhewn boulders, has been reconstructed. Carp used to be sold out of the fountain's waters before Christmas every year. It is said to be good luck to kiss the statue of the god Amphitrites on top of it! The whole area around here, including Star á Radnice, had to be reconstructed. There are tunnels everywhere underneath the area from old sewers. There are different levels of sewers from different ages. The buildings started sinking into them, necessitating reconstruction. In slang the sewer system is known as 'ementál', because of the holes in it. Mozart performed in the Reduta Theatre, also on nám. 25 Unora, in 1767. Built in neo-Classicist style, Reduta is the oldest theatre in Brno, and is now used for operetta.

In the Capuchin tombs (Kapucínská Hrobka) on Kapucínské nám. near the railway station are housed the mummified bodies of Capuchin monks and local dignitaries. An air passage was specially designed to keep the bodies in a dry state. Open Tuesday to Saturday 9am to 4pm, Sunday 11am to 4pm. Closed

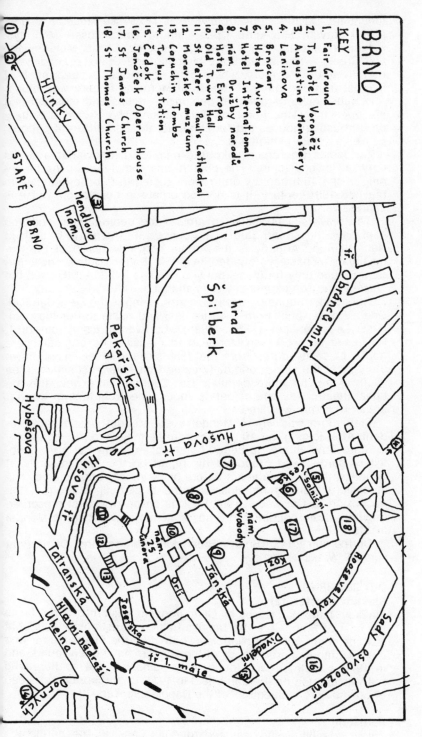

BRNO

KEY

1. Fair Ground
2. To Hotel Voroněž
3. Augustine Monastery
4. Leninova
5. Brnocar
6. Hotel Avion
7. Hotel International
8. nám. Družby národů
9. Hotel Evropa
10. Old Town Hall
11. St Peter & Paul's Cathedral
12. Moravské muzeum
13. Capuchin Tombs
14. To bus station
15. Čedok
16. Janáček Opera House
17. St James' Church
18. St Thomas' Church

lunchtime. Up the steps from here is Moravské Muzeum v Brno (the Moravian Museum). Open 9am to 6pm, closed Mondays. Exhibitions include coins, geology, zoology, Ciril & Metodej, the two Greeks who helped unify Moravia, and Uherské Hradiště in the 8th and 9th century, where gold was produced, and much of interest from the days of the Great Moravian Empire was found. The Kapucínske gardens lie behind the tombs and museum and are open the same hours as the museum. The Moravian Gallery on ul. Husova houses old furniture etc. through different periods, as well as other exhibitions.

St. James Church at Jakubské nám. is distinguishable by its very tall slender spire. The church was completed in the beginning of the 16th century and reconstructed in neo-Gothic style in the late 19th century. It is not too ornate in decoration, but it is impressive.

The university is scattered around the central area, and you can mark the strong student influence. St. Thomas's Church at Náměstí Rudé Armady is the former convent church of the Augustinian Monastery founded in 1350. Earlier Gothic, now Baroque. Open only for mass, but you can see a little bit through the glass doors. The ex-monastery is attached.

One modern building in Brno worth seeing is the Leoš Janácek Opera House, built from 1960 to 1965 and named after the composer Leoš Janácek (1854 - 1928) who lived in Brno from 1881. He based his works on Moravian folk-music. The original opera house close by dates from the 1880's. Bata shoes, now known throughout the world, originally came from Czechoslovakia. (See 'Gottwaldov' for more details). The Centrum store near the national theatre was one of Bata's shops. The archi tecture was far ahead of its pre-war time.

Staré Brno was where Mendel lived. Mendel was a poor student. After joining the Augustine order he moved to the monastery in Staré Brno where he began botanical experiments in the monastery garden and produced his report on the fundamentals of genetics. It was some years before his work was appreciated. The monastery building remains, and the brick-built Church of the Ascension of Our Lady, from 1322, is one of the best preserved original Gothic buildings in Brno. A memorial was built to Mendel in 1965.

On the outskirts of Brno is Brněnská přehrada (Brno Dam). Boat service. Walks.

OUTSIDE BRNO
Slavkov (Austerlitz)
Slavkov, better known by its German name Austerlitz, is not far to the east of Brno. Here the famous Battle of Austerlitz was fought in December 1805 with Napoleon defeating the Russian Tzar and the Austrian Emperor. Bones of the soldiers have been found, and in 1976 a skeleton was found. A monument to the soldiers who fell was erected on the battlefield in 1911. In the Baroque chateau of Slavkov are momentos of the Napoleonic wars.

Pernštejn
This medieval castle was regarded as unassailable during the

Brno: St. Peter's Cathedral

Middle Ages. The castle was modified from a fortress to a palatial residence over time. The oldest parts of the castle are the round tower and the ramparts which rise straight from the rocks on which the building stands. On a tour one can see amongst other things period furniture, Rococo wall paintings, and the dungeons. Open April to September, closed Mondays. North- west of Brno; get there by train or car. (see cover photo).

Other
The Moravian Karst, Stražnice and places to the south of Brno have their own section in this book.

ORGANISED TOURS
From May 15 to September 15 Čedok have half day bus tours to Slavkov every Tuesday, and bus tours of Brno every Saturday.

EVENTS
There are several international trade fairs in Brno: SALIMA (foodstuffs), February; consumer goods in April; the International Engineering Trade Fair in September. International music festival in September.

TO & FROM BRNO
There is now a motorway from Prague to Brno and on to Bratislava. Fast bus service on the motorway to Prague. There are no longer flights to Brno, except during exhibitions. Regular trains from Prague (48 kčs). Rychlík train to Bratislava takes about 2 hours and costs 38 kčs; osobní about 3 hours for 22 kčs. Brno to Stránice is 12 kčs osobní. For transport to the Moravian Karst see the 'Moravský kras' section. Best way to Tábor is by bus, which takes 2 1/2 to 3 1/2 hours and costs 45 kčs. By train to Tábor takes about 7 hours, except a once a day direct rychlík service which takes 4 hours and costs 48 kčs. The railway station is centrally located, but the bus station has recently moved a little outside the centre of town.

GETTING AROUND
Brno has a slightly different public transport system to the rest of the country. Tram and bus tickets cost 1 kčs per trip or 4 kčs per day. The tickets are narrower than the normal Czechoslovak tickets. Some routes operate rather strange hours, and some finish for the day between about 5pm and 7pm. The red colour means night service. Night buses run once an hour and they all meet outside the railway station. In Brno slang trams are called 'salina'.
Other details are the same as in the rest of Czechoslovakia.

PRACTICAL INFORMATION
Maps: Detailed map of Brno with public transport available for 9 kčs. Map of Brněnská přehrada 3 kčs.
Police: For registration or visa extensions, Leninova 20, morning only.
Changing money: at Státní banka československa at nám Svo-

body 21 or Rooseweltova 18; at Hotels International, Continental, Grand, Slavia & Slovan; at Čedok, Divadelní 3 or nám. Svobody 4.

Left luggage at the railway station if under 15kg.

Travel Agents: The Čedok office for foreigners is at Divadelni 3, open 9am to 5pm (summer to 6pm), 9am to 12am Saturday. Guides may he hired through Čedok. Sport-Turist are hopeless and send foreign visitors to Čedok. Rekrea, Radnick á 11. CKM, Česká 11, 657 04 Brno; tel. 236 41-3. Can issue the blue student card, but not ISIC.

Rental Cars from Brnocar; office on Solniční open Monday to Friday 7am to 7pm, Saturday 7am to 6pm, Sunday 8am to 8pm, all year. Their garage is under Hotel Intercontinental. For Czechs the price is 98 kcs per day, but for you it is around US$4.50 per hour or US$23 per day, US$145 per week, plus 23c. per kilometre. Unlimited mileage costs US$62 per day, US$290 per week. 15 per cent tax is charged on top of these prices. Only the person who signs the contract can drive. The car is insured, but you are not unless you pay extra for that. The car can be used in Czechoslovakia and Austria only. If you want to pick it up or drop it off somewhere else there are delivery and collection fees. To rent a car you need your passport, visa and driving licence. You cannot pay in Czechoslovak kcs, except for the odd times when Brnocar cannot bank your dollars! During holiday periods reservation is necessary.

Late night shopping: There is a shop open till 9pm in Česká and Solnicní.

Showers: Cheap showers in the railway station.

Post Office: The post office at the main railway station is open around the clock.

SLEEPING
Hotels
Continental, ****, Leninova 20, 657 64 Brno; tel. 75 05 01, 75 07 27. Central. Up to US$40 per person.

International, A*, Husova 16, 656 67 Brno; tel. 264 11- 9, 266 11-9. Central. Modern.

Voroněž I, A*, Křížkovského 47, 603 73 Brno; tel. 33 63 43, 33 31 35. A little out of the centre. Very nice hotel built by Polish workers. About US$30 to US$40 per person per night.

Voroněž II, B*, next door to the above at no. 49.

Avion, B*, Česká 20, 602 00 Brno; tel. 276 06, 277 97, 266 75. Smaller than any of the above which all sleep hundreds. Central.

Europa,B, nám. Svobody 13, 602 00 Brno; tel. 266 21, 278 51. On the corner of Jánská. Central.

Private Accommodation
Private accommodation is cheaper than hotels, but you must be staying for 3 days or longer. Book through Čedok. Singles 100 kcs, doubles 150 kcs. You must register at the police yourself.

Hostels
In July and August CKM operate temporary hostels in student halls of residence. As the hostels they use tend to vary from year to year, it is best to check first with their office at Česká 11. If

they are closed, you could try Kolej VUT, L eninova 88 & 90, or Kolej SČSP, Purkyňova ulice, Brno - Královo Pole, PSČPO600 00. The price for YHA members is 27 kčs, non-members 65 kčs. Booked from abroad, price is about £10 full board. Some beds at one of the hostels are reserved for foreign travellers who turn up, so there should be a bed, but may not be. The other hostels are for CKM groups only, but if there is space the door-keeper has discretion to allow you to sleep there.

If you have the *International Youth Hostel Handbook*, you may notice a hostel listed at Brněnská Přehrada. In practice, if there is a group there you can't stay there, if there is not a group it is closed. In exceptional circumstances you may be allowed in when there is a group there, but not if it is a children's group. In this case you must first get a voucher from CKM, but they probably won't know about these vouchers! Cost, if you haven't given up already, 50 kčs per night.

Other hostels in Brno send you to Sport-Turist first to get a voucher. But Sport-Turist will only issue vouchers for groups, and will send you on to Čedok to be booked into an expensive hotel.

Camping
Camping Bobrava, A, 664 42 Modřice; tel. Brno 32 01 10. South of Brno. Open about June to September, sometimes longer. Tram 2 to last stop (Modřice), then 1km walk. Also motel and cabins.

Obora, A, 635 00 Brno; tel. 49 42 84. At Brněnská přehrada. Camping and cabins. Open all year. Accessible by bus (roughly hourly), or in summer only by bus and boat.

Other
Trains stop in Brno at various strange hours of the night, so many people sleep in the station. If you follow suit, sleep in the waiting room, or you may be woken by a friendly policeman's foot.

EATING & EVENINGS
The centre of Brno is very alive by Czechoslovak standards, with theatre, concerts, opera, pubs, wine bars etc. The booking office for modern concerts, student clubs etc. is on Dvořakovo. The booking office for classical concerts, theatre, opera etc. is between Maheno and Janaček theatres.

Various places to eat or spend an evening on the street Česká. At Na České Grill Bar on the corner of Česká and Jakubská there tend to be foreign students. The Sputnik food complex includes a sk. I vinána open till the small hours.

At the **Hotel International** restaurant you should have a tie and suit on, but you may get away without. Clean toilets! 'Interclub' open 9pm to 3am, closed Sunday & Monday.

Udobrého kata (the good executioner) is a pivnice full of raucous crowds. Open till 11pm, closed Saturday. On Josefská. From the road opposite the station, it is the first turning on the right.

Vinárna Baroko (sk. II) is a nice wine cellar at Orlí 17. Open 7pm to 2am, closed Sundays.

Apetit Grill on Kozi is a popular place for a drink. Wine and spirits in modern surroundings.

Hotel Evropa (nám. Svobody 13) has a kávarná with dancing to live music Monday to Saturday 8pm to 3am.

The vinárna **U Královny Elišky** (At the Queen Eliska) is an interesting looking place in the historical wine cellars of the monastery at Mendel Square. Sk. II. Open 7pm to 2am, closed Sunday. Live music.

Student Clubs

'V' Club, ul. Gorke'ho, open every day.
'Topas' club, Tanferovy kolej, open every day.
Two clubs at Leninovy kolej, Leninova 88.
Club of Kauniçovy kolej.
Club of Purkyňovy kolej, Purkyňova ulica.

JIHLAVA

Jihlava is the largest town on the Bohemian-Moravian Highlands, and is situated on the historic border between Bohemia and Moravia. The Czech community originated in the 12th century. In the 13th century a royal town of the same name, populate d mainly by Germans, originated to the south of the Czech community. At this time rich silver deposits were found in the area and the town underwent rapid development. The Royal Mint was situated here until the early 14th century. The composer Gustav Mahler spent his childhood here.

The town is an historic reserve. Many of Jihlava's old churches have survived, as have much of the interesting town walls. Jihlava's town square is the 2nd largest in Czechoslovakia and one of the largest in Europe. Part of the towns underground passages are accessible.

Hotels, UH & TU. Ubytovna TJ Modeta (UH, and TU A & B), Tyrsova 7, tel. 265 93, is signposted from the bus station.

ŽĎÁRSKÉ VRCHY

Žďárské Vrchy (Žďár Hills) are a 'protected landscape region' in the highest part of the Bohemian-Moravian Highlands. Apart from small remnants, the original pine and beech forests have been replaced with spruce forests. The watershed between the North and Black Seas passes through here. Good cross-country skiing.

The main centre is Nové Město na Moravě, where the Horácké Museum includes an exhibition on skiing and ski production.

There are many nice small ubytovací hostinec in the area, but they are always booked up.

ZNOJMO

An ancient South Moravian town. In the 11th century a Přemyslid stronghold, of which the Romanesque Rotunda of St Catherine is the only remnant to have been preserved. Old churches. Beautiful Baroque and Renaissance houses. Underground passages under 15th to 17th century houses open to the public. South Moravian museum, Přemyslovců ul. 6, open Tues. to Sun. 9am to 4pm.

Emergency breakdown service for motorists at Přímetice 156; tel. 752 37.

MORAVSKÝ KRAS (MORAVIAN KARST)

Moravský kras (the Moravian Karst) is a real wonderland, the most interesting part of which lies about 30km north of Brno. With its many limestone caves, the huge Machoca Abyss and boat trips on the underground Punkva River, it is well worth a visit.

Machoca is a 138 metre deep vertical sided abyss. You can drive to the top. The most popular cave is Punkevní. Via this system of caves you walk to the bottom of Machoca Abyss, and so take a boat for nearly half a kilometre down the underground Punkva River, a breathtakingly beautiful trip. Open all year: April to Sept. 7am to last tour at 3.15pm (2.45pm at weekends); Oct. to March 7.30am to last tour at 1.45pm (2.45pm on Sun.). Tour takes approx. 1 hour.

Balcarka Cave lies on the eastern edge of Moravský kras. Stalactites and stalagmites and underground pools. Open April to Sept. 7.30am to last tour 3.30pm, Oct. to March 7.30am to last tour 2.30pm.

Kateřinská Cave is where the Punkva River surfaces. A huge underground 'cathedral', 100 metre long, 20m high and 40m wide. Interesting stalactite and stalagmite formations. Open April to Sept. 7.30am to last tour 3.45pm; Oct. to March 8.30 am to last tour 3.45pm.

North of this area is the Sloup-Šošůvka cave system, forming an extensive maze on two levels connected by holes. Includes a famous stalagmite known as 'candlestick'. During the tourist season concerts are held in Eliščina Cave, which has excellent acoustics.

Tours of the caves are conducted in Czech and German, but at the entrance to each cave you can borrow a description of the cave in English, which you take with you on the tour and return when you come out again.

The caves are very popular, so expect queues and crowds in summertime.

There are walking tracks around Moravský kras.

SLEEPING

Camping at Autokemp Olžovec, 679 06 Jedovnice; tel. Blansko 931 34. Open 15/5 to 15/10. On a lake. Can drive to, or walk about 2km from the bus stop in Jedovnice.

Hotel Riviera, C, 679 06 Jedovnice; tel. 932 09. Sk. III restaurant.

Hotel Dukla, B, nám. Vítězného února, 678 01 Blansko; tel. 50 01-3. Doubles only.

PUBLIC TRANSPORT

In summer there is a bus leaving from Blansko Bus Station in the morning which takes you to Punkevní, Kateřinská and Balcarka Caves as well as the top of Machoca Abyss, waiting for you at each place. Bus ticket includes cave entrance fees.

There are trains to Blansko from Brno, but many are replaced by buses because of the reconstruction of railway tunnels that has been going on over the last few years. Buses to Jedovnice from Blansko and Brno.

PODYJÍ

A pleasant rural district south of Brno near the Austrian border. Castles, lakes and old hunting estates. In Lednice is one of the most visited chateaux in Czechoslovakia. This area was in the hands of the Lichtenstein family from the 13th century until the end of the Second World War. Hunting lodges and various follies were built on the estate. The little map 'Pavlovské vrchy' (3 kčs) is excellent for those wanting to explore this area.

Břeclav

The town of Břeclav is an important railway junction. The exchange office at the railway station is open 24 hours. There is no longer a rail service between Břeclav and Lednice. Just off the road towards Lednice is a castle which was restored in the 19th century. It is now used for offices etc. Its tower is in ruins. There is a camping ground beside the castle open mid April to the end of September. From Břeclav one can walk to Lednice by following the green marked track through the wet lowland forests of the river Dyje.

In Postorná, just out of Břeclav on the road to Lednice is a late 19th century octagonal church built by the Lichtenstein family.

Lednické rybn'ky

Lednické rybníky are lakes created for fishing in the 15th century. The road from Břeclav to Lednice passes by one of them. From this point it is a short walk to the pseudo 'Temple of Apollo', one of the follies. The area is a nature reserve for nesting birds, so some of it is closed. Nice for picnics. One may swim where marked by buoys, but not out to the island which is a nature reserve. No windsurfing. Sk. III self service restaurant & accommodation in season. Camping on the other side of the road.

The road from Lednice to Valtice also passes the lakes.

Lednice

The castle in Lednice is open from the 1 May to 31 October, weekends only in October. The medieval castle was modified over time to its present form. The rooms, with their beautiful wooden interiors, may be seen with a guide. The other part of the castle houses a museum. The original Church of St James was demolished and replaced with living quarters and the present St James Chapel. Down the lake from the castle you can see the 60 metre high minaret built between 1798 and 1802.

From Lednice it is a 3km walk (follow the green or yellow markers) to Jånov hrad, a castle built as a ruin! One can continue from here following the green markers to Břeclav, 10.5km altogether. From Lednice the red marked route takes walke rs to Valtice via Apollo, the lake and woods (13.5km). In a westerly direction the red markers lead to Mikulov (16km).

Across the road from Lednice Castle is Zámecký Hotel (tel. 98220). Singles/doubles are 90/130 kčs without bath, 120/160 kčs with bath. In season booked out by Čedok; out of season you may be able to get a room, but the castle is closed! Better than average sk III restaurant. Sk II snackbar, sometimes with live music. Cukraren.

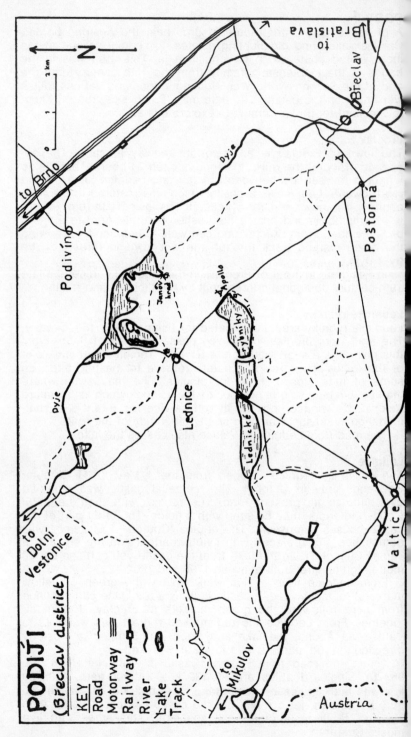

Cukravna
There is turistická ubytovna 1km towards Mikulov with 200 beds.
Owned by a sports club. In summer it is full with student brigades
and seasonal fruit factory workers. In Lednice is the 'Fruta'
factory, which makes salads, kompots (stewed fruit) etc.

Valtice
Wine producing. Valtice Chateau open April to October (in April &
October at weekends only). Early Baroque style throughout.
   Hotel Hubertus (B*) at the castle (tel. 945 37). UH & TU B at
Besední dům, Mikulovská 173 (tel. 941 20). Train service to
Břeclav. There are two railway stations in Valtice.

Dolní Vestonice
South Moravia was populated by mammoth hunters 30,000 years
ago. Mammoth bones and other artifacts have been found in
Dolní Vestonice. The museum here is open May to September 8am
to 12, 1pm to 4pm, closed Monday. Rest of year open weekends
only, same hours. Děvín (550m) is a nice mountain to climb. One
can follow the same track along the length of Pavlovské vrchy to
Mikulov.

Mikulov
Old town with chateau dating from the 13th century when Mikulov
was an important strongpoint on the South Moravian border. Jewish ghetto and old Jewish cemetry. Border crossing point on the
E7 from Brno to Vienna.

STRÁŽNICE
Strážnice is best known for its folk-lore festival, the biggest in
Bohemia and Moravia, where folk traditions are not as well pre-
served as in Slovakia. This is a festival of living folk tradition,
with costumes, dances, songs and customs from the Moravian
Slovácko area. Usually held in the last weekend of June, but can
vary.
   In the 17th century Strážnice was the third largest town in
Moravia. The towers of the town gates remain, but the walls are
gone. The town's late Gothic castle was changed to Baroque in
the 19th century. It is in its grounds that the folk festival is held.
The museum in the castle includes a display of mostly home-
made folk instruments. Open 1 May to 31 October: Tuesday to
Saturday 8am to 12, 1pm to 5pm; Sunday 9am to 12, 2pm to 5pm;
last entry 4pm. Also at the castle is the Zám ecká vinárna, a wine
restaurant open Tues. to Thurs 5pm to midnight, Fri. & Sat. 5pm to
1am, with live music on Friday & Saturday.
   Muzeum Vesnice Jihovýchodní Moravy is a Skansen museum
covering a large area. Open Tues. to Sat. 8am to 5pm, Sunday
10am to 6pm.
   The railway station is painted with folk art.

TO & FROM STRAŽNICE
By train or bus. To Bratislava 14 kčs osobní train, change at Kúty.
Strážnice to Kúty is railcar.

SLEEPING

Strážnice Autokemping, behind the castle in the castle grounds. Nice surroundings. Motel, chata and tent camping. Chata & motel open all year. The camping area is open 1/5 to 31/10, but you can camp in the chata area in winter. Chata are 2, 3 or 4 person. Motel: all twin rooms. In holiday periods beds are booked up, but some beds are reserved for one night people. Outside holiday periods there should be free beds. Restaurant open mealtimes, but not always in winter. Beside the camping ground is a swimming pool & mini golf.

The town's two hotels are across the square from each other. **Černý orel** (B) is the older of the two. Singles 100 kcs, doubles 136 kcs, 3 people in a double room 186 kcs. 40 kcs per person in a 6 bed dorm. Normally full Thurs. to Sat. One or two free rooms. Tel. 94 21 28. **Hotel Strážnice**, *** (B*), tel. 94 22 06. From 1/4 to 31/10 problem to get a room without reservation. Singles 120 kcs, doubles 180 kcs, both with shower. The town's turistická ubytovna is only available for footballers. Try the dorm at Čierny orel instead.

BUCHLOVICE & VELEHRAD

Buchlovice lies east of Brno on highway 50, just before Uherské Hradiste. It has a very nice Baroque chateau and gardens. The chateau was built in Italian style from the beginning of the 17th century and is adorned with sculptures. The park was originally laid out in formal Italian style, but later transformed into a French garden, and finally an English park. In 1908 Buchlovice Chateau played host to the Austrian and Russian foreign ministers who were negotiating the Austrian annexation of Bosnia and Herzegovina. Swimming.

Velehrad lies a few kilometres to the east of Buchlovice, off the main road. Archeologists think it may be a centre of the Great Moravian Empire. In the nearby town of Uherské Hradiste is a museum with artifacts from the Great Moravian Empire.

There is a ubytovací hostinec and camping ground (open summer only) in Buchlovice. Hotels in Uherské Hradiste.

GOTTWALDOV (ZLÍN)

The home of Bata shoes. Zlín was a small village when Bata introduced one of the factories he set up in places where people were poor. Another was in Svit, that was once called Batovany and is now called Partizanske. He built housing and schools for the workers in a progressive style for his time and built Bata shops in the centre of each town in the country. But he was a bit of a tyrant although he treated his workers well by the standards of the time. He banned the Communist Party at his factory. In 1938 going to Dresden on business, the pilot said there was too much fog to fly. Bata replied 'I'm the employer, do as I say'. The plane crashed and they were both killed. His brother took over Bata's empire until it was nationalized after the Second World War. Bata left Czechoslovakia but Bata factories still exist all over the world under the Bata name.

Zlín (renamed Gottwaldov) is still the centre of Czechoslovakia's shoe making industry. Museum of shoe making. Hotel, chalet (summer only) and hostel type accommodation.

NORTHERN MORAVIA
Northern Moravia is a horrible polluted industrial agglomorate. Ostrava is the centre of Czechoslovakia's iron and steel industry, where coal and iron ore are extracted and utilized. There has been rapid industrial expansion here since the Second World War. But the area around its periphery has nice natural beauty, including lakes and the Moravskoslezské Beskydy. It was not so long ago that the Beskydy had their original forest cover. But the demand for wood led to its destruction and the planting of spruce. Much of this happened in the 1820s, when industry began to develop in the region. Some small areas of original forest cover remain.

Addresses
Čedok, Dimitrovovo 9, 728 93 Ostrava; tel. 231424, 234287.
CKM, Gottwaldova 102, 702 99 Ostrava; tel. 23 46 81.
Autoturist breakdown service, Obrancu miru 30, Ostrava-Vitkovice; tel. 33672.
Pragocar (rental cars), Harantova 25, Ostrava; tel. 236675.

BÍLÉ (BIELE) KARRPATY (WHITE CARPATHIANS)
The highest point in this part of the Carpathian mountain chain is Velká Javorina at 970 metres. The road up on the Moravian side is closed in winter, but the road up from Cetuna on the Slovak side is open all year round. On Javorina is a TV transmitter, ski field, and Holubyho chata.

In the village of Velká nad Veličkou there is a 3 day long traditional folk festival on about the 3rd week of July. Vápenky is a nice small village below Velka Javorina on the Moravian side. Stráni-kvetná has a factory producing strik ing glass.

Access to these places from Strážnice or Nové Mesto nad Váhom. Trenc gives access to the northern part of the hills. I recommend you buy the map 'Biele Karpaty' even if you don't intend to tramp, as the little villages and roads between them are not marked on road maps.

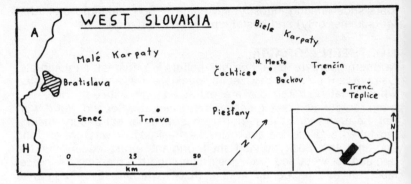

Trenčín Castle, Slovakia

WEST SLOVAKIA

BRATISLAVA

Bratislava, with a population of 410,000, is the second largest city in Czechoslovakia, and, since 1969, the capital of Slovakia. It lies on the River Danube, at the western extremity of the long arch of the Carpathian mountain chain. Its suburbs border the fortifications along the Austrian border, and it is only a few short kilometres north of the Hungarian border. In fact there used to be a tram to Vienna, and older people may have memories of riding there by bicycle, but today it is difficult for Czechoslovaks to cross the border.

Bratislava lies rather out on a limb in the south-west corner of Slovakia, so with all the beautiful old towns and wonders of nature in other parts of Czechoslovakia, it may not be worth a special trip to see. But if you are passing that way anyway, or have enough time, there is a lot to see, and it is interesting to feel the effects of the proximity of Austria and Hungary.

HISTORY
The first human traces here date from the late Stone Age. In the 1st century BC a Celtic tribe built a settlement here. Later it became a part of the Roman Empire. The first Slavs arrived here in the 5th and 6th centuries AD. In the 9th century Bratislava was part of the Great Moravian Empire. In the 11th and 12th centuries Bratislava castle was a frontier bastion of the Magyar State. In 1241 the Tatars plundered the settlement, but failed to take the castle. Budapest was under threat by the Turks, so in 1536 Bratislava became the capital of Hungary. The Turks never occupied Bratislava. In 1773 the census showed that 26,845 people lived in the city, making it the largest in Hungary. In 1811 the castle was burnt down due to the carelessness of soldiers. In 1938 Slovakia was granted autonomy. The government banned all activities of the Communist party. On 4/4/45 Bratislava was liberated from the Germans by the Soviets.

BRATISLAVA TODAY
Bratislava has undergone rapid expansion, and is very much a mixture of old and new. The town is overlooked by its castle, which has undergone extensive reconstruction, and below it lies the old town, which is definitely worth exploring. On the hill above the castle lived the affluent citizens. But many of the new suburbs, Petržalka on the other side of the Danube in particular, look like architectural and sociological disaster areas.

It can be beautiful along the Danube which is fast flowing here, and there are many Czechoslovak patrol boats. You'll probably either like or detest Most SNP, the modern bridge, obviously designed as a showpiece, which connects the two sides of the

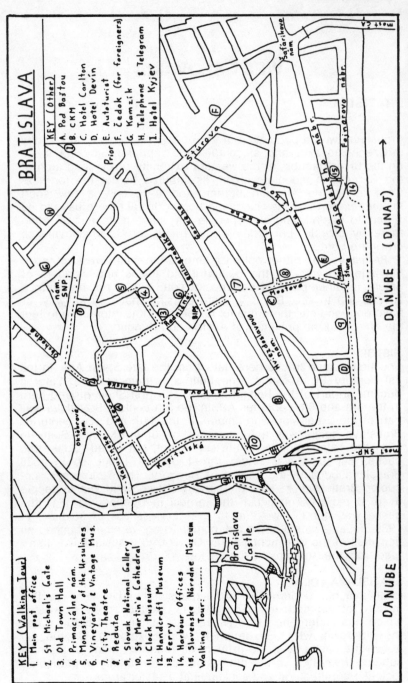

BRATISLAVA

KEY (Other)
A. Pod Baštou
B. CKM
C. Hotel Carlton
D. Hotel Devín
E. Autoturist
F. Čedok (for foreigners)
G. Kamzík
H. Telephone & Telegram
I. Hotel Kyjev

KEY (Walking Tour)
1. Main post office
2. St Michael's Gate
3. Old Town Hall
4. Primaciálne nám.
5. Monastery of the Ursulines
6. Vineyards & Vintage Mus.
7. City Theatre
8. Reduta
9. Slovak National Gallery
10. St Martin's Cathedral
11. Clock Museum
12. Handcraft Museum
13. Ferry
14. Harbour Offices
15. Slovenské Národne Múzeum
Walking Tour: ....

Bratislava Castle

DANUBE (DUNAJ)

DANUBE

river. The old bridge was re-built by Soviet sappers after the Germans damaged the original in 1945. It is presently again under reconstruction, and closed to the public. There are plans to build a fourth bridge west of the castle, so that the main road will cross to Petržalka and bypass the centre of Bratislava before crossing back over most Hrdinov Dukly.

Mosquitoes are very bad in Bratislava, particularly by the Danube where they breed in pools caused by its rise and fall.

The Malé Karpaty foothills begin right in the town, so peaceful woods are only a walk from the centre and vineyards on the slopes stretch right down into the town.

Today Bratislava has 8 per cent of Slovakia's population, and 10 per cent of its industry, the most important of which is chemical industry.

Radio and television can be received from three countries. It is popular to listen to Austrian radio, mainly because it broadcasts good music. The large Hungarian minority can watch television from Budapest. You'll see a lot of jeans in Bratislava, in contrast to the more conservative eastern part of the country. There are a lot of expensive things in the shops that you don't see in the rest of Slovakia.

TO SEE
A Walking Tour of Bratislava
I have described the following in the form of a walking tour which you may or may not choose to follow. The tour is by no means comprehensive, but does take in many of the main sights, and gives one a look at the various sides to the city. The tour is set out in a continuous form, but it is not necessarily intended as a one day tour. I would recommend at least 2 days; longer if you like to browse in museums etc.

The main square in the centre of town is námestie SNP, the square of the Slovak national uprising. A group of statues erected to commemorate the 30th anniversary of the uprising, dominates the square and features flames to keep 'ever alive' the message of the Slovak national uprising. Using the area around the statues and flames for relaxing is likely to be frowned upon by the police. The square was previously called Stalin Square.

Across the road from the square is the main post office. Following this street uphill, then taking the first turning left (Michalská) leads one into the old town. Michalská crosses a bridge, under which the city moat ran. Travelling actors' companies gave performances here in the 18th century. At Michalská 26, in what was one of the oldest pharmacies in Bratislava, is the Pharmacy Múzeum. St Michael's Gate, originally built in the 14th century, is the only gate left today. In it is the Armament and City Fortification Museum. Both museums are open 10 am to 5 pm, Tuesday to Sunday.

Turning left into Zámočnícka and continuing on along Dibrovovo nám. brings you to Radnicna and on the left, the Old Town Hall. It is a nice building, especially the courtyard where there are concerts in summer. On the first floor is the town museum, and in the cellar in the former cells the Museum of Feudal Justice. Open Tuesday to Sunday, 10 am to 5 pm. On the opposite side of the Old Town Hall is Primaciálne nám., with Primaciálny Palác (Primate's Palace) at no. 2. Built in 1781 as the archbishop's palace, from 1903 the building was used as the town hall. Today it houses representative rooms of the National Committee of Bratislava. At Ursulínska 5, by Primaciálne nám. is the monastery of the Ursulines, erected in 1687 together with a school. The well in the square was discovered in 1977! Back on Radnična, at no. 1, is the Vineyards & Vintage Museum in the Palace of the Apponyi Family (1762).

At the end of Radnična, turn right into Leningradská and first left into Rybárska brána. Across the road at the bottom of this street is the City Theatre built in 1888 in Neo- Renaissance style. Today it is the opera and ballet scene of the Slovak National Theatre. Near the other side of the theatre is a turning, Mostová. A little way down here, on the corner of Palackého, is Reduta, the concert hall of the Slovak Philharmonic Orchestra. This Neo-Baroque building from 1914 is very ornate, and worth a look inside if it is possible.

Continuing down Mostová brings you to the Danube waterfront. If you haven't seen it before, you can now see Most SNP, the bridge that the city sacrificed much of its heritage to build. The oldest part of the town, including the Jewish Synagogue was demolished to build the access road and remains of the old town walls were found while excavating for the road. Turning to the right brings one to the Slovak National Gallery (Slovenská Národná Galeria). This is in the restored building of the former Water Barracks, built 1759-66. Judge for yourself what has been done to the building. Open 10 am to 5 pm, closed Mondays. 4 kčs, 2 kčs students.

Walking up beside the bridge access road will bring you to St Martin's Cathedral. Originally built in the 14th & 15th century on the site of an older church, it underwent various additions and reconstructions. The tower was built in the moat of the castle, and had a defensive function until the end of the 15th century. From 1563 to 1830 the cathedral was the coronation church of 10 Hungarian kings and 8 queens. At present it is open only rather odd hours, as there is strengthening work underway, because vibration from the new road to Most SNP is weakening the building. From the church follow Kapitulská, where some of the Gothic and Baroque houses have been restored. Kapitulská 4 is the reconstructed executioner's house.

Turn right at the end of Kapitulská, left into Klariská, and right again at the top of the stairs. This brings you to Októbrové námestie. On this square is the church of the Trinitaries, built from 1717-27. The interior is decorated by the Italian painter Galli Bibiena. The monastery was rebuilt to become the county hall in 1844. Today it houses offices of the Slovak National Council. The column in the middle of Októbrové námestie dates from 1723 and is of the Madonna, commemorating the plague epidemic the town suffered in 1712-13. Behind the column lies the little Capuchin church, modest in decoration, and small and quiet with people coming in to pray. Built 1708- 11.

From Októbrové námestie head back along Kapucinska towards the castle. After crossing the access road to Most SNP, turn left and follow Židovská along above it. At the bottom end of the street, at Židovská 1, is the House of the Good Shepherd, built in 1760. Today it is the Clock Museum, the only museum in Bratislava to have any written material available in English. Open daily except Monday 10am to 5pm. Across the road from here is the Handcraft Museum, which is open 10am to 5pm, closed Tuesday.

From here one can climb up the hill to Bratislava Castle. Various castles have existed on this site over the centuries. It was an important site for the Great Moravian Empire, when a castle built of clay and wood existed here. After the fall of the Great Moravian Empire, Hungarian kings continued to fortify the site. In 1526 Hungary became part of the Habsburg empire, and the castle was used as the governor's residence, protecting the empire against the Turks and disgruntled Transylvanian princes. The castle was rebuilt several times during the Habsburg rule. Later reconstruction made it more a place to live in than a fortress. In 1802 the castle became soldiers' barracks, and in 1811 it was destroyed by fire. In 1954 reconstruction work began, and stretched over the next decade. Today the castle houses Slovak Government offices and a museum. Open 9am to 4pm, but the grounds are open outside these hours.

Dropping down from the castle the same way you came up, walk across the Danube over Most SNP. On the other side you can pay 3 kcs to go up in the lift to the cafe Bystrica, with excellent views and high prices. If it is clear you should be able to see Austria and Hungary. There is only the kaviareň up there; there is no viewing deck as such (though there is a good view of Petržalka from the toilets!). Open 1 May to 31 August 10am to 11pm; rest of year closes at 10pm; Mondays open from 1pm. Just past here on the upstream side of Viedenská cesta the closed border area begins. Walking downstream from here brings one to a ferry back across the river. See 'Getting Around' for operating schedule. If the ferry is not operating, return across the bridge.

On the town side of the river are the water transport offices. From early April to late October there are cruises on the Danube at 9am every day. The cruise costs 5 kcs, and is 10km long. Opposite the harbour offices, on the corner of Vaja nského nábrežie & Fajnorova nábr. is Slovenske Národne Múzeum (the Slovak National Museum), open 9am to 5pm, closed Mondays. And so ends our tour!

Still Within Walking Distance
The street Obrancov mieru has many old buildings and palaces along it. At no. 25 is Múzeum V. I. Lenin, open Tuesday to Friday 8am to 6pm, weekends 9am to 3pm, closed Mondays. On Tolstého ul., a side street to Obrancov mieru, the buildings have nice facades and statuary. On the hill above here is the impressive Slavín War Memorial, built in honour of the Soviet soldiers who lost their lives when they drove the Nazis out of Slovakia. It shows the dates different towns were liberated.

It is a nice walk out along Banskobystrická, with gardens and buildings including the Government Building of the Slovak Socialist Republic, but most of the grounds and buildings are closed to the public. This leads one to Gottwaldovo nám. on the right, not bad for a modern square. It has a fountain, memorial, grass and seats, and even toilets. On the other side of Banskobystrická is a smaller shadier park. In Sovietske nám. is another plague monument.

ON THE OUTSKIRTS OF BRATISLAVA

Zlaté piesky iṣ a lake with swimming and boating. Entrance to the lake costs 3 kcs. In 1976 a plane crashed into the lake in summer and many people were killed.

Kamzík is a 440m Malé Karpaty peak above Bratislava, with a television tower on top. One can drive to the top, walk from the main railway station by following the red markers (3/4 hour), or take bus no. 213 to the last stop and then walk (1/2 hour). The buses run late, and when they finish night bus 143 runs down from the same stop. There is no bus to the top. At the top there are restaurants open in the evening, and a bufet open daytime only. One of the restaurants is the class I Expo Koliba. In the television tower is a coffee bar which is supposed to revolve hourly. There are also ski tows.

Železná studnička is the valley behind Kamzík. There are four natural lakes, one of which you can hire boats on, but they are no good for swimming. There is a chairlift up to Kamzík which operates at weekends, or every day in winter if the snow is good. Železná studnička is also a starting point for hikes. Accessible by bus no. 33.

The Zoo. At the time of writing the zoo in Mlynská dolina was being extended to 11 times its previous size, so that the animals could have more natural surroundings.

Devín. The impressive ruins of Devín Castle sit upon a promontory overlooking the point where the river Morava enters the Danube. In theory the castle can be visited by taking bus 29 from underneath most SNP to the last stop and then following the signs. The castle closes at 6pm. Photography is forbidden. When I tried to visit the castle I was stopped and taken away for questioning for a couple of hours. The end result was that, yes, I could visit the castle, but I should come back the next day because by that time it was too late! If you do want to visit the castle follow the route I have described which is the way the border police told me one must approach the castle, and don't wander around the rest of the village. The bus trip out is rather depressing, as it follows what some call the Iron Curtain, a high fence etc. to stop people approaching the Danube, which has Austria on the other side. If you do travel along the Danube by boat between Bratislava and Vienna, you get a good view of Devín Castle.

Rusovce. The village of Rusovce lies south of Bratislava near the Austrian and Hungarian borders. Its attractions are a chateau, a Roman Museum, and a nudist swimming lake. The chateau was built in the English neo-Gothic style and is surrounded by an English style park. The building is now used by the Slovak Folk Ensemble and is closed to the public, but you are free to wander in the grounds. The small Roman Museum is open from May to September, 10am to 5pm, closed Mondays. Nude swimming is practised in a nearby lake formed in an old gravel pit. Rusovce is accessible by car or bus no. 116.

The Danube. There were some nice spots downstream on the Danube, but two huge dams jointly built by Czechoslovakia and Hungary are going to flood this area, and according to Hungarian and Austrian protesters the ecological consequences will be devastating. Hungary's economy has found the cost too much to bear, so Austria has come to the rescue with US$500 million in credits in exchange for the total estimated electricity output of one of the dams over a 20 year period.

OUTSIDE BRATISLAVA

The Malé Karpaty (Little Carpathian Mountains) stretch north from Bratislava, and are a popular destination for trampers at weekends. There are caves, Driny jaskyňa, open to the public near the top end of the hills. The cave is of tectonic origin and was not formed by underground water flow. Tours from 1/4 to 15/5 and 16/9 to 31/10 at 9am, 11 and 2pm. 16/5 to 15/9 hourly from 9am until the last tour at 4pm. Rest of year closed. 6 kčs, 3 kčs children under 15 & students.

The area to the east of Bratislava is not very interesting, with lots of towns and industry.

ORGANISED TOURS

The following 3 tours operate every Wednesday from May 15 to September 15, and in July & August on Saturday also. Pickup from some hotels and Čedok. Book at Čedok.

Sightseeing Tour of Bratislava: afternoon tour, 3 hours, 60 kčs.

Malé Karpaty(Little Carpathians), evening tour, finishing with dinner at Zochova chalet with Gypsy music. Return to Bratislava about 10pm. 161 kčs.

Sightseeing Tour of Bratislava with Malé Karpaty. From early afternoon till about 10pm. 178 kčs. Including dinner.

EVENTS

The Bratislava lyre

International pop song festival held in May.

Grape Harvest

The foothills of Malé Karpaty are covered with vines. The grapes are harvested in early autumn. Shortly afterwards, for a period of only about 2 to 3 weeks, the delicious young wine 'burciak' is available in Bratislava.

Biennials of Illustrations Bratislava (BIB)

Held in September and October every odd numbered year (i.e. 1989, 1991). An international exhibition of illustrations for children's books, with entries from all over the world. This is really worth seeing if you are in Bratislava at the right time. In the House of Culture, just down from ná. SNP towards Prior.

The Bratislava Music Festival

An international music festival lasting two weeks and starting about the end of September.

SPORT
Sporting complexes are not normally open for the general public in Czechoslovakia, but they can be hired by groups. Here are some exceptions which are open to the public some of the time:

Swimming
Outdoor swimming pools are open from June to mid September. On Vajnorská ulica is a heated indoor swimming pool. At 50m it is the largest in Bratislava. Open 7.30am to 10pm, closed Mondays. In daytime available for schools only, and sometimes open only for professionals. Can hire bathing clothes.

Ice Skating
There are two ice skating stadiums next door to each other on Trnavskó cesta. Sometimes closed for training. Another stadium on Bajkalskó ulica.

Tennis
One can play tennis and hire rackets at Zlaté piesky.

Boating
Rowing boats, windsurfers and water bicycles can be hired at Zlaté piesky.
   It is possible, but only for experienced sportsmen, to borrow canoes, 7 man dinghies or kayaks from T.J. Vinohrady at Nabr. L. Svobodu 17, 841 01 Bratislava (tel. 329661). The boats may be used on the small branch of the Danube by the club-house. The Danube itself is dangerous because of its swift flow and barge traffic: The club is open all year round, but when it is very cold the boats are taken to the Malý Dunaj. Boats may only be taken away to other areas if arranged beforehand. Groups wanting to use boats must ask in advance, in which case the club's committee decide whether or not to lend the boats.
   Every year TID, an international Danube trip from West Germany to Bulgaria is held. See the general 'Boating' section for details.

TO & FROM BRATISLAVA
By Car
Bratislava is connected with Prague by motorway, and has main road connections to Vienna and Budapest.

By Bus & Train
Prague: by rýchlik train 64 kčs, 5 hours. Often late as many of them are international trains which don't begin from Bratislava. Trains on the same route stop at Brno, and many travel on to East Berlin. By bus 115 kčs, 4 hours.
   Žilina: by rýchlik train 48 kčs; by bus 57 kčs. There are trains to **Budapest** at 1.09, 6.00, 12.00, 14.20 and 18.00.
   Vienna: Bus leaves Bratislava at 7.00 and 17.30, takes about 2

hours, and costs 50 kčs. Buy tickets at the Mlynské Nivy Bus Station. Bus from Vienna leaves at 8.00 and 17.00, costs 74OS. Train leaves Bratislava at 9.30 and 17.20, and takes about 3 hours. Buy ticket (about US$4) at station or Čedok. Both must be paid for in western currency.

By Boat
There is a boat service to **Budapest** 3 or 4 times a week from early May to early September. US$10 one way, US$20 return, must be paid in western currency. The boat leaves Bratislava early in the morning, and takes 3 1/2 hours to reach Budapest. From Budapest it leaves late afternoon, taking 4 1/2 hours for the return trip upstream.

There is also a boat service to **Vienna**, but Čedok in Vienna book it up with their one day package tours to Bratislava. For these package tours you can get a special visa on the boat. The boat leaves Bratislava at 5pm daily. The only way you can get on it if you are not on the package tour is to ask the captain if he can take you. If he does, it may be on the understanding that you will have to stand. Fare (105 kčs) must be paid in western money. There are some interesting views along the river. The Czechoslovak side is horrible with its barbed wire, guards etc, but you do get a good view of the ruins of Devín.

From early April to late September there is a daily boat service between Bratislava and **Komárno**. Fare 30 kčs one way. The boat leaves Bratislava at 4pm and arrives in Komárno at 5.30pm. From Komárno it leaves at 6.30am, arriving in Bratislava at 8.30pm, but on Sundays it leaves 1 hour later from Komárno.

By Air
There are international flights to Moscow, Leningrad, Sofia and Berlin. There are several direct flights a day to Prague, two per day to Košice, and one per day to Poprad. ČSA's office is at Mostová 3. Their airport bus leaves one hour before domestic flights and two hours before international flights; free for domestic flights, 5 kčs for international. To the airport from Hlavná stanica (the main railway station) take bus no. 24.

Hitch-hiking
Difficult on the Bratislava-Brno-Prague route. Try from somewhere along Viedenská cesta for Vienna. Hitching to Hungary is difficult.

GETTING AROUND
Efficient public transport service by tram, bus and trolley bus. Buy street map (see below) which shows all local transport routes. But there are lots of public works all the time, so the streets, and bus and tram routes are always changing. The tunnel under the castle is only open for trams. Buy tickets beforehand from kiosks, and punch them yourself as you enter the bus. For buses to the airport see above. Night buses run from nám. SNP hourly from 12.45am until the last bus at 4.45am to most parts of the city. The night bus to Zlaté piesky is no. 132 which leaves at 12.40, 1.40 and 2.35am. 'ZZ' at bus stops means night bus.

There is a ferry service across the river. It operates from about early April to early October from 10am to 8pm Tuesday to Friday, 10am to 9pm Saturday and 9am to 8pm Sunday. From early September, until it stops operating for the season, it finishes at 6pm every day, and starts at 10am on Sundays. Trip costs 1 kčs and is on an open boat.

MAPS & GUIDEBOOKS

Bratislava, Town Plan, detailed map of Bratislava including suburbs, public transport and index, 12 kčs.

Bratislava, Town-Monuments, map of town centre and information on historic buildings, museums etc in various languages, including English.

Bratislava Guide, by O. Došek, D. Učníková & M. Murín, Šport, Bratislava, 1978. English edition out of print. Thorough guide to Bratislava. Bit dated, but good background information.

TRAVEL AGENTS

Čedok have a special office for foreigners at Štúrova 13 (tel. 520 81, 552 80). Speak English. Helpful. Open 9am to 6pm Monday to Friday, 9am to 12 on Saturday. Currency exchange. Guides can be hired through them. I was quoted 150 kčs for 3 hours.

CKM, Hviezdoslavovo nám. 16, 814 16 Bratislava; tel. 33 16 07. Open Monday to Friday.

Tatratour, Dibrovovo námestie 7, 815 09 Bratislava; tel. 335 852. In the old town. Can help with information on Bratislava. Open Monday, Wednesday, Thursday & Friday 8.30am to 4.30pm, Tuesday 9am to 6pm, Saturdays from 15/5 to 15/9 only 9am to 12.

Autoturist, Štúrovo nám 1; tel. 337381-4. Entrance from alleyway. Open Monday, Tuesday and Thursday 9am to 12 and 1pm to 4pm; Wednesday 10am to 12, 1pm to 4pm; Friday 9am to 12, 1pm to 2.30pm. The exchange office is open Monday to F riday 9am to 12 (from 10am Wednesdays).

OTHER PRACTICAL INFORMATION & ADDRESSES

Bratislava Informačná a Propagačná Služba (BIPS), the Bratislava information and publicity service, is at Leningradska 1. Information on Bratislava, cultural programmes, events, guides, tours.

For registering at the police if you are staying with friends, or for visa extensions, visit **Pasové oddelenie**, the District Passport & Visa Dept., at Legerského 1. Take tram no. 3, 5, 7 or 11 towards Rača. Open 8am to 1pm. Tel. 663 51.

Hlavná pošta, the main post office, is at nám. SNP 34. Poste Restante is open every day. On Saturday open 7am to 5pm, Sunday 9am to 4pm in summer.

The exchange office on the road to Vienna is open 24 hours. There is an exchange office in the harbour building.

If transferring money to Czechoslovakia, transfer it to Československá obchodní banka, Ul. Lehotského 3. A bit out of the centre. Look for the upside-down triangle.

The following countries have consulates in Bratislava: Austria,

Bulgaria, Cuba, Finland, East Germany, Hungary, Poland, Roumania, Yugoslavia and USSR.

Cars may be rented from Čedok. Price for Škoda: US$25 per day, US$137 per week, plus 21c. per km. Insurance US$5 per day, US$30 per week. With unlimited mileage: US$61 per day, US$270 per week, extra days US$39, including insurance. 15 per cent is added to all charges. A car can be picked up or dropped off in other parts of Czechoslovakia, but if so an extra charge of 20c. per km will be added. Must be paid in foreign currency or by credit card.

Emergency breakdown service phone 24 40 13.

SLEEPING
Camping & Bungalows
There are two camping grounds out at **Zlaté piesky**(which means Golden Sands). Hotel Flora's camp is the largest, and is on the lake. Bungalows for 4 people 187 kčs or 250 kčs depending on quality of building. If less than 4 people, must still pay same price. Tent camping 21 kčs per person, 8 kčs per tent. Cars 8 kčs. Area tax 3 kčs. Open for tents May to September, bungalows all year. From June to mid September there is a disco club, restaurant and many bufets. From May to the end of September Golf Club (sk III plus 10 per cent) is open 11am to 10pm, with drinks and some food. Mini golf. Nice surroundings. Noise from main road, so try to keep your distance from it. Facilities in a bad state of repair, but has hot water & cooking elements. Can hire rowing boats, windsurfers and water bicycles from May to September.

The other camp is a little further down the same road. It has the same facilities in the same state of disrepair. It is smaller, also has bungalows, but is not as nice as Flora, and has no direct access to the lake. 21 kčs per tent, 21 kčs per person plus 21 kčs per car. 3 bed bungalows with hot & cold water, toilet, communal shower, 270 kčs, best to book them through Čedok. For tents open 15 June to 15 September, for bungalows to 30 October. Tel. 651 70.

Zlaté piesky is a long way out, but there are fast buses. From Monday to Friday during rush hours only take bus 110 to the last stop. Otherwise take bus 32 from nám. Fr. Zupku at the beginning of Trnavská cesta, and get off just past a petrol station. From the railway station to nám. Fr. Zupku you can take bus 22, 23 or 24. Time from the centre of town to Zlaté piesky including changing bus about 40 minutes.

There is a chalet camp (B) at **Koliba**. Tel. 421 75. Open summer season only. 4 person bungalows 115 kčs. Trolley bus 213 to last stop.

The camps at Zrkadlový háj you may see mentioned in the *1983 Camping* book closed down about 10 years ago!

Hostels
CKM have some sort of arrangement for YHA members and others that their own staff don't seem to understand. The following is a rough guide to this chaotic system.

CKM have a hostel from about early July to late August in

Studentský domov J Jronca, Bernolákova 3, 800 00 Bratislava; tel. 42612. 27 kčs for YHA members. 45 kcs- 80 kčs for others. There is another hostel at Šd L. Štúra, Osmolovova ulica, 800 00 Bratislava - Mlynská Dolina open in the same period. But if possible it is best to check with the local CKM office first, and find out what is open where, if they know themselves, which they didn't when I asked them! The hostels are in student dorms, and CKM really intend them for their package tourists, but you can stay there if you can find out where there is a spare bed. Booked from abroad the hostels cost £8.60 per night full board.

There is also a YHA member price of 27 kčs at CKM's **Juniorhotel Sputnik**, Drienova ul, 801 00 Bratislava; tel. 227883, 222604, but it is usually full. Sk. III restaurant. Disco: 15 kcs entry, must spend at least another 30 kčs.

T.J. Vinohrady, Nabr. L. Svobodu 17, 841 01; tel. 239661 have accommodation in 4 bed rooms for about 60 kčs per person. Preference is given to sportsmen, but if it is not full others may stay there. Communal toilets, showers & kitchen. No restaurant. Open all year. Heated in winter.

There are also T.J. Vinohrady dorms near Juniorhotel Sputnik. Slovakoturist use them for groups, but you could try and get a bed.

Motel
Motel Zlaté piesky (Interhotel), Kat. A, tel. 651 70. At the end of the road to the camping grounds. 30 doubles at 440 kcs, with shower etc. Open 1/3 to 30/10. See 'Camping' for more on Zlaté piesky.

Hotels
The majority of hotels in Bratislava are B* category. There are no cheap hotels (C class).

Hotel Flora, B*, Zlaté piesky; tel. 672 841. Doubles 273 kčs; apartments (sleep 3) 684 kčs. Sk. II plus 10 per cent restaurant. Best to reserve through Čedok. See 'Camping' for more info. on Zlaté piesky.

Hotel Carlton, B*, Interhotel, Hviezdoslavovo nám. 7, 816 09 Bratislava; tel. 582 09, 331 851. Very central.

Tatra, B*, nám. 1. mája 7, 811 06 Bratislava; tel. 512 78. Expensive sk.II restaurant, kaviaren & bar.

Hotel Bratislava, B*, Urxova 9, 821 03 Bratislava; tel. 295641 or 293523, telex 092336. Outside the centre. Largest hotel in Bratislava. US$30 single, US$50 double.

Juniorhotel Sputnik, B*, (see 'Hostels'), with shower single/double 156 kčs/234 kčs, with bath 182 kcs/273 kčs. Best to book through CKM in Prague. Usually full of package tourists. Booked from UK: about £15 full board, £13 half board.

Private
Accommodation in private homes through Čedok, Štúrova 13.

EATING & EVENINGS
There are eateries everywhere in the centre. The many wine

cellars evoke memories of Vienna, but they are maybe classier in Bratislava. They usually close at midnight. Vináreň with Gypsy music are a Bratislava trademark. In the summer there are a lot of places to take a drink outdoors.

Vináreňc, sk. III, downstairs in Kamzík, nám SNP. Nice. Open midday to midnight. Closed Monday. 3 kčs entry after 5.30pm. On street level in the same building is a large standup place with many counters with different food. Sk. III. Open Monday to Friday 6.30am to 8.30pm; Saturday till 2pm.

There is a collection of various types of eateries opposite Štatna banka čs on Štúrova.

Vináreň pod Baštou (Under the Bastion), Bastova ulica, signposted from inside Michael's Gate. Quite nice, but non- smokers might find the air a bit thick. Open Monday to Friday 11am to midnight, Saturday to 3am. Cover 5 kčs after 6pm. Sk. II.

Cukráreň next to Čedok for those with sweet tooth. Jukebox. Monday to Sat. 8am to 8pm, Sunday 10am to 6pm.

Kaviareň in the tower of most SNP (see walking tour).

Kaviareň Danubius, sk. II, on the first floor in the harbour building, with a balcony over the Danube.

Mount Kamz´k: revolving Kaviáreň in TV tower; Koliba, nice, sk. I; another restaurant where it is possible to sit outdoors.

Stará Sladovňa (the Old Malt House). Seating 1500 people, it is the 2nd biggest restaurant in Europe. Find it on Cintoriska. From 1872 to 1976 this was a malt-house, where malt barley used to ripen in dark malt rooms. Now it has become a large capacity restaurant complex, so large that the locals have dubbed it 'The Mammoth'. A beer restaurant, while most others in Bratislava are wine restaurants. Nice place, despite its size. Various restaurants and beer garden. Sk. II plus 10 per cent. Cover charge sometimes. Traditional jazz on Thursday nights.

Cheap sk. IV sit down cafeteria:**Rest. Charitas**, Heydukova 12, basement. Open for lunch only. Closed Sunday. Mostly people who work in the area and receive lunch vouchers to eat here. Also dietary food. First pay at the cashier for your food, then collect it at the window. Drinks from another window—pay there. Take back your own plates, glasses etc.

Velký Františkáni, vináren, 10 Dibrovo nám., sk. I, foreigners and non-conformists hangout, young people, often speak English.

Other evening hangouts: Kyjev Klub in Kjev Hotel, sk. I open till 3am; Kláštorná vináreň, 1 Pugačevova; there are not many discos, Hotel Carlton has one from 9pm to 3am. Mierové nám. is an evening meeting place of the young.

BRATISLAVA TO ŽILINA
Whether one travels by rail or by road on the E16 (highway 61), all except the first part of the trip from Bratislava to Žilina follows up the valley of the river Váh. There are lots of legends associated with the castles of the valley.

Senec
25km by road out of Bratislava is Senec, with a lake with swimming and watersports. (The Bratislava-Žilina railway does not

pass through Senec.)

Piešťany
A popular tourist resort and Slovakia's most famous spa. The springs here were known to the Romans. Kayaking in the river, and boating on the dam lake Slnava. Bus service from Vienna. Air service from Prague. Camping & chalets on Slnava open May to September. Hotels from cheap to luxury.

Čachtice
A little off the main road and railway, near the town of Nové Mesto nad Váhom. Ruins of Čachtice Castle accessible from here. In the 13th century the castle was an important strong-point on the Hungarian border. At the turn of the 16th- 17th centuries there lived here 'the cruel lady of Čachtice', Alzbeta Nádasdy-Báthory, who murdered no less than 651 young girls to bathe in their warm blood, believing this would bring her eternal youth. She was eventually brought to justice. The castle has been uninhabited since a fire in 1708. Interesting limestone country with caves and springs. The area around the castle is a nature reserve with some rare species of lime- tolerating plants.

Biele Karpaty (White Carpathians)
See Bilé Karpaty, under Moravia.

BECKOV
Near Nové Mesto nad Váhom, on the opposite side of the river Váh. The ruins of Beckov Castle lie on chalky rocks. The first fortified castle replaced an earlier building here in 1208. It is said that before the castle was built a nobleman and his wife lived in a mansion near the site. After the woman gave birth to twins, she decided to employ a wet nurse. But she couldn't find anyone she wanted, until a giantess appeared at the gate. The giantess was very good with the children, and there were no problems until the woman felt that the children were becoming too close to the giantess. She persuaded her husband to sack her. But the nobleman had dreams about a castle. The giantess wagered that if she could build a castle within a year, she could keep the children. The nobleman laughlingly signed. Every night more of the castle appeared, until, before the year was up, it was finished and the giantess claimed the children. The nobleman said he would give her all the money he had and the servants too, instead. But returning to the house, he found the giantess and children gone. Before the year was up, the noblewoman poisoned her husband in revenge for the grief he had caused her.

The best known owner was 'the lord of the Váh valley and the Tatras', Matúš Čák, who rebuilt the castle in the 14th century.

It is said that Beckov was given to the Fool. But the owner threw the Fool from the castle. As the Fool fell he said: 'to the year, to the day'. Exactly a year later the owner went crazy and jumped from the castle.

Destroyed in 1729, and never rebuilt. The ruins of the Renaissance palace, chapel and parts of the fortifications are all that survive. Good view.

In the village of Beckov are a former monastery and 14th century Gothic church. Walking in the Považský Inovec Hills. Chalets & ubytovací hostinec.

Trenčín

The town of Trenčín is overlooked by its castle. The castle originated as an 11th century fortress. This castle was also owned by Matúš Čáks, who had a residential palace built in it. In the 16th century it played an important defensive role against the Turks. The castle had no water. A legend associated with this concerns the period when the Turks were here. The castle owner got rather attached to the Turk Fatimah, whom he had imprisoned. The owner was told that he would have to dig a well to get her back. A look at the position of the castle, high on a rock, shows how difficult a demand this was to meet. The castle was severly damaged by fire in 1790. Reconstruction began in 1954.

Today a town of 48,000 inhabitants, Trenčín was at one time on the border of the Roman Empire. The rock on which the castle stands bears one of the oldest Roman inscriptions in Czechoslovakia (from 179 AD), recording the victory of the Second Roman Legion over the Quadi. In the town are remains of its fortifications and several Gothic and Baroque buildings. Walking in the Bielé Karparty. Hotels, hostels, camping.

Trenčianske Teplice

One of Slovakia's better known spas, situated in a valley surrounded by forest covered hills, a little way off the main Váh valley. On the southern outskirts of the town is an area known as Zelená žaba (the Green Frog), with a natural warm water pool.

By train change to the narrow gauge electric railway at Trenčianska Teplá. Buses from Vienna & Bratislava. By road, 5km off the E16, turn off at Trenčianska Teplá. Two cat. C hotels, and one cat. B*.

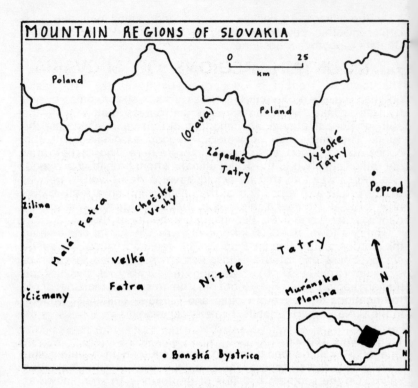

ŽILINA (sketch map)

KEY

1. Pošta 2 (post office)
2. Hotel Metropol
3. Hotel Polom
4. Bookshop
5. Prior dept. store
6. Hotel Slovan
7. Church of the Most Holy Trinity
8. CKM
9. Čedok
10. Hlavná Pošta (Main post office)
11. Grand Hotel
12. Tatratour
13. Kino Úsvit
14. Malá Fatra ubytovňa
15. Police (tall grey building)
16. Market - place
17. Hotel Dukla
18. State Bank of Czechoslovakia
19. Hotel Slovakia
Railway: ▬ ▬ ▬

MOUNTAIN REGIONS OF SLOVAKIA

MALÁ FATRA & ŽILINA

Malá Fatra (the Little Fatras) are a mountain range in Central Slovakia. They encompass Vrátna dolina, said to be the most beautiful valley in Slovakia. The entrance to the valley from Terchová passes between spectacular rocky crags. Malá Fatra cover a small area, so the views tend to be out over villages farms and towns. But a lot of variety is to be found in this area. Some of the tops are open and flattish; others steep and craggy. Lower down one can find anything from pleasant forest to precipitous little ravines. It's an excellent tramping area. The main town is Žilina.

Malá Fatra are very popular with German tourists, but the further you get away from Vrátna dolina the more peace and quiet you are likely to be able to find, and the more likely you are to meet the native Slovaks.

Terchová is the birthplace of the Slovak folk hero, Juro Jánosík, the local Robin Hood. Jánosík studied to be a priest. When he came home, he found that his father had been beaten by a rich man, so he became a highwayman, taking only from the rich, and giving to the poor. He was eventually captured and hung by his ribs. He refused to say where his hiding places were, and Slovaks believe his treasures are still to be found.

GETTING THERE & TRAVELLING ON

Žilina lies at the cross of the E85 and E16. The most convenient public transport is train. Žilina is a major railway station. There are rýchlik trains to Bratislava at 2.07, 3.15, 4.06, 4.52, 10.45, 12.05, 14.05, 16.23, 17.00, 17.12, 17.4 0 and 19.24; fare 48 kčs; travel time about 3 3/4 hours. Also good service on to Poprad and Košice. From Prague by train about 8 hours.

GETTING AROUND

To Vrátna in Malá Fatra there are buses from platform 9 or 10 at Žilina bus station roughly hourly from 6am to about 6pm. Hitch-hiking is reasonable. The bus station is close to the railway station. There is a local bus service around Žilina, but it is possible to walk around the central part of the town.

PRACTICAL INFORMATION

Žilina can be a bit confusing to find one's way around, but it isn't so bad if you stick to the station and central areas. A new edition of the map of Žilina is expected, but count yourself lucky if you can find one.

Good detailed map 'Malá Fatra', 6 kčs, not always available, so keep your eye out for it. Map of Javorniky Kysuce (7 kčs) covers area to the west of Žilina. Bookshop on the corner of ulica SNP and nám. SNP has a better selection of maps than normal. But

they didn't have 'Malá Fatra' when I was there! There is a book
on Malá Fatra but it isn't available in any foreign languages.
Many shops in Žilina are closed at lunchtime.
The main post office holds mail only 2 weeks.
Čedok are at Hadzova 9, on the corner of Na Priekope. Open
M-F 9am to 6pm, Sat. 9am to 12. Tel. 22510. Friendly & helpful.
CKM are at nám. Dukla 10; tel. 235 21.
Left luggage at the railway station, usually only if it weighs
less than 15kg (depends on who is working there at the time).

SLEEPING
Žilina
There is no camping in Žilina. The cheapest place to stay is **T.J.
Slovan Malá Fatra ubytovňa'**, ul. Veldá okruzná 26, 010 01 Žilina;
tel. 206 92. Tur. ub. B (12 bed dorm) costs 42 kcs plus 2 kcs per
night tax if you stay long er than 1 night. There is also tur. ub. A
(5 bed dorm) and Hotel C (doubles). Check in from 2pm to 8pm.
Just a place to crash. Nothing there, but has the basics one
needs. Often full, especially at weekends.
All the following hotels have post code 010 01. **Hotel Slovakia**,
B*, nám. V. I. Lenina, tel. 46572-3, telex 75606, is the best and
largest hotel. Horizont-Club on the 7th floor with a view. Swimming pool & sauna in basement. **Hotel Polom**, B*, Volgogradské
nám., tel. 208 38, is just across the road from the railway station.
Rooms with shower: single US$23, double US$38. **Hotel Metropol**,
B, is also opposite the station. 132 kcs double without bath, 24
kcs to use the shower. But I don't recommend it for its noise if
nothing else. **Grand Hotel**, B, Sládkovicova ulice 1, by (nám.
Dukla, the Town Square); tel. 210 56. Sk. II restaurant & kav. **Hotel
Slovan**, B, Šafárikova ul. 16, (be hind Prior). **Hotel Dukla**, C,
Dimitrovova ul. 3; tel. 202 34.

Camping
Autokemping Stop, 013 24 Strecno; tel. Žilina 925 84. Camping
and cabins. Open all year. Footbridge access from Strecno to
Malá Fatra.
Campsite at Varín by the bridge on the Žilina-Terchová road.
Also walking access into Malá Fatra from here: **Verejné táborisko**,
013 03 Varín. Open 1 July to 31 August.
Campsite near Branica also on the road from Žilina to Vrátna,
between Belá and Terchová. Not all buses stop here. First bus
stop after Branica is the closest to reception. Only facilities are pit
toilets & drinking water taps. Strung out along the road, between
the road and the river. Noise from road, but not too much traffic.
Open 15 June to 15 September.
There is a Čedok camp in Vrátna dolina itself. **Autokemping
Vrátna**, 013 26 Terchová; tel. Žilina 952 20. Open 15 May to 30
September. Also bungalows.
Note that Verejné táborisko Starhrad near Nezbudská Lúčka
and the campsite at the bottom of Dolné diery have been closed
down.

Mountain Hotels and Chalets
In Terchová is **Hotel Jánošík**, named after the hero of the legend.

'C' grade. Tel. Žilina 951 85. Address 016 06 Terchová.

Hotel Boboty, B*, 013 06 Terchová-Vrátna; tel. Žilina 952 27. On a turning off the road to Štefanová. Sauna. Singles US$23, doubles US$38.

Chata pod Sokolím, hotel C & TU A, 013 06 Terchová- Vrátna; tel. Žilina 953 26. Cold water only. Central heating. Access for cars, or 5 minutes walk from the bus.

Chata Vrátna, Hotel B & TU A, 013 06 Terchová-Vrátna; tel. Žilina 952 23. At the top of Vrátna dolina. Singles 125 kcs, doubles 187-234 kcs, no bath. Use of shower 32 kcs! Posh sk. II restaurant. TU and cheaper eatery underneath. Closed October-November.

Chata pod Suchým, 013 13 Varín, no telephone. Access by foot only: about 2 1/2 hours from Varín or Strecno. Closed April and November, rest of year open. Nice. Friendly people. 1075 m.a.s.l. Dorm 46 kcs, double 144 kcs. There is bedding. Sk. III eatery with nice wooden tables & chairs, decorated with deer antlers.

Note that chata pod Chlebom and chata pod Rozcutcom have both burnt down.

EATING
See also 'Sleeping' above.

Žilina
There are a lot of possibilities around the railway station and nám. Dukla areas.

The restaurant in Žilina railway station (sk. II) is open till 10pm. A stand-up bufet is open all the time, except 11pm to 1am. Hot food, salad, drinks, etc. A raging place full of drunks in the evening, but they don't cause too much problem !

Grilované Kurcatá, Zápotockého ul. 29, near the bus station. Pleasant enough little grill and drink bar, but lots of smokers, as one can smoke anytime, unlike most catering establishments in Czechoslovakia. Next door at no. 31 is a pivá ren.

EVENINGS
Žilina is a town of 83,000 people, with only 1 cinema! Try the hotels, or Restaurant Junior. Grand Hotel has a night bar, entrance 20 kcs. There are also night bars in Hotel Metropol & Hotel Slovakia.

EVENTS
At the end of June there is a folk festival in Terchová.

TO SEE
Žilina
Between nám. SNP and nám. Dukla (often called just námestie) is the Gothic church of the Most Holy Trinity. Its history can be read in English. Today it seems to have a young congregation. In the suburb of Závodie (take bus no. 1) is the late Romanesque church of St. Stephen, with fresco decoration. In the suburb of Budatín, at the confluence of the Kysuca and Váh rivers, is a chateau dating from the 14th century. It guarded the road leading from Hungary to Silesia near a ford where a toll was levied. Partly

ruined by fire in the mid-19th century. Reconstructed in its present form 1920-22. Now now serves as a regional museum of the Váh region.

Terchová
Jánošík Museum. The entrance to Vrátna dolina, with its spectacular rocky crags.

Vrátna
From Chata Vrátna at the top of the road up Vrátna dolina there a chairlift takes you to within easy walking distance of the peaks Chleb (1647m) and Velký Kriván (1709m). Expect queues. Open all year except October-November.

Strečno
The ruins of Strečno Castle stand high atop a steep craggy peak at the entrance to the Strečno Gorge. Founded in 1321, it was an important position on the trade route leading through the Váh Valley. Often in the hands of anti-royalists, the castle was destroyed in 1678. Today a major reconstruction project is underway, so the castle is covered with scaffolding. The idea is to maintain the skyline as it is, but to build a museum inside, showing the castle's development, and especially to house an exhibition of the Slovak National Uprising.

Near Strečno is a monument to French partisans who fought here in the second world war.

Bytča
In Bytča is a Renaissance manor house (1571-74).

Súlovské Skaly
South-west of Žilina is Súlovské Skaly, a nature reserve of beautiful rock outcrops, including the ruins of the medieval Súlov Castle. Access via Bytča.

TRAMPING
Tracks are well marked.

Walking times from chata Vratná(750m.a.s.l.):
to top of chairlift (green): 1 3/4 hours.
Chata na Grúni (yellow markers). 45 minutes. Food available here.
Chata pod Chlebum (burnt down, green): 2 1/4 hours.
Šutovo railway station (green): 4 3/4 hours.
Poludňový Grún, 1460m. (yellow): 2 hours.

But most people come to Vrátna to ride up in the chairlift, which costs 10 kcs one way or 15 kcs return. At the top of the lift it can be very cold compared to Vrátna. There is a sk.IV bufet at very inflated prices. From here it is a 5 minute walk to the Snilovské saddle on the main ridge or a 3 hour walk on the blue marked track along a side ridge finishing up at Starý Dvor bus stop in Vrátna dolina.

The ridge track at Snilovské sedlo is part of 'Mezinárodna

Horská Cesta Priatelstva' from Eisenach to Budapest, but this route is more symbolic than anything else, and not many people seem to have heard of it. From Snilovské sedlo (1520m.) it is 25 minutes to the top of Chleb or 35 minutes to the top of Velký Kriváň. Other walking times along the main ridge: to the left: Medziholie 3 3/4 hours, Zázrivá 7 3/4 hours; to the right: Suchy 3 1/2 hours, Strečno railway station 6 1/2 hours.

Snilovské sedlo to Strečno & adjoining tracks
This is a nice walk, beginning on an open rounded ridge, then becoming more craggy until it drops into the forest after Suchý. Interesting castle ruins.

Taking the track to the right brings one to Bublen (1605m) after 1 1/4 hours. From here it is 5 1/4 hours on to Strecno, or 2 3/4 hours down the green track to Branica, by the campsite. (Uphill this track takes 3 1/4 hours.) About 15 minutes on the Strecno side of Bublen there are some small springs, which you may be able to drink out of if there is enough water and not too many people churning them up. Continuing on the red marked track towards Strecno, the next peak one crosses is Priehyb (1462m). From here one can cut out to Krasnany on the blue track (2 hours to the bus stop), and it is now 2 1/4 hours back to the chairlift. The next fork brings a choice of following the red track over Suchý (1468m), or cutting und er it on the yellow track. The first choice takes 1 hour 5 minutes to where the tracks meet again, the second 25 minutes. The route now begins to descend to chata pod Suchým, the last 5 minutes steeply. The chalet is a welcome little retreat (see 'Sleeping').

From chata pod Suchým it is 2 1/4 hours down the green marked track to Varín, or 2 hours on the red marked track to Strecno. By now you are in a more friendly area, with fewer tourists and more local people. The red marked track follows a ridge a little way from the chalet, then drops steeply down, past a crucifix where you'll probably see fresh as well as plastic flowers, to Starý Hrad. This castle was built in the 13th century to guard a ford over the river Vaň. Its ruins are a fantastic sight, high above the river and surrounded by trees. From the castle it is only 50 minutes to Strecno railway station. 5 minutes after the castle the track hits a roadway. There are nice picnic spots on the way down. Down in the main valley the track leaves the roadway again, and cuts across above the railway. From the station there are trains back to Žilina stopping at Varín on the way. At the end of the day there are trains at 17.09, 18.14 and 19.49, but best check the train timetable before you set out. Otherwise the main road is just across the footbridge in Strecno.

Štefanová-Velký Rozsutec-Horné Diery-Dolné Diery
About 7 hours. A really good trip. One can drive to Šefanová (625m), hitch-hike or catch the Vrátna bus. Follow the green marked track from Štefanová to Medziholie (1 1/2 hours). This part is a real 'highway', a wide track with lots of people. Steep as far as Šlahorka, then not so steep. Nice scenery. From Medziholie (1185m) the red track to the right leads to the top of Stoh after 1 1/4 hours. Our route is the red track to the left, a STEEP, popular,

but satisfying climb to the top of Velký Rozsutec (1610m), from where there is a good view (1 1/4 hour, 1 hour if you are FAST). Velký Rozsutec is a craggy peak, unlike most Malá Fatra peaks which are rounded. The descent to Medzirozsutce saddle (1200m) takes just under an hour. There is a water source just below the saddle. Other walking times from here: Malý Rozsutec, green, 25 minutes; Zázrivá, red, 2 hours; back to Medziholie on the blue track behind Velký Rozsutec, 1 hour.

Our route leads down Tesná rizna and Horné diery to Podžiar (1 1/2 hours, blue). Horné Diery is beautiful, like the valleys in Slovenský Raj. Now you are in the part of Malá Fatra where Jánosík is thought to have hidden his booty. Podžiar is an open grassy area 715 metres above sea level. From here our route leads down Dolné Diery and out to the road at Biely Potok in 40 minutes, but it is possible to cut back to Štefanová from Podžiar in 25 minutes. Another alternative is to walk down Dolné Diery to the bottom of Nové diery (25 minutes), then follow the yellow marked track up Nové diery and back to Podžiar (35 minutes) before returning to Štefanová. From the bottom of Dolné diery at Biely Potok it is a 20 minute walk to Hotel Jánosík, or 30 minutes to Terchová.

You might prefer to walk this trip in the opposite direction. In some ways it is nicer walking up the little ravines, but if you walk in this direction it is a very steep downhill drop off Velký Rozsutec. Times in this direction: Biely Poto k-Podžiar 40 minutes; Podžiar-Medzirozsutce 1 3/4 hours; Medzirozsutce- Veký Rozsutec 1 3/4 hours; Velký Rozsutec-Medziholie 1 hour; Medziholie-Štefanová 1 1/4 hours.

SKIING
There are ski lifts and tows in Vrátna dolina for downhill skiing, e.g. by the camping ground. The chairlift from Vrátna to Snilovské sedlo leads one to another downhill skiing area. Cross country ski tracks are also marked from here. In ideal weather and snow conditions it is possible to ski from the top of the chairlift via the peaks along the main ridge to Medziholie in about 4 hours.

THERMAL SWIMMING
There are thermal swimming pools at Rajecké-Teplice, about 1/2 an hour south of Žilina by bus.

ČIČMANY
Čičmany is a quiet little mountain village south of Žilina where beautifully decorated wooden houses are still preserved in the lower part of the town. Some of the best houses burnt down in 1923, but they were later restored by the Institute of Ethnography. There is a museum, but it is not always open. Čičmany is quite high up, and can be cool even in summer.

Buses to Čičmany leave from Žilina bus station from platform 17, but there are not very many, and the timetable differs on different days of the week, so check it carefully. Access from other directions is difficult without a private car.

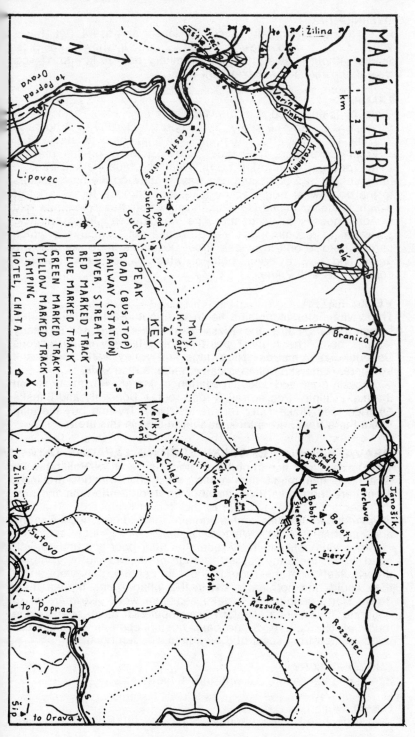

OVERNIGHTING
Hotel (B) and dormitory accommodation at Kaštiel (tel. Rajec 9297). Double with shower 195 kčs, without shower 156 kčs. Single without shower 104 kčs. Dormitory bed 39 kčs to 47 kčs. Use of shower 21 kčs. Restaurant & bar.

TRAMPING
Čičmany is on the edge of the Malá Fatra map. From Čičmany it is 5 hours to Fačkovské sedlo, 3 1/4 hours to Tužina or 3 hours to Pružina. There are buses from all 3, but best check timetable first.

From the village of Fačkov, below Čičmany on the road to Žilina, one can climb Klak by following the blue marked track to the south-east (2 3/4 hours one way). Following the blue markers to the north-west from Fačkov takes one through forest, a lot of which is being milled, to Domaniža, which has some nice old wooden houses in its centre. The walk doesn't have anything particular to recommend it. Keep an eye out for markers, which can be hard to find in places. From Domaniža there are buses to Rajec and Pov. Bystrica, both of which have public transport connections with Žilina.

VELKÁ FATRA
The Velká Fatra mountains lie to the south-east of Malá Fatra, between Malá Fatra and Nízke Tatry. There are not so many tourists here. The highest point is the relatively inconspicuous Ostredok (1592 metres). Nice ridge and valley walks. Bears still live here. Gaderská dolina is canyon-like: a nice walk.

Access from and accommodation in Martin, Ružomberok (on the main Žilina - Poprad rail & road route), Donovaly and Banská Bystrica (see Nízke Tatry for the last two). Try and buy the map Velká Fatra if you are interested in tramping in this area.

ORAVA, including CHOCSKÉ VRCHY & ZÁPADNÉ TATRY
The Orava region lies in northern Slovakia. Near the Polish border is a huge man-made dam, under which five villages drowned. From here the Orava River flows down through the hills and past the spectacular Orava Castle to the Váh at Kralovany. The area is surrounded by hills and mountains, including Chočské vrchy and Západné Tatry (the Western Tatras).

Orava was until relatively recently rather poor and underdeveloped. When the army passed through on the way to help Vienna defend itself from the Turks in the 17th century, they were angry they could find nothing to eat in the villages and burned them down. Many people left to take seasonal work elsewhere or to emigrate to America. Modern developments have swept aside much of the culture of the past, but an open-air museum has been created from some of the original wooden homes.

CHOČSKE VRCHY
Interesting tramping area, with forest, bluffs etc.

Podslip
Was a deserted village. Today people are rebuilding the houses

in their original style. From Kralovany on the main Žilina-Poprad railway line take the train up the branch line to Kralovany zastávka railway station. The trains run about once every 2 hours, so it may be quicker to walk the 3 km. From Kralovany zastávka (accessible by car) a yellow marked track leads you up to Pošíp. It is a nice walk, and you can continue on to the summit of Šíp (1169m).

Kvačianska and Prosiecka dolina
These two karst valleys lie at the other end of Chočské vrchy. A nice round trip can be made by walking up Prosiecka dolina then down Kvacianska dolina. The round trip is best in this direction. An old mill has been reconstructed here.

ORAVSKÝ HRAD
Oravský Hrad (Orava Castle) is a dramatic sight, and really worth visiting if you like castles. It sits imposingly at various levels on a rock which rises spectacularly 112 metres up from the Orava river at the village of Oravský Podzámok. Built about 1267 and rebuilt and extended at various times over the centuries. In 1800 the entire complex was destroyed by fire, leaving only walls standing. It was roofed over again and in 1895 reconstruction began, but was interrupted by the First World War. Reconstruction began again in 1953, resulting in the present state of the castle.

Open June to August 8am to 6pm, May, September & October 8am to 4.30pm. 4 kčs. You must go around with a group, which takes 90 minutes, and requires a minimum of 15 people. Hopefully there will be enough people around—otherwise find out when a bus load is expected. There is no leaflet available in English, only in German, Russian and Hungarian. Part of the castle is devoted to a museum of the area.

ORAVA LAKE
The dam creating Orava Lake was completed in 1954. Of the five villages that were submerged, the church of one of them, Slanice, remains above water level on an island which can be reached by boat from Slanická Osada. The Baroque church (1766 - 69) was restored in the 19th century, and today serves as a museum of Slovak villagers art and sculpture. The lake is used for swimming, fishing and water sports.

ZAPADNE TATRY
The West Tatras form a chain from Orava to the High Tatras. There is not so much development and roading in the West Tatras as in the High Tatras. There are normally longer walks up valleys to the ascents. Gacial lakes are common. The most popular area is Roháče, and Roháčska dolina is the most developed area, with roading, camping etc. This area was glaciated. Roháče Glacier was 12 km long and over 100 metres thick.

Tramping Routes
Turn off the Roháče valley road at Adamcula and follow the blue marked track up Spálená dolina to a mountain tarn. Follow the green marked track past three more tarns before dropping back

down to the end of the road.

The peaks Tri kopy, Hrubá kopa and Banilov are difficult to climb but popular. Accessible by marked tourist track.

To the west the limestone bluffs of Sivý Vrch can be climbed by taking the track up from the village of Mysicková.

Juránova dolina: one can walk up through the gorge from Oravice.

MAPS & GUIDES

A new edition of the map 'Západné Tatry Roháče' should be published at about the same time as this book. There was a map of Orava including the lake and the whole Orava Valley, but it is now hard to find. A tourist guide book is available in German for 19 kcs.

ACCESS

Public transport services are not as good here as is usual in Czechoslovakia. Kralovany is on the main Žilina-Poprad railway line and road. From here there is a highway right up the Orava valley, and on into Poland via the Trstená-Chyzne crossing, which may be used by foreigners. The highway is parallelled by a railway as far as Trstená, with slow local trains about every couple of hours. They are the best way to get up and down the valley by public transport. Dolný Kubín is the main town of the area. There is one direct bus connection between Dolný Kubín and Liptovský Mikuláš per day. From Liptovský Mikuláš this leaves at 8.30am. If you come in on this bus, you must then wait over an hour in Dolný Kubín for the next train up the valley, which leaves at 10.29am. There are a lot of buses between Dolný Kubín and Ruzomberok, but not at weekends. From Terchová in Malá Fatra there are two buses a day to Dolný Kubín. In the tourist season there may be some direct buses from main centres.

Access to Roháče is from a side road turning off the main valley road at Podbiel. For Oravice turn off at Trstená.

Access to Kvacianska and Prosiecka valleys is easiest from the other side of the mountains, from Liptovský Mikuláš for example.

SLEEPING & EATING
Dolný Kubín
Camping and bungalows: Autokemping Gäcel, 026 01 Dolný Kubín; tel 3445. Camping 15 June to 15 September. Bungalows all year. There are also hotels in Dolný Kubín.

Oravský Podzámok
Hotel Odboj: C class hotel and turistická ubytovňa B. Tel. Dolný Kubín 931 15. Various places to eat & drink in hotel.

Orava Lake
Two camping grounds.

Roháče
Camp at Zverovka mid June to mid September. Chata Zverovka, TU A, 027 32 Zuberec; tel. Dolný Kubín 951 06; also cabins. Book

Čedok, Dolný Kubín.

Traditional wooden houses

At Bobrová rala, a part of Podbiel, typical wooden houses have been renovated and refurnished to be used as tourist accommodation. Bookings through District Management of Tourism, Dolný Kubín.

NIZKE TATRY (Low Tatras)

Nízke Tatry is the second highest mountain range in Czechoslovakia, after Vysoké Tatry. But Nízke Tatry covers a much greater area than Vysoké Tatry: the main range alone is about 80 km long. The characters of the two mountain ranges are also different. Nízke Tatry is more rounded in shape than the jagged peaks of Vysoké Tatry, but sometimes end in steep limestone valleys in their lower reaches. The highest peaks are Ďumbier (2,043 m) and Chopok (2,024m). The upper mountains are granite, while the Demänovská Wall is limestone. There were valley glaciers on the northern side. One can see moraine and glacial lakes, but these are more marked in the Vysoké Tatry. There has been a lot of tourist development in Nízke Tatry in recent years, with hotels, chair lifts and ski runs. But in spite of this, some of the quietest and most unspoilt areas in Czechoslovakia lie in the Nízke Tatry, especially in the eastern part. Bears and lynx still live here.

Nízke Tatry offer all sorts of possibilities for walking and tramping. There is a track all the way along the main ridge. The mountain chalets don't get as full as those in the High Tatras. I was told it was possible to find somewhere to sleep if you just turn up. The summer season for walking in the mountains is from the end of May until October, while the skiing season runs from the end of November until April. Jasná is the pride of Czechoslovak ski resorts. There is angling in the river Čierny Váh, especially for trout, and fishing also in Liptovská Mara, the large hydro lake by Liptovský Mikuláš. Like Vysoké Tatry, the Nízke Tatry is more expensive.

The main towns in the area are Liptovský Mikuláš in the north and Banská Bystrica in the south-west. The main resort areas are Demänovská dolina and Jasná near Liptovský Mikuláš, Bystria dolina on the opposite side of the main range to Jasná, Donovaly on the saddle on the Ružomberok-Banská Bystrica road at the western end of Nízke Tatry, and Čertovica mountain station again on the main divide but half way along Nízke Tatry between the eastern and western parts.

A detailed map of the area, 'Nízke Tatry', is available for 11 kčs. There is a guide in German, 'Niedere Tatra', costing 21 kčs.

LIPTOVSKY MIKULAŠ

Liptovský Mikuláš is a good centre for access to Nízke Tatry. A town of 24,000 people, it lies on the main road and railway between Žilina and Poprad. The town played a role in Slovakia's political and cultural life in the 19th century.

There is a museum of the Slovak Kras, Múzeum Slovneského Krasu, on ulica Školská No. 4 (the road turning off opposite

Slovakoturist). It has exhibits on cave mapping and exploration, and samples from caves. What's more, it has a clean toilet with hot water, toilet paper etc! Open 1/4 to 31/10 Monday to Friday 8 am to 4 pm, weekends 9 am to 12 noon. Rest of year Monday to Friday only 8 am to 4 pm. In the Literárnohistorické múzeum Janko' Krála, nám. Osloboditelov 30, are exhibits on the literary and revolutionary traditions of Slovakia, and on local history. Open Tuesday to Friday 9 am to 4 pm, weekends 9 am to 12 noon, entry 2 kcs.

Fishing in Liptovská Mara. Windsurfing school.

Public Transport
Liptovský Mikuláš lies on the main Žilina-Košice railway line, with regular trains. There is also one bus a day to Žilina, leaving at 9.35 am. Bus service up Demänovská dolina to Jasná; last bus 22.30. One bus a day to Dolný Kubín on the river Orava at 8.30 am.

Practical Information
A map of Liptovský Mikuláš is planned. In the meantime I hope the sketch map is of help.

Čedok: Námastie Osloboditelov 7.

Slovakoturist: Ulica 1 maja 34.

If your gear is showing the worse for wear, you can have sports clothing, tents etc repaired at Oprava Športových odevov, and bags etc at Oprava kozeného tavaru, both on the same side of the square as Čedok (go through an alley and up the stairs). Explain that you are a tourist and can't wait the usual 3 weeks, months or whatever. They were very helpful to me.

Left Luggage
At the railway station. Shouldn't be a problem if you carry it in your self. 1 kčs per day.

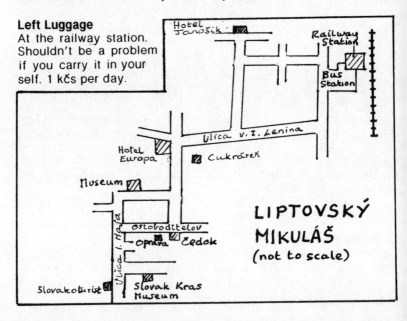

Sleeping

Post code for Liptovský Mikuláš is 031 01.

Hotels: The flashest hotel in town is Čedok's **Hotel Jánošík**, B class, a multi storey hotel on Jánošíkovo nábrezie (ph. 227 26). Prices booked from abroad: doubles without bath US$17 in season; single US$21 without bath , US$26 with bath. Cheaper in off season. Liptovský Mikuláš's largest hotel, with 128 beds. Nearer the central square, at Šturova 13, is **Hotel Europa**, C class. There are 12 double rooms at 156 kčs, one 3 bed room at 234 kčs, four 4 bed rooms at 265 kčs and one 5 bed room at 296 kčs. Price for one person 94 kčs.

Hostels: (1) Hotel Lodenica, ph. 223 49. Turistická Ubytovňa A & B. (2) Partizán, Vajanskeho 23, ph. 222 20. TU B. (3) Dynamo, Palúdzka, ph. 240 61-2.

Eating

Sk. II restaurant, plus stand-up self-service food and grog bufet in Hotel Europa. Opposite the hotel is a very comfy cukráren.

DEMÄNOVSKÁ DOLINA & JASNA

Demänovská dolina is full of German and other tourists, but notwithstanding that, it is beautiful and has many attractions. Čedok arrange day trips here from the High Tatras (see under 'Vysoké Tatry'). But it you have more time it is worth spending a few days in the area.

There are two limestone caves in Demänovská dolina open to the public. Demänovská ladová jaskyňa (Demänová Ice Cave) is situated in the limestone massif under the rock Bašta. It is the oldest known cave in Slovakia. The whole Demänová cave system has over 20 km of passages and 500 metres are open to the public. The cave was created when the Demänovka River flowed underground. The higher parts of the cave have normal limestone formations, while the lower parts are permanently ice covered. The best time to visit is in spring, when new ice and icicles are formed by water getting in through cracks. Worth seeing. Open 16/5 to 15/9, rest of year and Mondays closed. First tour 9 am, then hourly till last tour at 4 p m. 6 kčs, 3 kčs children under 15 and students. The entrance is 15 minutes strolling pace up the hill from the car park and bus stop on the road.

Higher up the valley is Demänovská Jaskyňa Slobody (The Demänová Cave of Liberty) with its beautiful limestone formations and lakelets. During the Slovak National Uprising partisans had their arms and food stored in this cave. From 16/5 to 15/9 there are hourly tours from 8 am to the last tour at 4 pm. Rest of the year tours at 9 am, 11, and 2 pm. Closed Mondays. 8 kčs, 4 kčs children under 15 and students. Accessible from car park and bus stop by walking or by chairlift.

From Jasná one can travel by chairlift right across the mountains, via Chopok, the second highest peak in Nízke Tatry. If the weather is good enough the chairlift from Jasná to Chopok operates from 8.30 to 16.30. From Chopok there is another chairlift down the other side of the mountains to Srdiečko Hotel.

TRAMPING

There are many possiblities for tramping in the area. One can start directly from the camping ground at the bottom of Demänovská dolina. (Track open only in season). From here it is a 1 3/4 hour climb to the peak directly above, Demänovska Hora (1304 m.a.s.l.). From here it is another 1 1/2 hours to Ilanovské saddle (1253 m.a.s.l.). From the saddle you can continue following the yellow markers to the top of Krakova Hola (1751 m.a.s.l.), which takes 5 hours altogether from the camping ground. Alternatively you can drop down the green marked track to the right from Ilanovské sedlo, finishing up on the Demänovská dolina road.

It is popular to take the chairlift up to Chopok, then to tramp in one direction or the other along the main ridge of the Low Tatras. For example it is 2 to 3 hour tramp along the main ridge track (red markers) to ch. Hrdinov SNP, a mountain chalet. One can also walk to Chopok from Jasná.

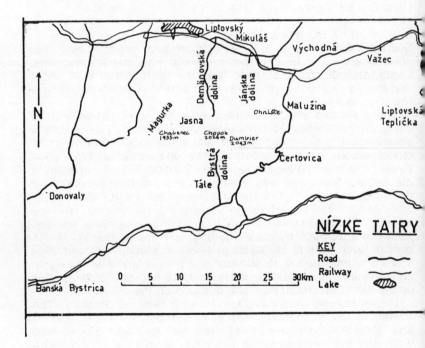

SKIING

Jasná is a good winter sports area. Čedok can arrange group or individual ski instruction. Skiing is possible here from early November until May. There is no avalanche danger around Jasná. Many of the hotels and lodges have small ski runs right next to them. More experienced skiers can take the chairlift up. The greatest choice of runs is from Luková, the intermediate stop on the way up to Chopok. With the chairlifts up both sides of Chopok, it is of course possible to ski on both sides of the mountains. Some runs in the area are rather difficult; others are more suitable for average skiers.

Cross-country skiers can take the chairlift up to Chopok and follow the poles along the main ridge to chata Hrdinov SNP, below Ďumbier (about 3 hours), and from here continue to Čertovica (another 3 hours). In the other direction from Chopok one can ski across Chabenec peak (1955 m) to Ďurková saddle (5 to 6 hours), and so descend down to the village of Magurka. These trips should only be undertaken by those experienced with cross country skiing in mountainous terrain, and only under ideal weather and snow conditions, usually in spring.

Practical Information
Slovakoturist has an office in Jasná. The bus service between Liptovský Mikuláš and Jasná runs roughly once an hour. It stops at both caves. Hitch-hiking in the valley is difficult.

SLEEPING & EATING
There are many hotels, bungalows, turistické ubytovne etc in the valley, and especially up at Jasná. If writing to any of these places, the post code for Demänovská dolina is 032 51, and if phoning the telephone exchange is Liptovský Mikuláš.

The only camping is at the Čedok camp at the bottom of Demänovská dolina. Address: Autokemping, 03251 Demänovská dolina; tel. 221 85. Open May to September. A few minutes walk from the bus stop. Overpriced. Fee for one person alone 44 kčs; the only facilities are handbasins and toilets. There is occasionally hot water for short periods. One can shower at the adjacent hotel for 21 kčs. The hotel is class B, is open all year, and has doubles for 187 kčs. Address: Hotel Bystrina, 03251 Demänovská dolina; tel. Liptovský Mikuláš 221 83. Unhelpful staff. There is a sk. II restaurant on the grounds, open from 7.00 to 21.00 daily, but don't bother going there within an hour or two of closing time, or you'll be ignored. Sk. IV outdoors hostinec, open 8.00 to 20.00, sells mainly beer, but also a few odds & ends such as biscuits and salami. To buy groceries, follow the turnoff opposite the camp entrance to the nearby village of Pavčina Lehota. Turn right at the 'T' junction in the village, and you'll find a small shop. If you follow the main valley road just a little way up from the camp entrance, you'll come to Tri Studničky which has a nice little restaurant (sk.III plus 10 per cent) open 10.00 to 20.00, but often reserved by groups.

Horský Hotel Jaskyňa Slobody, C plus TU A, 51 beds, sk. III restaurant, tel. 916 71.

Jasná: CKM have a 'C' grade hotel, also with dormitories, 'Junior Hotel B. Björnson', named after the Norwegian writer who lived here for a few years. From the bus stop, the hotel is on the way to the Chopok chairlift. Usually full. Dorms: 3 bed room 72 kčs per bed, 6 or 8 bed room 46 kčs per bed. Also annex used for YHA members. Quite nice sk. III restaurant. Can hire winter sports equipment. Hotel Družba, B*, sk. II restaurant, tel. 915 55. Hotel

Liptov, B*, sk. II restaurant, tel. 915 06. Mikulášska chata, C plus
TU A, sk. II restaurant, nice building, tel. 916 72. Chata na
Záhradkách, dormitory accommodation, sk. III restaurant. There
are various places to eat in Jasná.

JANSKA DOLINA
Jánska dolina is the next main valley to the east of Demänovská
dolina. From the valley bottom at Liptovský Ján one can walk all
the way up valley and so to the top of Ďumbier in 5 hours.
Another trip is to follow the blue marked track up the valley as
far as Pred Bystrou. From here branch left up Púchalka valley
(yellow). The green marked track to the left from the saddle leads
up to the karst tableland, Ohnište. Good view from the summit.
The plateau is a nature reserve with interesting rock formations
and beautiful flowers in summer. Continuing along the track takes
one to the peak Slemä via Michalské saddle. From Slemä keep
following the track down to a junction, from where various possiblities are open, including going back to Liptovský Ján over the
peak Smrekovica. This roundtrip takes 9 hours.

MALUŽINA
Maluzina is a village on Highway 72, the road crossing between
the eastern and western part of Nízke Tatry. Worth mentioning
because it has a nice campsite, and is a convenient access point
for those interested in walking up to Ohnište. The campsite's
address is Verejné táborisko Zväzarmu, 032 34 Maluzina. Open 15
June to 15 September. Access by bus from Králova Lehota railway station.

ČERTOVICA
Čertovica (1238 m.a.s.l.) is on the road saddle between the eastern and western Nízke Tatry. Access: see 'Maluzina'. Tramping in
summer. Good access to the central part of Nízke Tatry, especially the highest mountain, Ďumbier. Two ski tows. Skiing best
suited for beginners, or for those experienced with long distance
ski touring. To ski up to Chata Hrdinov SNP takes about 4 hours.
Accommodation in Chata Čertovica, (C class hotel and TU A).
Address: 032 34 Maluzina; tel. Maluzina 9259. Other accommodation and small ski fields in Vyšná Boca and Nizná Boca, between
Čertovica and Maluzina.

VÝCHODNA
Východná is on the main road between Liptovský Mikuláš and
Poprad. The largest folk festival in Slovakia is held here about
the first weekend of July, with amateur groups from villages
dressed in their costumes and demonstrating such events as
wedding rituals, the welcoming of spring, etc. People sleep in
sleeping bags in haysheds. Ask the owners first!

VAŽEC
Vazec is a small village between Východná and Poprad. In 1931
fire completely destroyed the pretty village which attracted writers artists and photographers. Today its main appeal is Vazecká
jaskyňa, a cave formed by the underground flow of the river Biely

Váh, and especially interesting for its stalactites and stalagmites. Only recently opened to the public. From 16/5 to 15/9 the first hourly tour leaves at 9.00 and the last at 16.00. From 1/4 to 15/5 and 16/9 to 31/10 there are tours at 9.00, 11.00 and 14.00. Rest of the year and Mondays: closed. 6 kčs, 3 kčs children under 15 & students. Hotel and turistická ubytovňa.

LIPTOVSKA-TEPLIČKA
This village in north-east Nízke Tatry used to be very isolated. The two roads into it didn't exist. Access was by track or bush railway up the Čierny Váh. The villagers speak their own dialect. There was terraced farming here. Collectivization led to erosion through the destruction of the terraces. There are now new houses here too. The villagers say that they do not want to become museum pieces. Today the village is accessible by bus from Štrba, Svit and Poprad. Accommodation: Turistická Ubytovňa a Váh, 059 40 Liptovská Teplička, tel. Poprad 925 30. 27 beds, hot & cold water, central heating. One can climb Kráľova hoľa (1948 m) from here (green marked track southwards).

BYSTRA DOLINA & TALE
Bystrá dolina is the valley opposite Jasná on the south side of the mountains. Near the bottom of the valley is Bystrianska jaskyňa, a cave created by the river Bystrá. Same opening hours, seasons, and prices as Važecká jaskyňa (see above). On the way up the valley is Tále, an accommodation centre with a little ski field, suitable for beginners or cross country, and a tobogganing course. The road up the valley ends at Hotel Srdiečko, from where the chairlift rises via the mid- way stop at Kosodrevina to Chopok, giving access across to Jasná and Demänovská dolina and to the ski fields on both sides of Chopok. On the southern slopes of Chopok the ski season lasts from December to April. From Kosodrevina it is possible to ski cross country to ch. Hrdinov SNP in about 1 1/2 hours. See 'Demänovská dolina & Jasná' for other possiblities.

Access
By car turn off Highway 66 at Podbrezová. Public transport: train to Podbrezová station, then bus service up to Hotel Srdiečko. By chairlift from Jasná!

Sleeping
If you don't have a prior booking Čedok in Banská Bystrica may be able to help you.
   Hotel Srdiečko, B, (1330 m). At the top of the road and bottom of the chairlift. Singles US$12 to 15, doubles US$18 to 22. Lowest prices only out of season. Address: Mýto pod Ďumbierom - Chopok Juh, 977 01 Brezno; tel. Brezno 951 21 .
   Hotel Kosodrevina, B*, (1690 m). At the mid-way stop on the chairlift from Srdiečko to Chopok. Singles US$9 to 14, doubles US$16 to 26. Lowest prices only out of season. Access by chairlift. Postal address same as Hotel Srdiečko. Tel. Brezno 951 05.
   Chata Hrdinov SNP pod Ďumbierom, TU A, (1740 m). Access by foot or skiing only. 2 hour from top of chairlift, or follow the green

marked track turning off the road a bit below Hotel Srdiečko. Tel.
Brezno 051 20.
Motel Tále: B grade motel, A grade camping ground, and B
grade chalets. Chalets open all year round, motel & camping open
in summer season only. Motel doubles with shower US$28. Tel.
Brezno 951 91. Also at Tále is Hotel Partizán, B* . Singles without
bath US$9 low season, US$13 high season. Doubles US$16 to
US$26 depending on washing facilities and season. Tel. Brezno
951 31.

BANSKÁ BYSTRICA
Banská Bystrica is a beautiful town lying below the south- west
corner of the Low Tatras. In medieval times it prospered due to
silver and copper mines. In the following centuries the town
declined, until 1918 when new industry began to grow here. On
the 29 August, 1944, the town's freed radio station declared the
beginning of the Slovak uprising against the Nazis. Today Banská
Bystrica has a population of 66,200, and is Central Slovakia's
political, economic and cultural centre.
The most interesting part of town is around Red Army Square.
Part of the old castle has been preserved. The main town gate is
one of the few relics of the fortifications that remain. The 15th
century town hall is now a museum. The town's Gothic churches
are worth seeing. There are houses with richly decorated facades
in the old town dating from the 15th & 16th centuries.
Čedok here control a lot of the hotel rooms on the southern
side of Nízke Tatry.

Travel Agents
Čedok, Nám. ČA 26, 974 75 Banská Bystrica; tel. 223 14.
CKM, Horná 65, 974 58 Banská Bystrica; tel. 258 46.

Sleeping
Camping   A class Čedok camp open 15 May to 15 September.
Tel. 330 12. 4 berth chalets and tent sites.

YHA Hostel: YHA members can stay at CKM's Junior Hotel for the
special hosteller's rate. Address: ul Februároveho vítazstva 12,
947 58 Banská Bystrica; tel. 233 67. 500 m from bus.

Hotels:
Hotel Lux, B* (***), Nové námestie 6, 975 92 Banská Bystrica;
tel. 241 41. 200 beds. Singles & doubles.
Národný Dom, B*, ul. Februárového vítazstva 7, 974 00 Banská
Bystrica; tel. 237 37. 48 beds.
Urpʼn, B*, Nejedlého ul. 5, 974 00 Banská Bystrica; tel. 245 56.
72 beds.
Prices for the last 2 hotels, which may be booked through
Čedok: singles with shower US$23, without shower US$21; dou-
bles with shower US$38, without US$34; in Národný dom only,
doubles with bath US$42.
CKM Junior Hotel, B, see under YHA hostel.

DONOVALY

Donovaly (960 m) lies between Nízke Tatry and Velká Fatra on Highway 59 between Ruzomberok and Banská Bystrica. Bus service from Banská Bystrica. Donovaly is a summer and winter holiday resort. Ski season from December to April. A couple of chairlifts and some shorter ski tows. Cross country skiing. Sledging. Donovaly is at the westerly end of the marked route along the crest of the Low Tatras.

Sleeping

Športhotel Donovaly, B, 976 39 Donovaly; tel. Banská Bystrica 991 20. Doubles US$21 in season. Autokemping, tel. Banská Bystrica 991 35, camping & chalets. Open January to March, and 15 June to 15 September.

MAGURKA

Magurka lies just below the main ridge of Nízke Tatra on the north side between Donovaly and Chopok. Accommodation in Chata Magurka (TU B) or in chalets. Chalets open only in season. Access by train to Ruzomberok, then bus to Železného, from where it is about a half hour walk to Magurka. In summer it may be possible to drive in. From Chopok it is about a 4 to 5 hour tramp along the main ridge, dropping down the green marked track from Durkovej saddle to Magurka. Small ski lift.

VYSOKÉ TATRY (High Tatras)

The highlight of Slovakia for most people is the towering majestic Vysoké Tatry (High Tatras), the highest mountains in Czechoslovakia. This alpine area, with its jagged rocky peaks and beautiful mountain lakes, offers excellent tramping in summer, and skiing in winter. But it can get rather crowded.

The Vysoké Tatry are the northernmost part of the 1200 km long arch formed by the Carpathian Mountains. They lie in the north of Slovakia, on the Polish border. In fact a smaller part of them lies in Poland. You are not allowed to cross the border. The area is protected as a national park.

Gerlachovský štít (2655 m) and Lomnický štít (2632 m) are the highest mountains in Czechoslovakia. Other important peaks are Slavlovský štít (2452 m), Konćistá (2535 m) and Kriváň (2494 m).

In the Quaternary era the Vysoké Tatry were covered for the most part by alpine glaciers. The present landscape is a result of glacial erosion.

Coniferous trees predominate, by far the most common being the spruce. Higher up the dwarf pine predominates. Picking flowers is forbidden. Berries abound. Roe deer are found at lower altitudes, and red deer higher up. Among the wildlife, if you are lucky, you may see chamois or marmot.

One of the first and most prominent scientists to devote attention to the Tatras was Robert Townson, an Edinburgh physician, geographer and traveller. He studied the area, and was the first to ascend some of its peaks. He published his experiences and impressions in a work entitled 'Travels in Hungary in the year 1793'.

The oldest tourist centre, Starý Smokovec, was established in 1793. Tourism began to flourish in the late 1800s. It is now one of Czechoslovakia's main tourist areas, and prices are higher than in the rest of the country.

SEASONS

In winter the temperatures are below zero, but there is not much precipitation. The first snow usually comes in November, and the last in April. The first signs of spring arrive in April, and the snow thaws on the southern slopes by the middle of May.

In the Tatra resorts the temperature is about 12°C to 15°C in summer, but higher up it averages only 4°C. Summer is the wettest time of year. On a typical summer day it will be clear in the morning, then clouds will gradually gather resulting in thunderstorms in the middle of the day. By the late afternoon it will be clear again.

Early autumn can be the most pleasant time in the Vysoké Tatry. The weather tends to be more settled, it is not as hot and crowded as in summer, and apart from late night frosts it is warmer than in spring. Late autumn is typically rainy.

BOOKS & MAPS

Vysoké Tatry, by Vladimír Adamec & Radek Roubal, Šport, Bratislava. An excellent guide book to the Vysoké Tatry, but unfortunately the English edition (called *High Tatras* and published in 1974) is out of print, and there are no plans to reprint it. But the book is available in Slovak, German (*Hohe Tatra* 27 kčs), Russian and Hungarian.

The first detailed map of Vysoké Tatry was produced by army cartographers in 1870, but if you would like something more up to date, 'Vysoke' Tatry, Letná Turistická Mapa' is an indispensable map for hiking. 8 kcs. There is also a skiing map of Vysoké Tatry for 4.50 kčs.

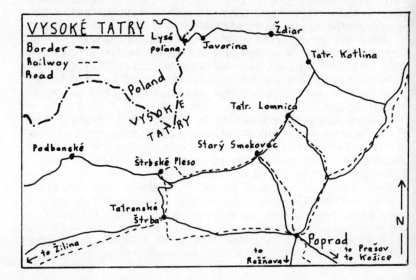

GETTING THERE & LEAVING AGAIN
By Air
There is a ČSA flight about once a day from Prague via Bratislava to Tatry/Poprad. Fare each way from Prague: 480 kčs. Airport open all year.

By Rail
Regular trains on the main line between Žilina and Košice stop at Poprad. If you're heading for Štrbské-Pleso, get off at Tatranská-Štrba. Connections or direct trains from Prague and Bratislava.

By Bus
Buses tend to be secondary to trains as a means of access to the area, but there are also buses, especially connecting with places to the south, where there is no railway. The main bus station is in Poprad, but there are also some long distance buses from Starý Smokovec. Bus is the best means of transport between Vysoké Tatry (from Poprad or Starý Smokovec) and Prešov. To cross to the Polish part of the Tatras, take a bus to Javorina, walk over the bridge to customs, and catch a Polish bus to Zakopane. You must have first obtained a Polish visa from a Polish consulate. There is an exchange office there where you can change your compulsory minimum exchange for Poland, but if entering Czechoslovakia at the same crossing there is no Czechoslovak bank at the border.

By Car
Poprad is accessible by main highways, including the E85. From Poprad there are good roads up to the mountain resorts.

GETTING AROUND BY PUBLIC TRANSPORT
The main means of transport is by electric train. From Tatranský Štrba there is a rack railway which climbs the 425 m to Štrbské Pleso in 4.8 km. From Poprad there are rail services to Starý Smokovec and Tatranská Lomnica (2 kčs). To Tatranská Lomnica one must sometimes change trains at Studený Potok. All of the main resorts are connected by rail. There are ski racks on the Tatran Railway. If boarding at an unmanned station, buy your ticket from the conductor. There are some buses also, and when these run they are usually quicker than the trains (e.g. Stary Smokovec to Poprad 20 min. as against 40 min. by train). Travelling north of Tatranská Lomnica to Tatranská Kotlina, Ždiar and Javorina one must use buses. The last buses from the Polish border at Lysa Polana leave at 18.25 and 19.40, and from Javorina post office 5 minutes later. There are more buses from Ždiar. Sample bus fares: Javorina - Ždiar 4 kčs, Ždiar - Tatranská Kotlina 2 kčs, Ždiar - Starý Smokovec 7 kčs. Most public transport runs about once an hour.

USEFUL INFORMATION
Čedok in Starý Smokovec (tel. 24020) is the best source of information. The office is open Monday to Friday from 8 am to 6 pm, and from 8 am to 12 am on Saturdays. They have a leaflet in English entitled 'With Čedok in the High Tatras in Summer', describing some of the attractions and walks in the area. The

exchange office is open slightly shorter hours. There is someone who speaks English and my impression was that the staff were helpful. The Čedok office in Poprad opens from 9 am to 5 pm (6 pm on Wednesdays, and 12 am on Saturdays). The exchange office closes half and hour earlier, and is closed between 1 pm and 1.30 pm. Čedok's Poprad address is nám. Dukelských hrdinov 60, 058 01 Poprad (tel. 23 287).

Mail sent to Poste Restante in Poprad should be collected from the telephone and telegraph office just outside the main post office at Marxova ul. 11.

Money can be changed at either Čedok office, or at the bank in Poprad at Marxova ul. 9, open M-F 7.30-11.30, and 12.30 to 15.30, or on Thursday to 17.00.

Horska Služba, the mountain service, is next door to Čedok in Starý Smokovec. They can give you advice, and hopefully rescue you should the need arise!

There is a left luggage service at both the bus and railway stations in Poprad (1 kcs per day). One can also eat at both stations.

ACCOMMODATION

It probably won't be very easy to find anywhere to stay, and many places are much of a muchness, so just find *somewhere*, then get out of it and into the mountains! A tent is your best bet if it is warm enough, otherwise it may be easiest to ask Čedok in Starý Smokovec to find you somewhere to stay. Try not to let them hoodwink you into something more expensive than what you intended. The aim seems to be to herd western travellers into the more expensive hotels.

Camping

(Poprad): There are no camps in Poprad; the one you may see on maps is closed.

Tatranská Štrba: a Čedok camp within walking distance of the Tatranská štrba - Štrbské Pleso rack railway. But dirty and no hot water. Open June to August. Tel. 9713 Poprad.

Dolný Smokovec: 'Tatracamp pod Lesom', 059 81 Dolný Smokovec, tel. Starý Smokovec 2406. A new camp 2.5 km before Starý Smokovec on the road up from Poprad (get off at Podlesom stop on the Poprad - Starý Smokovec railway line). Camping. Bungalows. Class 3 restaurant. Open 15 May to 30 September.

Stará Lesná: Stanový tábor Stará Lesná, 059 60 Tatranská Lomnica. Cheaper but crowded camp. Open 15 June to 15 September. 3 km from Tatranská Lomnica, 1 km from Stará Lesná station.

Tatranská Lomnica: (1) Eurocamp FICC, 059 60 Tatranská Lomnica, tel. Starý Smokovec 967 741-5. A huge expensive camp, open all year round. Camping or bungalows. About 3 km down from Tatranská Lomnica (bus service, or Tatranská Lo mnica-Eurocamp stop on the train).

(2) Autokemping Tatranec, 059 60 Tatranská Lomnica, tel. Starý Smokovec 967 704. Up the road from Eurocamp. Open 15 June to 15 September. Friendly. Cheaper than Eurocamp. Camping 19 kcs

per person, 25 kcs per tent. Bungalows. The showers are sometimes hot!

Turistická Ubytovňa
Horný Smokovec: turistická ubytovna in Juniorhotel (see below)
    Tatranská Lomnica: Alpínka (TU B), 059 60 Tatranská Lomnica, tel. 96376. About 80 kcs per night. Book through Čedok.
    Ždiar: Protežka (TU B), 059 55 Ždiar. Tel. Starý Smokovec 9891. Sleeps 47 in 3 to 7 bed rooms. About 80 kcs per night. Hot and cold water. Central heating.

'YHA Hostel'
YHA members can get a special price of 27 kčs at CKM's Juniorhotel, 06201 Horný Smokovec (tel. 2661-3), if there is any space, which there rarely is. Bus and train stop nearby. If booked from abroad price becomes about £11.50 with full board, £9.50 with half board, nothing cheaper possible.

Hotels
    Poprad : (1) Hotel Europa, Wolkrova ul., by the railway station. Tel. 269 41. B*.
    (2) Hotel Gerlach, Hviezdoslavovo nám, tel. 231 11. B*.
    Štrbské Pleso: (1) Hotel Patria A*, 059 85 Štrbské Pleso, tel. Starý Smokovec 925 91, telex 078255. US$14 to 20 per person in double rooms with bath. Beautifully located by lake.
    (2) Hotel Panoráma B*, 059 85 Štrbské Pleso, tel. 021 11. A rather strange example of Czechoslovak modern architecture! By the railway. US$10 to 20 per person.
    (3) Hotel Fis B*, 059 85 Štrbské Pleso, tel. Starý Smokovec 922 21. 15 minutes walk from the railway station. Used by Czechoslovak sportsmen.
    Nový Smokovec (post code 062 01): (1) Park Hotel B*, tel. 2342-5. Interesting shape. Close to railway station. US$17 to 30 per person.
    (2) Hotel Tokajík B*, tel. 2061. Small traditional style building. US$15 to 30 per person.
    (3) Hotel Bystrina C, tel. 2618. 300 m from station. Double rooms with shower. Only breakfast and light refreshments served.
    (4) MS Hotel B, tel 2976, 2972. 300 m from station. 2 & 4 bed rooms. Class III restaurant.
    Starý Smokovec(post code 062 01): (1) Grandhotel A*, tel. 2501-3, telex 078270. Central. Nice exterior. US$20 to 40 per person half board.
    (2) Hotel Úderník B, tel. 2458.
    Horný Smokovec(post code 062 01): (1) Bellevue Hotel A* B*, tel. 2941-5, telex 078269. 500 m from station. US$17 to 40 per person half board.
    (2) Hotel Šport B, tel. 2361. 500 m from station.
    (3) Juniorhotel CKM B, tel 2661. Prices per room: single 109 kčs, double 182 kčs, 3 bed 278 kčs, 4 bunks 352 kčs. If writing to book, write 2 months before.
    Tatranská Lomnica(post code 059 60): (1) Grandhotel Praha B* (some rooms upgraded to A*), tel. 967941-6, telex 78271. 1 km from station.

(2) Hotel Slovan B*, tel. 967 851.
(3) Hotel Lomnica B, tel. 967251. 100 m from station. Older style. Outdoor cafe in summer.
(4) Hotel Mier C, tel. Starý Smokovec 967 936.

Private Accommodation

There is private accommodation in the area, but only citizens of 'socialist countries' are allowed to stay there. If you do manage it, expect to pay around 35 kcs single, 60 kcs double, and don't register at that address! Čedok might arrange private accommodation for you if there were nothing else available.

Mountain Huts

One can't just walk into the mountain huts in the Vysoké Tatry and expect to be able to sleep there. They tend more to be bases for climbers. Others may be able to stay there if they book in advance through Slovakoturist. Their local office is in Hotel MS in Nový Smokovec, behind the circular Park Hotel. The huts are named after the first climbers in the Tatry.

FOOD & DRINK

Generally I have no particular recommendations. But the following have been recommended to me: Zbojnicka Koliba (Highwaymen's Den) in Tatranská Lomnica, a 1st class wine restaurant in a log cabin, a few minutes walk from Grandhotel Praha, where reservations may be made; Hotel Lomnica in Tatranská Lomnica; and both the Grandhotels. The local beer is Pivo Tatra, costs 4.60 kcs for a half litre draught, and packs a punch.

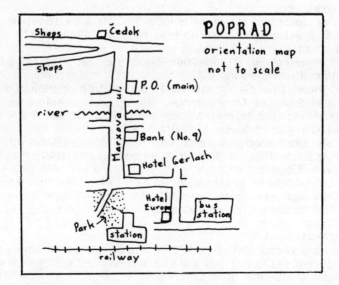

THE SETTLEMENTS AND THEIR ATTRACTIONS

Popradis not so interesting although it is the main centre in the area. Most people arrive by train. Hotel Europa is just outside the station to the right. A little further along in the same direction is the bus station. If instead of leaving the station by the exit to the right, you head away at right angles to the railway line, another exit leads out into a park. If you keep heading in the same direction you'll come out opposite the end of Marxova ul. Hotel Gerlach is across the road on the right. Following Marxova ul., the bank is on your right before the street crosses the river, and the post office also on the right on the other side of the river. Turning left at the far end of Marxova ul. brings you to a shopping street. Čedok is on your right just after you turn. (See map)

The resort towns of **Štrbské Pleso**, **Starý Smokovec**, and **Tatranská Lomnica** are pleasant, nicely laid out towns with a lot of greenery and parks. Štrbské Pleso is situated on the lake of the same name. Above the town is a ski jump. Starý Smokovec is the main tourist centre, and forms one entity together with Nový Smokovec and Horný Smokovec which are within walking distance. From Tatranská Lomnica there is an aerial cableway to Lomnický štít (2632) via Skalnaté pleso. It may be necessary to book to get on it. One can be on the summit until the next car arrives. There is another aerial cableway up to Skalnaté pleso. In Tatranská Lomnica is the Tatra National Park (TANAP) Museum. It's open Monday to Friday 8 am to 12 noon and from 1 pm to 5 pm, and on Saturdays and Sundays 8 am to 12 noon.

Tatranská Kotlina's attraction is Belanská jaskyňa, a cave 15 to 20 minutes walk uphill from the road. From mid-May to mid-September there are tours every 1 1/2 hours from 9.30 am until the last tour which leaves at 3.30 pm. For the rest of the year there are tours at 9.30 am, 11 am and 2.30 pm. Like most things in Czechoslovakia it is closed on Mondays, but unlike most things it is open all year. Take enough clothing as it may be rather cold (15°C in summer and -4°C in winter).

Ždiar is a fair way away from the main resorts, and sprawls several kilometres along the valley between the Belianske Tatry and the Spišská Magura range. The village was founded by Walachian colonists in the 15th century. It is notable for its architecture and folklore, but unfortunately both are dying out. It has beautiful wooden houses with finely painted facades. The traditional style house was built around a courtyard, which is typical of highland communities in the Carpathians. More recently houses were built in the style found in the Zakopane area in Poland. Until recently the villagers used to wear their local costume, but today you'd be lucky to see them.

TRAMPING
Within the Tatra National Park, one is obliged keep to routes well marked and trodden. Many tracks are closed from 1 November to 30 June every year. This is because of danger of avalanches, because the chamois arrive at that time of year, and as a nature protection measure. But they are still open for climbers (see 'Climbing' below). The Belianske Tatry, between the main part of

Vysoké Tatry and Ždiar are completely closed to everyone, including climbers.

The main thing you must remember is that the weather can change very rapidly. So be prepared with a good parka and something warm. Wool clothing keeps you much warmer than other clothing if it should become wet. Good walking boots with ankle support and vibram soles protect your ankles and are more comfortable to walk in, as long as they are worn in first. Puttees can be very useful, and keep you from having to stop to get stones out of your boots. Don't go above the bushline unless there is good visibility and never in bad weather. Here tracks are not marked with poles, though there may occasionally be painted markers on rocks to help you find the way. If clouds begin to close in on you while you are up there, get down quickly. Snowstorms can occur at these higher altitudes even in summer. Horska Sluzba (the mountain rescue service) in Starý Smokovec can help you plan trips, and advise you about weather conditions. Insects can become unbearable to those who are troubled by them but are not common above the bushline.

There are a multitude of possible trips and variations on them. Here are some ideas, some route guides and some walking times. 'Gun trampers', who don't stop for rests or taking photos will not take as long as the times quoted. The figures are altitudes in metres.

From Štrbské Pleso

Štrbské Pleso, at 1355 m above sea level is the highest of the Tatran resorts. Among other tramps, it is possible to ascend two of the Tatran peaks from here.

It is a 1 hour walk to **Jamské pleso** (1447 m), on a red marked track leading to the west from Štrbské Pleso. From here a blue marked track leads to the top of **Kriváň** (2494 m). The complete trip to Kriváň and back to Štrbské Pleso takes about 7 hours. The track above Jamské pleso is closed in winter.

There is a chairlift from Štrbské Pleso to **Solisko**, where refreshments are available. From here one can ascend **Predné Solisko** (2093). Alternatively, follow the blue marked track to the left from the top of the chairlift to **Furkotská dolina**. Heading up the valley (yellow markers) takes one past some beautiful lakes, then up a steep climb to the saddle, **Bystré sedlo**, at the top of the valley. From here there is a side track to the top of a hill, where the view includes frozen lakes. The descent to **Mlynicka dolina** on the other side is again steep. Following the valley down brings one back to Strbské Pleso, passing a waterfall on the way. A whole day is required to enjoy this round trip. One can walk to Furkotska dolina from Štrbské Pleso by two different routes, instead of taking the chairlift up. In winter most of this trip is closed. The ridge between the two valleys forms the watershed between the Váh and Poprad river systems, and thus of the Black and Baltic Seas.

One of the best views in the Tatras is from the summit of **Rysy** (2499) on the Polish border. From Štrbské Pleso follow the red marked track to **Popradské pleso** (you don't have time to pick the raspberries!), the blue track from here up **Mengusovská dolina**,

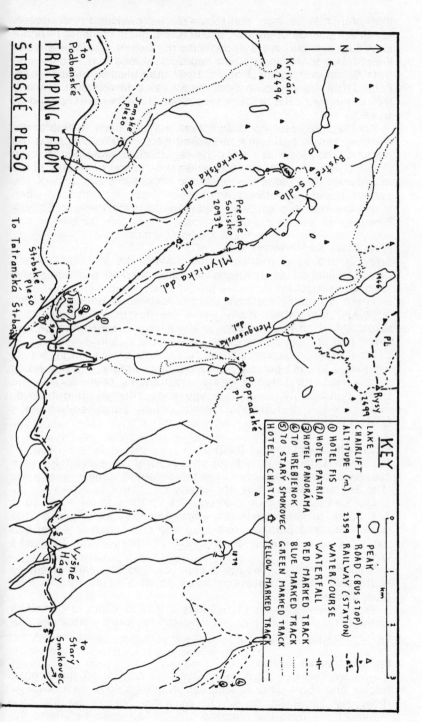

TRAMPING FROM
ŠTRBSKÉ PLESO

to Podbanské

Kriváň 2494

Jamské pleso

Turkotská dol.

Bystré (Sedlo)

Predné Solisko 2093

Mlynická dol.

Štrbské pleso
To Tatranská Štrba

Mengusovská dol.

Popradské Pl.

Rysy 2499

PL.

1350

1466

1474

Vyšné Hágy

to Starý Smokovec

KEY

○   LAKE
●━━■   CHAIRLIFT
2359   ALTITUDE (m)
▲   PEAK
▬◉▬   ROAD (BUS STOP)
╪╪   RAILWAY (STATION)
⌇   WATERCOURSE
)   WATERFALL
――― RED MARKED TRACK
--- BLUE MARKED TRACK
····· GREEN MARKED TRACK
―‧― YELLOW MARKED TRACK

① HOTEL FIS
② HOTEL PATRIA
③ HOTEL PANORÁMA
④ TO HREBIENOK
⑤ TO STARÝ SMOKOVEC
HOTEL CHATA

0   1   2   3
km

N →

then branch to the right and follow the red markers to the summit. The track passes **Chata pod Rysmi**, the highest chalet in Czechoslovakia, and crosses a snowfield. The return trip from Štrbské Pleso takes 8 1/2 hours, from Popradské pleso 6 1/2 hours, and from Chata pod Rysmi 2 hours. Rysy may also be climbed from Poland, but if you ascend from the Slovak side you must descend the same way. The track above Popradské pleso is closed in winter.

Another possible trip is to follow the red track to Popradské pleso as above, but from Popradské pleso, keep following the red markers. They lead up a steep zig-zag climb to **sedlo pod Ostrvou** (1959). From here you can follow the red marked track around the mountain slopes near the bushline, dropping down one of the various tracks to the Starý Smokovec - Štrbské Pleso road when you have had enough, and catching the train back to Štrbské Pleso.

From Starý Smokovec (1010)

Starý Smokovec is overlooked by **Slavkovský štít**(2452), which may be climbed by following the blue marked track from the town. 9 hours return.

There is a cable car from Starý Smokovec to **Hrebienok** (1263 m, 2 km) from where many walks are possible. Alternatively it takes 3/4 of an hour to walk to Hrebienok. From Hrebienok one saves half an hour on the climb up Slavkovský s̆ t̆.

From Starý Smokovec it takes 10 1/2 hours to walk right across the Tatras to **Lysá polana** via **Bielovodská dolina**, or 9 1/2 hours to **Javorina** via **Terycho chata**. Both tracks open only in the summer season. These are one way times. You can return by bus.

A round trip Hrebienok-Téryho chata-Zbojnícka-Hrebienok takes 8 hours.

From Tatranská Lomnica (860)

Tatranská Lomnica is not such a good starting point for high altitude tramps, unless one takes the overhead cableway up. (See 'The Settlements and their Attractions').

One can take the blue marked track up through the forest for 1 3/4 hours to **Studenovodské vodopády**, the waterfalls on the stream **Studená potoka**. From here one can continue higher into the mountains, or drop down to Starý Smokovec or **Tatranská Lesná**.

Walking between Tatranská Lomnica and **Skalnaté pleso** via **sedlo pod Malou Svištovkou** takes about 3 hours (green, then blue, markers).

From Skalnaté pleso (1751) it is a 2 hour climb to **Lomnické sedlo** (2190). There is no marked tourist track from here, the saddle, to the summit.

From Tatranská Kotlina

If you would like to get away from the crowds on the popular tracks, and don't mind missing out on getting up quite as high as them, try Tatranská Kotlina to Javorina. Set off on the blue marked track from the opposite end of Tatranská Kotlina to the track up to the caves. After 1/2 hour turn right on the green marked track. Another 1 1/2 hours (3/4 hour if you are fast) brings you to Hviezdon. So far the track has been nicely graded. From here it is steeper for a while, then sidles around with mountain views, until after another small climb it comes to the track junction at Biele pl. by the ruins of Kežmarska chata. From here one can descend again to the left (2 1/2 hours to the road, or 3 hour to Tatranská Lomnica). The track straight ahead leads to Zelené pl. (1/2 hr) and on to Skalnaté pl. via Velka Svistovska (another 2 hours). To continue to Javorina turn right at the Biele pl. junction on the blue marked track. The last grind from here to the saddle (Kopské sedlo, 1749) between the Vysoké Tatry and the Belianske Tatry takes 1/2 hour. The ridge just before the saddle is actually higher than the saddle itself. In these upper parts of the trip there are beautiful alpine flowers in season . After another hour, the track arrives at a collection of tables and benches at a bridge over the river in the bottom of a pleasant valley. Then a 'supertrack' leads down, through bluffs, and turns right into Javorina dolina. Look back up the valley for good mountain views. The last 3/4 hour is on a roadway, and is not so interesting. From Javorina the last bus leaves at 19.45 for Poprad via Starý Smokovec. Hitch-hiking may be possible.

CLIMBING

To climb without a guide in the Vysoké Tatry one must be a member of a climbing club and have a membership card. One can climb anywhere except in the special nature reservations where climbing is forbidden; i.e. Slavkovska dol., Kolovi dol., Mlynár, Čierna Javoriná dolina and Nefcerka dolina. Climbing is also forbidden on any walls off Slavkovska and Kolovi dolinas. Nefcerka dolina is closed only up to the bushline. You may climb its walls, but you must enter it another way. Climbing walls must be reached by marked tourist track and then the shortest way to the wall. Anything from stage 2 difficulty and up may be climbed. Stage 1 climbs, which are easy, may not be climbed, but you can descend by a stage one route. The climbing area is a fairly small area of the mountains.

Guidebooks are all old, and available only in Slovak, Hungarian and Polish. A new guidebook is being prepared. This will be published in German as well.

People who are not members of a climbing club may climb only with a guide. A guide to climb Gerlach, the highest peak, costs 400 kčs and can take a maximum of 5 people. The more difficult the climb, the higher the price of the guide.

When climbing leave your intentions at the nearest mountain hut. Write the time you are leaving, when you expect to be back, what route you plan to take, and its difficulty. When you get back sign in again. If you don't arrive back the Mountain Rescue Service will be notified. If one is not a member of a club, one has no insurance cover, and must pay for any rescue.

Some of the most popular climbs are:

> west wall of Lomnicky štít
> south wall of Kežmarský stít
> north wall of little Kežmarský štít (at 900m,

this is the largest wall in the Vysoké Tatry)
Siroka veza
yellow wall of Prostredy hrot
north wall of Javorový štít (mainly in winter)
Batizovsky stít

Climbing in the Vysoké Tatry started at the end of the 19th
century. Now the 7th and 8th stages of difficulty are starting to be
climbed.
   Climbing is possible all year round. There is ice climbing as
well as rock climbing, skiing off peaks, and the new sport, ski
rally, is popular with climbers.

SKIING
It is best to have your own gear with you, but skiing gear can be
hired from Hotel Patria in Štrbské Pleso, and maybe from the
Grand Hotels in Starý Smokovec and Tatranská Lomnica.
   The skiing season is from December to May, the best period
being from Christmas to the end of March. In April skiing is
possible only at higher altitudes, specifically at Skalnaté Pleso
and on Predné Solisko mountain slopes. The weather tends to be
clearer in winter than in summer.
   'Cesta uzavretá—nebezpečenstvo lavin' means 'Path
Closed—Avalanche Danger'.
   Štrbské Pleso is the most important skiing centre, with downhill
skiing, cross country and two ski jumps. Other important ski
centres are Hrebienok above Starý Smokovec, and Skalnaté pleso
above Tatranská Lomnica. Ždiar is a good place for learners and
families. The snow conditions in Ždiar are good each year; not
much snow is needed as there is grass underneath. Lifts in Ždiar
cost about 1 - 3 kcs. The lift from Skalnaté pleso to Lomnické
sedlo costs 6 kcs. At Štrbské Pleso you will have the longest
waits for lifts (typically 30 - 40 minutes). At Lomnické sedlo and
Ždiar the waiting time is more like 5 - 10 minutes. A new centre is
being opened up at Jesersko, close by in the Spišská Magura
mountains, with new lifts and good skiing. See 'Skiing' in the
introductory section of the book for summer skiing.

TOURS
Čedok in Starý Smokovec arrange the following bus tours:
Jasna
A day trip for skiers to Jasná in the Low Tatras. Every Tuesday
from January 15 to March 31. Cost about 100 kcs, including lunch.
Demanovske Jaskyne - Jasna
A day trip every Tuesday from June 1 to September 30, including
tour of cave, lunch, and return chairlift up Chopok. All inclusive
price about 130 kcs.
Dunajec - Cerveny Klaštor
Every Tuesday, Wednesday, Thursday and Friday from June 1 to
September 30. This trip is to Pieniny, on the Polish border on the
other side of Spišská Magura. It consists of: a visit to the Carthusian monastery in Červený Kláštor, now a m useum; weather
permitting, a raft trip down the gorge of the river Dunajec; lunch
at Haligovce; and a visit to the skanzen at Stará Lubovna. All

inclusive price about 145 kčs.

With your own car you can visit Pieniny independently. If you travel up by the ordinary bus service instead of going on the tour, you may have trouble getting a bus out from the end of the raft trip. You could walk out again. There is a camp site at Červený Klástor. There is a detailed map of this area: 'Spišská Magura Pieniny' costing 8 kčs.

MURÁNSKA PLANINA (Muráň Tableland)

Muránska Planina (the Muráň Tableland) is situated south of the Low Tatras, and south-west of Slovenský Raj. It is a good area for tramping. One normally meets Czechoslovaks rather than tourists here. Although camping is not allowed, peop le sleep out here. As well as bluffs and karst, there are free running horses.

The map 'Slovenské Rudohorie - Stred' covers this area. There may be a new series of maps of Slovenské Rudohorie coming out, in which case this one will have another name. If you can't find a map of the area, the Nízke Tatry map covers part of Muránska Planina.

One can sleep at the hostinec, Jeleň, in the village of Muráň. 10 beds, cold water only. Tel. Revúca 694 54. Another starting point to Muránska Planina is Červená skala, a former smelting hamlet, but there is no accommodation.

Oravsky Zamek

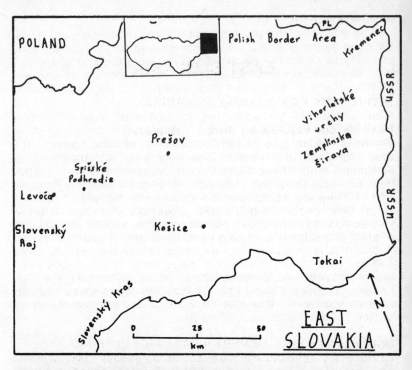

Spisske Podhradie, Slovakia

EAST SLOVAKIA

SLOVENSKÝ RAJ (SLOVAK PARADISE)

From a distance Slovenský Raj, located south-east of Poprad, looks deceptively like an area of gentle rolling hills. But in its depths is hidden an area of spectacularly beautiful scenery. The area consists of Triassic and mesozoic chemically pure limestones which have been eroded by streams to form narrow canyons, cascades and waterfalls. In the winter these become frozen. They are accessible to walkers, with the aid of ladders, steps and chains. Since 1964 Slovenský Raj has been a 'protected landscape zone'. Numerous protected and rare species of plant and wildlife are found here. There are beautiful flowers.

There is a detailed map of the area: 'Slovenský Raj', 2nd edition, 1986, 7 kcs. There is a guide book, but it is published only in Slovak and German. Other books: *Slovenský Raj* , by Ladislav Jirousek & Karol Hric, 94 kcs. *Slovenský Raj* by Ladislav Denes. Both have a resumé in English, but consist mainly of photos.

DOBŠINSKA LADOVA JASKYŇA (DOBŠINA ICE CAVE)

Of the many caves in the area, Dobsinská ladová jaskyňa is the only one open to the public. A visit to it is fascinating, but cold! Tours begin at 9 am, 11, 1 pm and 3 pm between 16 May and 15 September. During the rest of the year, and every Monday, the cave is closed. Cost: 8 kcs, 4 kcs students and children under 15. No information is available in English.

ACCESS, CENTRES, SLEEPING & EATING

Bases to explore this area from are Čingov, Dedinky, Dobšinská ladová jaskyňa, Klástorisko, Hrabusice- podlesok, Spisská Nová Ves, or if you have a car, even Poprad, the High Tatras or Levoca.

Hrabušice-Podlesok

Although not terribly easy to get to, I feel that Hrabusice- Podlesok is the most convenient place to stay. It is well- situated as far as the most interesting area to walk in is concerned, and although a long way from Dobsinská ladová jas kyna, a pleasant day trip can be made by walking over the hills to it.

There are some direct buses from Poprad. Otherwise one changes from a long distance bus at Spis. Stvrtok, to a local bus to Hrabusice-Podlesok. By train get off at Vydrník. There are occasional buses from Vydrník to Hrabusice-Podlesok, otherwise it's a one hour walk. If there is no bus to Hrabusice-Podlesok for a long time, one can catch another bus to Hrabusice razc. Betlanovce from where it is only 1 km further to walk. There are also buses between Podlesok and Spisska Nová Ves. Hitching may be possible. There is a car park at Hrabusice-Podlesok.

Autokemping Podlesok, 053 15 Hrabuzice, ph. Spisska Nova

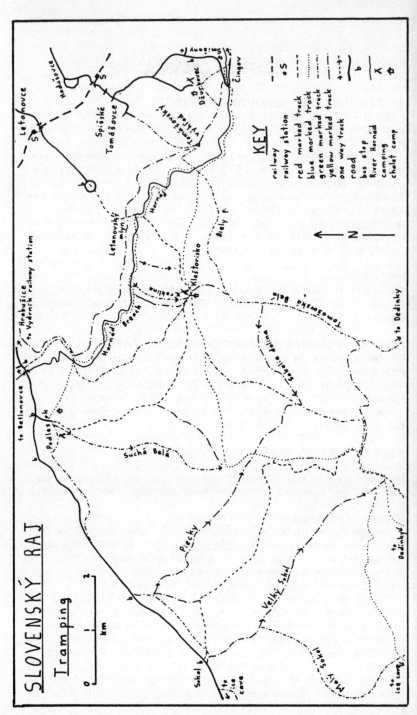

Ves 916 281 is the main accommodation centre. There has been building activity in the last few years, but there are still no showers, no hot water and no flush toilets. Compensation for these conditions are the friendly atmosphere of the place, the view of the Vysoké Tatry on a clear day, and the fact that you can walk straight out of the camp into the most interesting part of Slovenský Raj. Price for camping per night is 16 kcs per tent, plus 8 kcs per person, plus 2 kcs per person tax. For camping it is open from 1 June to 15 September. There are bungalows which are open all year round.

Spišska Koliba (CHO A, B), 053 15 Hrabušice-Podlesok, ph. Spišska Nová Ves 916 326. Chalets.

Eating: Meals are served in the restaurant Spišska Koliba (sk.III) from 7.30 to 9 am, 12 to 3 pm, and 6 pm to 9 pm. There is a little stall with some groceries behind the restaurant. There can be ·long queues here in the morning—quicker to eat breakfast in the restaurant. Between the camp and the koliba is a barrel shaped stall selling beer and sweets.

Kláštorisko

Kláštorisko is situated on a mountain meadow. The road up to it is closed to the public, who must walk the 1 1/4 hours up from Hrabušice-Podlesok. The people of the Spiš region found refuge here during the Tatar raids on Hungary in the period 1241- 42. In thanksgiving for their protection, they built a monastery here in the 14th century, which became a home for Carthusian monks. This was in the 15th century and local robbers camped in the ruins for many years, terrorizing the surrounding villages. An archeological excavation is underway. Skiing in winter.

Camping is possible at Kláštorisko from 15 June to 15 September. There is also a tourist hut and some chalets, which are usually full. Address: Verejné táborisko a chatová osada Kláštorisko, 053 15 Hrabušice, ph. Spišska Nová Ves 916 307.

Čingov

Car park. Some buses. 1/2 hour walk to Čingov-Ďurkovec from Spišské Tomášovce railway station.

The campsite at Čingov-Ďurkovec is not as crowded as the camping ground at Hrabušice-Podlesok. It is spread over a hill, with a view over the surrounding towns and farmland (not over Slovenský Raj). Cold water only, including shower. Cheaper than Hrabušice- Podlesok. Open 15 June to 15 September.

Besides the camp there are a couple of chalet colonies and dormitory accommodation. A restaurant is open some of the time, and there is a nice vinaren, also selling coffee and soft drinks, that seems too flash to wear tramping clothes in, but everyone does. The toilets under the restaurant have warm water. For accommodation bookings try Tatran or Čedok in Spišska Nová Ves.

In another part of Čingov, Smižany-Čingov, is Hotel Flora, a B class hotel, with A class chalets. Address: 053 11 Smižant- Čingov, ph. Spišska Nová Ves 932 27.

The place to go if you want more comfort is Hotel Metropol (B*), Dukelská ul. 1/1936, 052 01 Spišska Nová Ves, ph. 222 41. Spišska Nová Ves is the main centre for public transport to the northern part of Slovenský Raj.

Dedinky
There is tent camping in Dedinky, as well as chalets and a mountain hotel, Hotel Priehrada (B). The phone number for all of them is Rožnava 981 62, and the postal address is Dedinky, 049 25 Dobšiná.

Dobšinská ladová jaskyňa
There is no camping here. There are a couple of hotels, Hotel Jas, B class, by the track to the cave, and Hotel Ladová, C class, on the main road, and with a restaurant and bufet. There are also some A class chalets. The postal address for all 3 is Stratená-Dobšinská ladová jaskyňa, PSČ 049 71, and phone number for all 3: Rožnava 898 19.

TRAMPING
The key on the map is not in English. You may notice tracks with arrows on them. These are one way tracks, which may only be walked in the direction of the arrow. When you get there you'll see why! When a lot of people use them it can be rather hard to pass on the ladders and other aids to access. Those afraid of heights might need to avoid the most interesting tracks, though the steps, ladders, and chains etc. provided make it quite safe. The main rule to remember in tricky places is to move either one hand or one foot at a time. If you are afraid, look up, not down. There are also some beautiful easier walks: avoid one way tracks and canyons if you are looking for these. The walking times on the signposts are quite realistic, so if you found you were cutting the times in the Vysoké Tatry, don't necessarily expect to here. Don't judge times by distance on the map; there is a vast difference between the time it takes on some straight and flat tracks, to the time it takes on those that twist and clamber through canyons. A lot of the tracks are in stream beds, so be wary after lots of rain. I recommend boots for keeping your feet dry, even when you are in stream beds.

Part of the yellow marked track on the map through Kysel behind Kláštorisko has been closed, because a fire here made the boulders unstable. The blue marked track behind Kláštorisko is now 2 way.

The following is written using Hrabušice-Podlesok as a starting point, because of its convenient position.

From Podlesok you can get straight into an incredible gorge by following the green marked track up Suchá Belá. It takes 2 hours to the top, and can get crowded. It is a one way track, so from the top you must decide on another way back.

Another green marked track from Podlesok leads along the road below the camp, then up a valley. Part of it is a nice walk along the river, but a lot of it is along the road. When you come out on the entrance road to the youth camp, turn right. After 1 hour, one comes to the bottom of Piecky, and after 1 1/2 hours to the bottom of Velký Sokol. The road continues over to Dobšinská ladová jaskyňa, but the occasional bus service reaches only as far as Sokol. Hitch-hiking is difficult. Continuing on the green marked track from Sokol one comes to Dobšinská ladová jaskyňa after another 2 1/2 hours walking. There are many other possible walking routes to Dobšinská ladová jaskyňa, but this is the most simple. Coming back one could catch the Poprad bus as far as Vernár, then follow the red marked track over the hill then back to Podlesok via Sokol (3 1/4 hours).

The Piecky route leads up a stream. Suddenly there is a little canyon ahead. The track doesn't go up it, but turns to the left, where there is the first tall ladder up beside a little waterfall. People always gasp when they see it! When you reach the first roadway, you are not at the top. Cross it and keep climbing. Between here and Malá Polana (992m.a.s.l.) there are in season many raspberries, often each with its resident worm! Watch out for the nettles among them! This trip takes 2 hours, again on a one way track. From Malá Polana it is 1 1/4 hours to Klástorisko, or 3 1/2 hours right out to Smižany.

The Velký Sokol track is two way as far the junction where Malý Sokol enters it. As Malý Sokol is two way, a round trip is possible here, by going up Velký Sokol, following the blue marked track across the tops, and dropping down Malý Soko l (5 hour round trip). Malý Sokol is less developed, and not quite as spectacular as some of the other valleys, but it makes an interesting rock-hop. A lot of the stream is underground, but you may get your feet wet.

Heading in the opposite direction from Podlesok, past Spišská koliba, the blue marked track leads you, after 15 minutes, to Hrdlo Hornádu, the entrance to the Hornád Breach. Here is the rather strange sight of the Hornád River running in to the hills rather than out of them as rivers tend to do. The canyon used to be only accessible in winter on ice or in summer by boat. Now there is a track all the way down the river to Čingov (3 1/2 hours) or Smižany (4 1/4 hours) where there are more buses than from Čingov, and a railway station. Some of the way the track is on metal steps in bluffs far above the water. This is a good river for kayaking (permission is needed as it is in a nature reserve). Take something to drink with you, as the Hornád River flows into the hills from farmland, and is rather dirty. A good round trip is to follow the river down to Čingov, and return via the yellow marked track over Tomášovský Výhlad, a viewpoint on top of a bluff. This return route is quicker and very different, with wide open ridges and nice views, but it is quite a grunt where it drops down to Letanovský Mlyn then climbs back up again. Čingov to Podlesok on the yellow track takes 2 1/2 hours.

Other walking times(in hours) in the area of the Hornád Breach are:
From the bottom of Klástorisko Roklina, 1 hour downstream from Hrdlo Hornádu:
   Klástorisko, (green) 1; (yellow) 3/4
From Letanovský Mlyn, 2 hours downstream from Hrdlo Hornádu:
   Klástorisko (red) 1; Čingov (yellow) 1 1/4; Tomášovský Výhlad

(yellow) 3/4; Letanovce railway station (red) 1/2; Hrdlo Horna'du (yellow) 1; Hrabušice village (yellow) 1 1/2
From where Biely Potok meets the Hornád, 2 3/4 hours downstream from Hrdlo Hornádu:
The bottom of Kysel (green) 3/4; The bottom of Sokolia dolina (green) 1 1/4; Klauzy (green) 2; Kláštorisko (blue) 1 1/4; Tomášovský Výhlad (green) 3/4; Spišské Tomášovce railway station (green) 1 1/4
From the camp site at Čingov-Džurkovec:
Čingov (green) 1/4; Tomašovský Výhlad 3/4; Spišské Tomášovce railway station 1/2

LEVOCA

Levoča is a beautiful medieval walled town. It is worth at least a stop on the way from Poprad to Prešov. A lot of it is under restoration, a lot is falling down, and some is deserted, but there are some beautiful buildings, and it evokes an atmosphere of the past. Levoča was one of the most important towns in the Magyar Kingdom. Today it has a population of 11,000.

The church in the square is the second largest Gothic church in Slovakia, (the largest is in Košice). It houses a carved and gilded altar piece created by Master Pavol. At 18 metres high and 6 metres wide, it is the largest of its kind in the world. The altar piece dates from the early 16th century, and was restored in the 1950s. For 1 kčs you can hear a recording about it in English. The church is open in daytime from Monday to Saturday as a part of the museum, which is in the town hall. At the main entrance to the town from the main road, is Novy Minoritský kostel, another Gothic church which belonged to the monastery. Both churches date from the 14th century. There is another church in the forest on the hill above the town. The gymnázium, just east of the square, has a fantastic tower. In fact the building itself is worth a look at. There is a church, Gymnaziálny kostel, attached. The Town Hall, in the square, has a Gothic core surrounded by Renaissance extensions. You'll recognize it by its arches. The museum in it includes an art gallery and a history of Levoča. The square is surrounded by Renaissance houses.

In winter there is skiing in the valley.

PRACTICAL INFORMATION
Čedok and Slovakoturist both have offices on the square. Post code: 054 01.

GETTING THERE & AWAY AGAIN
The main bus stop is outside the walled town, just up the road from the main town entrance. Buses on the route Poprad- Prešov stop here. The last bus to Prešov leaves at 7.17 pm. The main road from Poprad to Prešov passes through the town, outside its walls. Easily visited as a day trip from Vysoké Tatry, Slovenský Raj or Prešov.

SLEEPING
Hotel Družba, cesta Slobody 22, tel. 2335. B class.

Hotel Biela pani, Nám. Mieru 36, tel. 2896. C class. The sign
outside just says 'Hotel C'. On the 2nd floor. Doubles 153 kcs,
same price for 1 person alone.
Autokemping Levočská dolina, tel. 727 01. Camping ground
and chalets 3 km up the valley from Levoca.

EATING
There are various places to eat and drink. For a quick feed, there
is a samoobsluha at the top of the square. Down the back streets
you'll find local pubs (hostinec).

SPIŠSKÉ–PODHRADIE
Overlooking the village of Spišské-Podhradie, atop a craggy hill,
lies the ruins of one of the most impressive castles in Czechoslovakia, Spišský Hrad. A fantastic sight! The oldest records of a
castle on this sight are from 1209. It was gradually developed,
and rebuilt several times between the 13th and 18th centuries.
The castle was of great strategic importance as the central point
of the Spiš region. It was the largest castle complex in Central
Europe, with five courtyards, extensive fortifications and a vast
outer bailey. In 1780 the castle was burnt out and since has
gradually fallen into decay. Restoration began in 1969.

In my opinion the castle is more impressive from a distance
than when you actually visit it. The entrance to the castle is from
a turning past Spišské-Podhradie on the main road to Prešov.
There is also a walking track up from Spišské- Podhradie. It is
open from 1 May to 31 October, daily except Mondays, from 9 am
to 5 pm (last entry 4.15 pm). There is an information leaflet in
English (or at least a valiant attempt at English!).

There are a number of legends attached to the castle. One of
them concerns Juraj Thurzo, the young lord of Spišský Hrad. He
was a man who loved company, good fun and, above all, pretty
girls. He decided to arrange a feast, and sent messengers to
invite all the local noblemen. During the feast Thurzo took a
fancy to Dorothy, the young daughter of the landlord Révay. The
more wine he drank, the more lustful he became. He asked her to
dance, and while they danced he planned to seduce her. 'It is
rather stuffy here. Would you like to take a stroll to catch a
breath of fresh air?' he asked with practised nonchalance. Once
outside he expected to see some sign of worry or fear, something
that never failed to excite him. But instead the girl calmly said:
'My mother asked me not to leave the hall. I have heard about
your amorous adventures. But I trust you.' At that moment something broke in Juraj Thurzo. He was overcome by a feeling of
shame, and a feeling of great love which he had not known
before. 'You are too good and too lovely for me to be worthy of
you' he whispered in her ear. The following month Spišský Hrad
was the scene of a grandiose wedding. (From 'Slovak Spas &
Health Resorts', No. 13).

The southern extension of the castle hill is the nature reserve
of Dreveník. An instructional path leads one around the more
interesting parts of it. Among the most remarkable formations are
the gorge Peklo (Hell) and Kamenný raj (Stoney Paradise) which

with imagination reminds one of a rocky townlet. There are a number of caves, often concealed. Cave men once lived here. In the southwest part of Dreveník is an ice cave.

Spišské-Podhradie itself developed from a settlement below the castle. Since the 12th century it was an important crafts centre.

Spišská Kapitula, now a part of Spišské-Podhradie, is a town built by ecclesiastical dignitaries. It is a fortified town, centred on its cathedral. Despite a few Gothic alterations the cathedral is a noteworthy example of Romanesque architecture. But count yourself lucky if you can get into it! The Renaissance bishop's palace was built in 1652.

Towards Prešov from Spišské-Podhradie the main road ascends Branisko via a series of hairpin bends. From here there are glimpses of Spišský Hrad. The marked tracks in this forested area are shown on a map at the highest point on the road.

GETTING THERE
Spišské-Podhradie is situated just off the main Poprad - Prešov road. Buses on this route stop there.

SLEEPING
The only accommodation is a C category hotel: Hotel Spiš, 053 04 Spišské-Podhradie, tel. 85 21. Has hot & cold water, and central heating.

PREŠOV
Prešov is an important Slovak and Ukrainian cultural centre. The first records of an urban settlement here date from 1247. Prešov attained the status of royal town in 1374. Today it has a population of 72,000 and is not overrun by tourists.

GETTING THERE & AWAY AGAIN
Straightforward driving from Poprad (European highway no. E85, Czechoslovak highway no. 18), Kosice (E85, 68) and Michalovce (18). Hitch-hiking is reasonable on these roads, but it is difficult to hitch out of Prešov itself. Buses are generally more convenient than trains. Bus service from Poprad, frequent buses between Prešov and Košice. Bus and train stations are across the road from each other.

GETTING AROUND
Buy tickets for local buses around the town beforehand from kiosks. Many of the local buses pass the railway station. At Trojica bus stop, in the centre, is a big bus orientation plan.

SLEEPING
Prešov's post code is 080 01 if writing to any of the following:

Hotels
Dukla B*, ul. Slov. republicky rád. 1, tel. 227 41, opposite Čedok. 122 beds. US$15 to 25 per person per night.
Šariš B*, Leningradská ul. č. 1, tel. 46353-54. 150 beds.

Savoy B, ul. Slov. republiky rád 50, tel. 310 62. 44 beds.
Verchovina B, Svätoplukova ul. 1, tel. 249 22. 30 beds. Next door to ČSA.
Hotel Sigord B*, 082 52 Kokošovce, tel. 983 02. Out of town.

Other
Motel Stop. 080 02 Prešov-Haniska. Tel. 252 20. B class motel plus camping. Note that is closed from 1/7 to 31/8 every year, when it is taken over by a children's camp. A few kilometres south of town on the road to Košice. Some buses.
   Autokemping, 082 33 Chminianska Nová Ves, tel 951 10. Open 1/7 to 30/9. 15 km west of Prešov on the road to Poprad. 2 km east of Chminianska Nová Ves village. Camping. Bungalows. Camping area floods if there is a lot of rain. Hot water! Bar. Washing machine & ironing in the 'Ladies'! - 5 kčs per hour. From Prešov 5 kčs by bus, buy ticket from driver. Bus stop is 10 minutes walk past camp entrance, but if you tell the driver you want the camp he might stop outside. Last bus out about 11 pm.
   Chatová osada B v Kúpeloch Išla, Prešov 080 01. Tel. Prešov 411 00. North east of Prešov. Bungalows only. Seasonally open.
   Tourist Hostel - Tatran, ul. Pod Kamennou baňou 6, tel. 492 52. 2, 3, 4 and 6 bed rooms. Bus 15 or 22.

EATING
Restaurants in the hotels. For something cheaper, but nothing special, there is a cl. III eatery at Slov. Republiky rád. 61, open daytime only. It has a toilet, but you have to ask for the key. In the same street, no. 21, is a class IV stand up 'bufet', open Monday to Friday 6 am to 8 pm, Saturday 8 am to 7 pm, Sunday 8 am to 6 pm. The locally bottled beer, Šariš, is good.

PRACTICAL INFORMATION
From Poprad follow the signs to 'Centrum' and they'll bring you to Slov. rep. rád., the main street for your purposes. No map of Prešov is available.
   Tatratour, Slov. rep. rád. 129, tel. 34300, 34301, 33962. For information and to change money.
   Čedok, same street, no. 1, tel. 24040, 24042, 33260. Opposite Dukla Hotel. Open weekdays 8 am to 4 pm, (Wednesdays 9 am to 6 pm), Saturday 9 am to 12 noon. Changing money weekdays 8 am to 3 pm, Wednesdays 9 am to 5 pm.
   Bank. Cnr ul. Leninova (the continuation of Slov. Rep. rád. leading towards the bus station) and ul. Partizánska.
   Public toilets. Ul. 29 Augusta.
   Tuzex, Slov. Rep. Rád. 38
   ČSA, same street no. 26.

TO SEE
There is a fantastic Greek Orthodox cathedral at Slov. rep. rád., next door to Čedok. It was founded in the 15th century, and rebuilt in Baroque style in 1754. In the centre of Slov. rep. rád. is the Gothic Church of St. Nicholas. It was built in the middle of the 14th century, with late Gothic extentions from 1502. On Svatoplukova is the Evangelical Church, dating from 1637 to

1642. All the churches in Presov are really worth a visit. People dress up to enter a church. The local people appear to be more church-going than the average Slovak, though it is mostly older people. On Saturdays there are weddings everywhere! Múzeum at Slov. rep. rád 86. Natural history section good. Political history section propoganda. Closed Monday. Open Tuesday to Friday 10 am to 6 pm, weekends 9 am to 1 pm. Entrance 2 kcs.

Presov is a town worth just wandering in. Some beautiful old buildings and houses are preserved here. Others are being demolished or left to fall down. They are generally typically rundown, but there are nice old buildings with some character. If you look through the old archways and into the damp back alleys, you could get another impression.

Presov can also be used as a base to visit other places. Day trips can be made to Kosice, Spisské-Podhradie, or Bardejov, a town to the north, retaining its medieval character.

FILMS
Presov has a lot of cinemas, with films from all over the world, some dubbed, some with subtitles; e.g. Mier Kino, Svatoplukova 4.

SLOVENSKÝ KRAS
Slovenský Kras, or the Slovakian Karst, covers 800 sq km, making it the largest karst region in Central Europe. Its attractions include wild gorges, abysses, dolines, blind valleys, ice grottos and limestone caves. The easiest accessible of these are the four caves, (Gombasecká, Domica, Jasovská and Ochtinská aragonitová) open to the public with guided tours, the beautiful Zadielská valley, and an ice grotto one may walk to from Silica. It is a good tramping area for those who find karst landscape fascinating, but more perserverance is required than normal in Czechoslovakia because the tracks in the area are generally poorly marked and maintained. There are also castles, both ruined and restored, in this peaceful and friendly part of Czechoslovakia. The tourist season starts early, as the weather is warmer, and it is very beautiful in spring.

The centre is Roznava, which was a mining town in the Middle Ages. Slovenský Kras borders Hungary, and many of the people are Hungarian speaking. Domica, Silická Brezová and Slavec, for example, are Hungarian villages. There are Hungarian schools as well as Slovak ones. During the second world war it was part of Hungary.

GETTING THERE & LEAVING AGAIN
Roznava lies just off Highway 50, which bypasses it, as does the railway. There is a good view from Jablonovské saddle on the road between Kosce and Roznava. The bus between Kosice and Roznava costs 21 kcs. Buses to Poprad pass alon g the southern edge of Slovenský Raj, stopping at Dobsinská ladová jaskyna. They leave every few hours, and take 2 hours 10 min. to Poprad. There is a bus connection with Budapest 3 times per week.

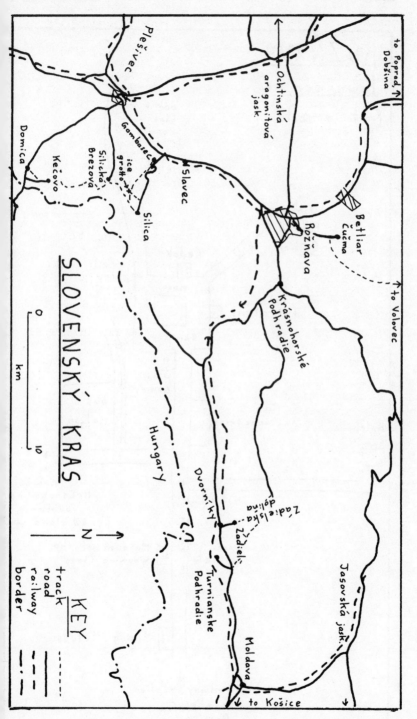

SLOVENSKÝ KRAS

Plešivec

Ochtinská
aragonitová
jask

to Poprad
Dobšina

Domica

Kečovo

Gombasec

Silicka
Brezová

ice
grotto

Slavec

Silica

Rožňava

Betliar
Čučma

Krásnohorské
Podhradie

to Volovec

N

Hungary

Dvorníky

Zádielska dolina

Zádiel

Turnianske
Podhradie

Jasovská jask

Moldava

to Košice

KEY

track
road
railway
border

0

km

10

GC-N

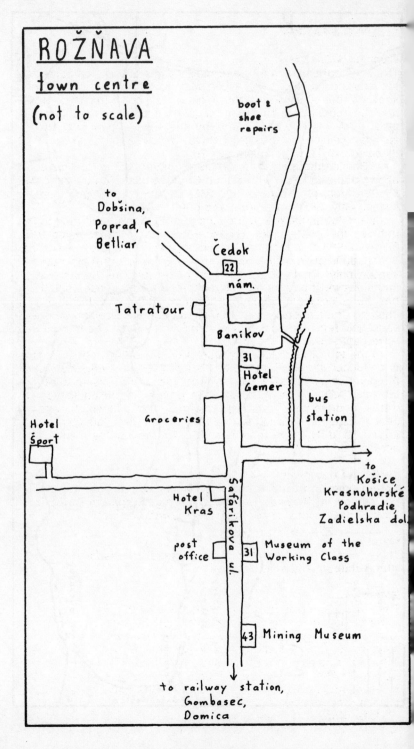

ROŽŇAVA
town centre
(not to scale)

boot &
shoe
repairs

to
Dobšina,
Poprad,
Betliar

Čedok
22

nám.

Tatratour

Baníkov

31

Hotel
Gemer

bus
station

Hotel
Šport

Groceries

to
Košice,
Krasnohorské
Podhradie,
Zadielska dol.

Hotel
Kras

Šafárikova ul.

post
office

31 Museum of the
Working Class

43 Mining Museum

to railway station,
Gombasec,
Domica

SLEEPING & EATING

Camping & Chalets

The only tent camping in the area is a camp site at Gombasec, by the entrance to the cave. Open May to September only. It has showers, but cold water only. A nice spot, apart from the racket one can sometimes hear from the quarry across the road. There is also an A class chalet camp by the cave, open only in the summer season. Address: Chatová Osada a pri Jaskyni, PSČ Plesivec 049 11, ph Roznava 921 76.

At Domica there are A and B class chalets, but the police won't allow people to camp with a tent: Chatová osada pri Jaskyni, 049 55 Dlhá Ves, ph. Roznava 928 915. Capacity 130. Open summer season only. Sk. III restaurant and bufet.

Up the hill at the top of the village of Betliar, up the road to the right of the chateau, is a peaceful B class chalet camp. (Ph. Roznava 983 07). It is a 10 minute walk from the main road. Reception is open only from about 4 or 5 pm to 7 or 8 pm, summer season only. Chalets cost 23 kcs per person, one person travelling alone must pay for a 2 room chalet (46 kcs). Since 1983 there has been no tent camping in Betliar. There is a bufet in the chateau grounds open from 7.30 am to 8 pm, and selling beer and sausages, reminding one of Germany. In the main street there is a restaurant above the shops.

At the top of Zádielska dolina is a chalet colony. Tent camping is no longer allowed here. There is a restaurant (sk.III), but out of the peak season there is no hot food, just drinks, biscuits, chocolate etc. As the road up Zádielska dolina is closed to vehicle traffic, to drive here you must drive in on the road which turns off near Krásnohorské Podhradie. From where this road comes into Zádielska dolina, the camp is 150 metres up the valley, left across a bridge.

Turistická Ubytovne

Hotel Gemer in Roznava has a dormitory with 8 beds for 32 kcs per person. In Plesivec Hotel Planina and Koruna hostinec both have B class dorms. (See 'Hotels' for addresses etc)

Motel

There is a B class motel in Krásnohorské Podhradie (ph 5230), with restaurant and snack bar.

Hotels

There are 3 hotels in Rožňava (post code 048 01).

Hotel Gemer (B), nám. Baníkov 31, (ph 28 29), is right on the town square. They charge foreigners 100 per cent more than the usual price, (unlike some hotels which charge them 160 per cent extra) i.e. singles 160 kcs, doubles 240 kcs, plus 40 kcs to use the bathroom! They tend to be full from March to August, especially in July & August. Reservations through Čedok. Class III restaurant, pivnice (beer cellar), 'pub' and a little shop.

Hotel Kras (B*), Šafárikova ul. (ph 2293-4), is a Čedok Interhotel. 152 kčs single, 234 kcs double. Class II and III restaurants. By the sports stadium is **Hotel Šport**, with restaurant and a pleasant class II kaviareñ. Both of these have car parks.

There are plenty of places to buy snacks around the centre of Rožnava. The local beer is no good.

In Plešivec (post code 049 11) is a hotel (Hotel Planina, C class, Železničná 483, ph 921 59) and a hostinec (Koruna, nám ČA 36, ph 921 58, cold water only).

GETTING AROUND
The main transport hub is the Rožnava bus station. Rožnava's railway station is out of town, though there is a closer station on a branch line.

To Domica
There is only an occasional bus to Domica. To walk there from Plešivec takes 3 hours. Hitching there is difficult.

Gombasec
The Silica bus from Rožnava stops right outside the caves and camp, and is the most convenient way to get there. Fare 4 kcs. It has a habit of running early, but also occasionally runs late. The last bus from Rožnava to Gombasec leaves at 22.50. Otherwise Gombasec is 15 minutes walk up the road to Silica from the main road, or a 30 minute walk from Slavec Jaskyna railway station if you do what the locals do and walk down the railway tracks (away from Rožnava) till you come to the road leading to the left to the caves. There is only one station at Slavec, despite what signs and maps may show.

Betliar
Various buses stop here. Also railway station on branch line.

Zádielska dolina
Catch bus to Zádielska Dvorníky.

Čedok
Nám Baníkov 22, Rožnava, ph 2343.

CAVES
Gombasecká jaskyňa is the easiest accessible of the caves for those without their own car. From 1/4 to 15/5 and 16/9 to 31/10 there are tours scheduled at 9 am 11, and 2 pm. From 16/5 to 15/9 there are tours hourly, with the first leaving at 9 am and the last 4 pm. The caves are closed on Mondays, and from 1/11 to 31/3 the caves are completely closed. The minimum number of people for a tour is 8, and some tours are cancelled because there are not enough people. 6 kcs, 3 kcs children and students. The tour commentary is in Slovak, with a German summary if requested. A leaflet in English is available. The cave was discovered in 1951. It is easy to walk through; in fact it has been rather overdeveloped for tourists, and one can see green growth around the lights. It is famous for its 'straws', created because the cave had no draught. These are stalactites up to 3 metres in length, but only 1/2 a centimetre wide. The red colour comes from oxidized

iron, and the black from oxidized manganese.

Domica is one of the 15 longest caves in the world. Only a small part of Domica jaskyňa is open to the public. It used to be possible to buy a special ticket and go underground to the Hungarian side, where the larger part of the cave system lies. As well as the usual limestone formations, this cave is interesting because of the remains found from when Neolithic man inhabited it nearly 5000 years ago. There are sometimes boat trips on the underground river Styx. Leaflet available in English. Open all year. Closed Mondays. From 16/5 to 15/9 tours at 9 am, 10.30, 12, 2 pm, and 3.30 pm. During the rest of the year: 9 am, 11, and 2 pm. Domica is very close to the Hungarian border. As a foreigner you may have your passport checked by the police.

Ochtinská aragonitová jaskyňa is to the west of Rožňava. I haven't seen it, but according to a tourist brochure it 'is the most precious gem among the subterranean treasures of the Slovak Socialist Republic. Beauteous, unprecedented shapes of aragonite flowers and crystallic patterns that appear as if made up of innumerable brilliants have grown on the walls of these morphologically interesting hollows'! Its season, tour times and prices are identical to Gombasec.

Jasovské jaskyňa is closer to Košice than Rožňava. It is not on the main road. Same times, etc as Gombasec.

For the ice cave Silická Ladnica see 'Tramping'.

OTHER ATTRACTIONS

Rožňava
This old mining town was already extracting ore in the 12th century. There is a mining museum at Šafárikovo č 43, and a museum of the working class at č31. It has a Gothic cathedral dating from about 1300, and other interesting old buildings. Around Rožňava lie forest clad hills.

Betliar
Betliar Chateau was founded in the 16th century, but has twice been extensively rebuilt. It now houses many collections, the most comprehensive being that of hunting trophies. At one time the chateau was a hunting lodge for the local nobility. Set in a large park.

Krásnohorské Podhradie
The mediaeval castle, Krásna Hôrka, dominates the landscape around Krásnohorské Podhradie from its position atop a cone shaped hill. Founded in the early 14th century, it belonged to several wealthy feudal families. In the 16th century it was enlarged and fortified at great expense by Peter Andrássy and was in the Andrássy family from this time on. They built several comfortable chateaux and, at the end of the 19th century, they installed a family museum in the castle. A few years later Dionysius Andrássy had a Jugendstil mausoleum built below the castle near the village.

CULTURE FESTIVAL

There is a Hungarian folk festival in Gombasek about the last weekend in June.

TRAMPING & WALKING

There was a map of Slovenský Kras some years ago, but it is very hard to find today. (Some people I met found a copy in a second hand bookshop in East Germany!) A new edition is not expected in the next few years. And if you do manage to find an old one, take it as a rough guide, because it is often inaccurate.

Walking times from Gombasec:
Plešivec (green) 1 hour
Silická Ladnica (ice grotto, yellow) 1 1/4 hours
Jablonovské Sedlo (yellow) 5 3/4 hours

Silická-ladnica

The most direct way to the ice grotto is to walk in from just before Silica on the yellow marked track (15 minutes). The sign at the top says 'Keep to the Path'. It is a spectacular drop from here down to the bottom. The path descends to the entrance of the cave - you can't actually go in, but can see the ice all around the entrance. If you are hot it is a cool retreat. The cave is also accessible by track from Silica (1/2 hour) and Gombasec. The track up from Gombasec goes up from behind the chalet camp, where it is a bit confusing, then it becomes a good track up the line of the power lines to Závozná. This is the top of the uphill grind (1/2 hour). The track then twists between dolines for some time, until suddenly one comes to a path with railings by the sign. (1 1/4 hours, yellow markers).

Domica - Kerčovo - Silická-Brezová - Silica

Red markers. It is not very easy to find the way, and the caves along the way are difficult to find. Be careful to stay on the track, as the Hungarian border is very close by. There is an occasional bus from Domica to Kerčovo. Otherwise it is a 30 minute walk. Kerčovo is an interesting looking little rural village. From Kerčovo it is 1 1/4 hours walk to Silická- Brezová. From the last bus stop in Kerčovo the way leads through the upper part of the village, then up a valley. When you come to the first building above the village, look up to your right, and you should see a marker on a tree which the track sidles up to. Walk along the top of the high fence. Pass the next building you come to on the left side, then veer slightly to the right. The track then passes through an area of dolines, generally keeping to right hand side of the open area, by the forest. When it enters the forest, there are still not many markers, but the route becomes easier to follow, and is level. This is a peaceful area, but criss-crossing tractor tracks and the karst landscape make route-finding a little difficult. When you are out of the forest again, the markers follow the right hand side of the open area. When you run out of markers, cut across to the village.

There is an occasional bus out from Silická Brezová, very

occasional! To continue to Silica, follow the red markers, if you can find them. When I was there this meant bashing ones way across a corn field. A short cut to Gombasec is to follow the power lines that the red track follows for a little way, until you come to the yellow track from Gombasec to Silická-ladnica, where you turn left. But this route is overgrown and thorny and difficult to follow. There are buses out from Silica. The red marked track continues from here all the way to Zádielska dolina via Jablonovské sedlo.

Volovec From Rožnava one can walk up the mountain Volovec, where there is a tourist hut. Or catch a bus to the village of Čučma, from where it's a 1 hour walk.

Zádielska dolina
There is a parking area just above the village of Zádiel, above which the road is closed to motor vehicles. The valley is a nature reserve. It is a beautiful 1 hour walk up what becomes a narrow canyon with limestone bluffs rising 100s of metres above. From the top of the valley it is 2 1/2 hours to Hrhov on the yellow marked track, or 8 hours all the way to Domica (if you can find the way) on the red marked track.

An interesting alternative route out from the top of Zádielska dolina is to follow the blue marked track to Turnianske-Podhradie (3 1/2 hours). This follows along the top of the bluffs you have been gazing up at, before dropping down to Turn ianske-Podhradie via the ruins of an old castle. This begins with a 1/2 hour grunt up an obvious track to a track junction (keep following blue). A little further along is a short deviation to a view point over Zádielska dolina. From here the track is quite level (which might surprise you if you'd looked up from the valley below), following along a plateau. Follow the markers, not the vehicle tracks they occasionally follow for a little way, or you'll get led astray. There is a wide area with no markers. Keep on at the direction of the last one, and you should find them again. Later the route comes out on the clifftop where there is a good view, and follows it to Zadielsky kamen, where there is a great view! Turn to the left: there are not many markers, but there is an obvious foot track. From here the way becomes slower as you descend over rocky terrain. Then climb up the ridge again towards the castle. The blue track heads off to the right, but keep going up the ridge if you want to inspect the castle ruins. They are most impressive at the far end - make your way there through the undergrowth. The modern fortifications are around the vineyards, not the castle: high fences and locked gates! When it reaches the highway, the marked route continues under it following village streets to the railway station.

EVENINGS
THE place to be is the Hotel Kras kaviareň in Rožnava. There is sometimes dancing, and on Fridays and Saturdays a band. But one must be correctly dressed, according to the sign at the entrance. All of the Rožnava hotels have nice kaviareň.

KOSICE

Košice, with a population of 203,000, is the second largest town in
Slovakia after Bratislava. Included in its population are about
15,000 gypsies. Košice is situated in East Slovakia, in the valley
of the River Hornád, 21 km north of the Hungarian border. Its
main attraction is its historic core.

Košice's history dates back to pre-historic times. In the Middle
Ages the town had 10,000 inhabitants. It was the second largest
city in old Hungary. Since the end of the First World War the town
has developed rapidly. At the end of the Second World War the
new government was formed here after Košice was liberated.

There was no interest in restoring the old town core before
1983, because Košice was a Hungarian city, and the Slovaks were
more interested in Slovak towns. Now the inhabitants of the inner
city are being moved out to satellite suburbs, so the old buildings
in the centre can be restored.

In the centre of Košice stands the most outstanding historic
building in Slovakia, the Gothic Cathedral of St. Elizabeth, completed in 1508. The exterior is especially impressive, bringing
back memories of St. Vitus's Cathedral in Prague. Ur ban Tower,
next to the cathedral, was built in the 15th century in Gothic style,
and reconstructed in Renaissance style in 1628. The inscriptions
on the old tomb stones around the wall are in German. The tower
is now part of Košce museum. Walking past the fountain from the
cathedral brings one to another impressive building, the State
Theatre.

At the corner of Leninova and Ulica Adyho, just across from
the theatre, is the Jesuit Church built between 1671 and 1681 in
early Baroque style. Walking down Adyho, and straight ahead at
the crossroads brings you to Ulica Pri Miklusovej Väznici. At no.
10, on the left, is Mikusova Väznici, two houses which now house
Košice's museum, with a permanent exhibition on the history of
the town. Until 1550 they were potters' houses. From this date, for
a period of about 250 years, they became a prison. They contain
cells, a torture chamber and the original interior decoration. Open
Tuesday to Saturday 9 am to 5 pm, Sunday 9 am to 1 pm. Near
Mikusova Väznici is Katova Basta, an old bastion dating from the
15th century. A little further out and to the right from here brings
one to Jacabov Palác on the corner of Gottwaldova & ul. gen.
Petrova. A rich Hungarian had this palace built in 1903 in pseudo-
Gothic style. Some of the stone came from the Gothic cathedral
during the cathedral's reconstruction. It became the residence of
Benes, Czechoslovakia's president, in 1944, after the liberation of
Košice. Now it is used for ceremonies etc.

There are a lot of interesting churches in Košice. One of these
lies in Dimitrovovo námestie. If you get off the main streets into
the back alleys you can see another side of the town. Frontages
of buildings that the public sees are painted and looked after,
while around the back is often 'grotty'.

There are nearby woods at Košice-krásna, Košický les (on the
road to Jahodná, bus 14), or Furca. There is kayaking at Anicka
(bus from the bus station).

There is an international organ festival in Košice about May -

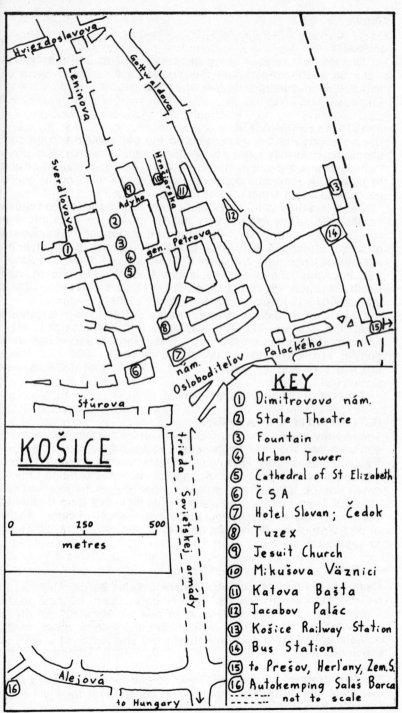

KOŠICE

0   250   500
metres

KEY

1. Dimitrovovo nám.
2. State Theatre
3. Fountain
4. Urban Tower
5. Cathedral of St Elizabeth
6. ČSA
7. Hotel Slovan; Čedok
8. Tuzex
9. Jesuit Church
10. Mikušova Väznici
11. Katova Bašta
12. Jacabov Palác
13. Košice Railway Station
14. Bus Station
15. to Prešov, Herľany, Zem.S.
16. Autokemping Salaš Barca
------- not to scale

June every year.

HERLANY
At Herlany is a geyser which once every 32 to 34 hours spurts water up to 30 metres above the ground for a period of about 20 minutes. Find out from Čedok when the geyser will be playing. There is a bus to it.

PRACTICAL INFORMATION
Ulica Leninova is the main street in the old centre, and offices, shops etc. you may need are on this street, or nearby. It is open to pedestrians and public transport only. There is a map of Kosice in nám. Osloboditelov, opposite Hotel Slovan. It is occasionally possible to buy a street map of Kosice.

Čedok's office is in the Hotel Slovan building at Rooseweltova 1, tel. 24079. They are not very helpful, and there is no information available in English, only in Russian or German. Tatratour are at Ulica Šrobárova 6, near the cathedral. They also have an exchange office, and are open from Moday to Friday, and Saturday mornings. Slovakoturist's address is: 040 01 Kosice, Ján Bacika 11, tel. 280 53, 277 40, 257 41, telex 077478. CKM's address: 042 12 Kosice, Leninova 82, tel. 207 37.

ČSA is at Pribinova 4, near Hotel Slovan. Their telephone number is 22578 or 22577, telegrams to AEROLINIE, telex 077216. The airport telephone number is 23568. Pragocar rental car company is at Ulica Vrátna 1, just off Leninova (tel. 205 3 5). There are taxi services at Pribinova 2 (tel. 222 44) and at the railway station (tel. 200 44).

Tuzex is at ulica Leninova no. 7.

GETTING THERE & AWAY AGAIN
The railway station and bus station adjoin each other between the old town and the river to the east (walking distance). There are frequent buses from Presov, and hitch-hiking shouldn't be too difficult. Bus connection to Michalovce. Buses and trains to Roznava (lot of international trucks, especially Rumanian on this stretch). Train from Poprad. Several flights a day from Bratislava and from Prague (mostly via Bratislava). Latest check-in at the airport 20 minutes before depart ure, or in town 45 minutes prior to departure.

SLEEPING
Camping at Kosice-Barca: **Autokemping Salaš Barca**, Alejová ul., 040 00 Kosice, tel. 583 09. 'A' category. Open 15 June to 15 September. Take tram no. 1 or 4, or bus no. 22 or 52, get off at Alejovául. If driving head south from the centre down trieda Sovietskej armády (direction Šebastovce) and turn right when you reach Alejovául.

Student hostels: Slovakoturist have double rooms in student hostels available for their groups, so you could see if they will book individuals in.

Hotels(all post code 040 00 Košice):
　Slovan, A* (****), Leninova ul. 1, tel. 273 78, telex 77416, 307 beds, all rooms with bath, singles US$22 to 30, doubles US$19 to 25 per person;
　Imperial, B* (***), ul. gen. Petrova 16, tel. 221 44, 60 beds, with bath US$14 to US$23 per person, without bath US$12 to 18.
　Hutn´k, B* (***), Tyršovo nábr. 6, tel. 377 80, 332 beds, rooms with shower & toilet.

EATING & DRINKING
At Leninova 16 Jednota have a complex of different class restaurants, vináren, pivnice and a night bar. There are also places to eat and drink near Jacabov Palác. There are numerous vináren around the old town. The markets are in Dimitro vovo námestie.

ZEMPLÍNSKA SIRAVA & VIHORLATSKÉ VRCHY
Zemplínska Širava is a 33.5 sq km artificial lake situated in the far east of Slovakia near the Soviet border. It is known as the Slovak Sea, because Slovakia doesn't have any sea. A few years ago, with its warm summer temperatures, it was a good place for swimming. Now it has become too polluted, although people do still swim in it. In the summer there are cruise boats. You may be able to borrow or rent canoes and dinghies, but not yachts—although you could try asking at club houses. At Vinné is Viniansky hrad, the ruins of a 13th century castle. The main centre in the area is Michalovce. It has some nice churches, and the Zemplín Museum is next to the bus station. If you walk out onto the road from the bus station, there is a map of Michalovce on your right. From Michalovce bus station there are buses out to the resorts along the northern shores of the lake. If you want to get away from the more developed resorts, head further out along the lake from Michalovce. At Kaluža 'high rise' development is starting. There is a Čedok office and a Tuzex shop in Michalovce.
　Vihorlatské Vrchy are the volcanic hills to the north of the lake. Although some of the area is now closed due to the military taking it over, there is still public access to Morské oko, a beautiful lake situated up in the forest, and Sninský-kamen, a rather spectacular peak.
　You may be able to buy a map of Slanské vrchy and Zemplínska Širava, but Vihorlatské Vrchy is not on this map. No map is planned at present, because the area is too close to USSR.

GETTING THERE & LEAVING AGAIN
There are a few buses a day between Prešov and Zemplínska Širava. The trip takes 2 hours 20 minutes. There are lots of buses between Michalovce and Košice. On this route one passes over Slanské Vrchy, where there is a huge memorial to Soviet soldiers. There is a direct bus once a day at 8 am from Michalovce to Rosnava, otherwise change buses at Košice.

SLEEPING & EATING
There are many camp sites along the lakeshore. Some have on-site tents, and some have bungalows. At Kamanec, there is camp-

ing behind the motel. If you go right down to just before the pier, there is a good spot for pup tents on the left. Also good blackberries. Strange looking chalet colony by the motel (ph 245 65). There is a camping area along the lake shore between Kamanec and Klokočoc, but it is rather exposed to the wind and close to the road. Camping at Palkov, just past Klokočov, is good. There is a large area available for tents, some of it sheltered, and it is not too close to the road. Most of the camping is open from mid May to mid September, and most have cold water only.

If you are looking for a roof over your head, rather than a camping spot, there are a couple of hostels in Horka, and a hostinec with sleeping for 20, cold water only, at Medvedia Hora. Kamanec Motel has B category accommodation. Cold water only. It is open all year (ph Michalovce 872 08). It has a cat. III restaurant, open from 8 am to 9 pm, but meals are served during more restricted hours. There is a B* class hotel, Merkur, in Horka (ph 752 70), otherwise there are 3 hotels in Michalovce.

VIHORLATSKE VRCHY

Morské oko is a beautiful lake surrounded by forest, a lovely peaceful spot formed when lava from a volcanic eruption blocked the stream running in the valley. It is now a nature reserve, and camping, fires, swimming and boating are all prohibited. Malé (Little) Morské oko is 1/2 to 1 hours walk from Morské oko itself, but it has been spoilt by logging operations. If you are a blackberry fan it might be worth walking up the first part of the track (season begins about late August).

Buses to Morské oko operate only in the holiday period between late June and late August. There are only one or two a day, and they run from Micholovce via Úbrež, not via the Zemplínska sirava resorts. There is one bus a day to Morské oko in the same season along the northern shore of Zemplínska sirava. It leaves Michalovce at 8.28, only stops at major stops (e.g. Kamanec Motel), and doesn't run at weekends. When there is no bus you must walk the last 9 km from Remetské Hámre (1 1/2 to 2 1/2 hours, following the blue markers along the road). Hitch-hiking is possible, but there is hardly any traffic outside the holiday period. At the parking area there is a 'bufet' and a map. From here it is a 15 minute walk up to the lake itself.

Sninský-kameň (1005 metres a.s.l.) is a fantastic sight. It is a large rock outcrop situated above Morské oko. To get there, follow the track to Tri Table (821 m.a.s.l.) from the top end of Morské oko, and then along the ridge to Sninský-kameň. Watch out for track markers on the way up, as logging roads criss-cross the hillside. A board at the bottom explains how the rock was formed. From the signs at the bottom, follow the red marked track around the rock, and you will come to steel steps leading to the top. Pollution and haze spoil the view, but one can see Morské oko below. From here the red track continues to Strihovké Sedlo, but it is not used much. Following the track towards Zemplíske Háre for a few minutes brings one to a ladder up onto the other promontory. From here it is possible to descend to the valley to the north.

The areas around Morské oko and Sninský-kameň are nature

reserves, but a lot of the rest of the forest has been spoilt by logging. Even so it is a beautiful area. While sitting on a log at Tri Table I had two species of beautiful butterflies sitting on me. One was camouflaged so that when it closed its wings it looked like a flake of bark.

The track from Tri Table to mount Vihorlat (1076 m.a.s.l.) is closed. Virhorlat can be climbed from Jovsa, on the north-east corner of Zemplínska širava. Coming out from Kamanec etc, turn left at the unsignposted road opposite a sign saying 'Svetu Mier' (which means 'World Peace'). With the military activity in the area, it may be wise to check first that this route is still open to the public.

Other walking times in the area
From the bottom end of Morské oko to:
Zemplínske Hámre, 2 hours; Tri Table, 3/4 hour
From Tri Table to:
Sninský-kameň, 1/2 hour; Strihovké Sedlo, 4 3/4 hours; Podhorod, 8 3/4 hours; Zemplínske Hámre via Sninský-kameň, 1 1/2 hours; Remetské Hámre, 2 1/2 hours; Zemplínske Hámre direct, 1 1/4 hours;
From Sninský-kameň to:
Remetské Hámre, 3 hours; Zemplínske Hámre, 1 hour; Strihovke sedlo, 4 1/4 hours.

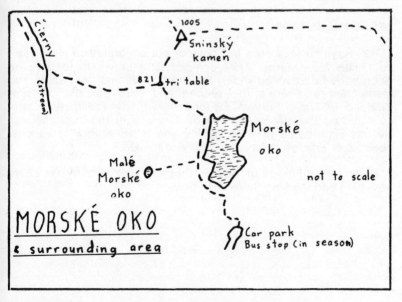

MORSKÉ OKO
& surrounding area

KREMENEC & THE POLISH BORDER AREA
North of Vihorlatské vrchy are the Bukovské vrchy, and at the point where Czechoslovakia, Poland and USSR meet is Kremenc (1221 m.a.s.l.). In this area there are old wooden churches in the valleys leading up to the border. In theory one may walk here on a red marked track, but I have heard of people being turned back by Russian border guards while on Czechoslovak territory. It is

possible to follow the Polish border from here, but not the Russian. But again one could have hassles, being a foreigner near the border. Today there is no border crossing to Poland between Kremenec and Dukla. There used to be both a road and railway crossing in this area.

TOKAI REGION
The Tokai region is in south-east Slovakia, and continues into Hungary. This is one of Slovakia's wine growing areas. Stredan. Bodrogom, Malá Tŕňa, Vinicky, Malý Hores and Král. Chlmec are all villages involved in wine making. The region has long fine autumns. According to an old Austro-Hungarian decree grape picking was permitted only after October 24, when the season was over in other areas. Today the picking season starts on St Simon and St Judes Day (October 28) at the earliest, and finishes in November, sometimes after the first snow has fallen.

ABOUT THE AUTHOR

Simon Hayman was born in England, but emigrated to New Zealand with his parents. After completing a university degree in Geography he travelled widely in Europe, Asia and the Pacific. He researched and wrote the second and third editions of *New Zealand—A Travel Survival Kit* for Lonely Planet Publications and co-authored the second edition of *Australia* in the same series. He has contributed to other guides and is the author of various newspaper articles in New Zealand and the UK.

Returning to Europe in 1983 for 'a short visit', Simon has been travelling and working there ever since.

INDEX OF PLACES

(See Table of Contents for other subjects)